American Attitudes

What Americans Think about the Issues That Shape Their Lives

BY THE EDITORS OF NEW STRATEGIST PUBLICATIONS

6th EDITION

New Strategist Publications, Inc.

Ithaca, New York

New Strategist Publications, Inc.
P.O. Box 242, Ithaca, New York 14851
800/848-0842; 607/273-0913
www.newstrategist.com

ISBN 978-1-935114-75-8 (hardcover)
ISBN 978-1-935114-76-5 (paper)

Printed in the United States of America

Table of Contents

List of Tables

Chapter 3. Science

Chapter 4. Religion

Chapter 5. Work and Money

Chapter 8.   Personal Outlook

Chapter 9.   Sexual Attitudes and Behavior

Introduction

Surveys and polls have become fixtures of American life, with each day bringing new findings and making new headlines. Some of the results are enlightening, while others serve only to muddy the water. Many surveys do not segment their findings by demographic characteristic, and most cannot be used to study trends in attitudes over time because methodologies and questions vary from survey to survey.

The General Social Survey is different. It has a long history. For more than 30 years, it has asked Americans many of the same questions, allowing researchers to compare attitudes not just over time, but also by demographic characteristic. The General Social Survey is one of the few resources that allow attitudinal differences and changes in attitudes to be explored in depth, often permitting researchers to pinpoint why change has occurred. The GSS is the mirror of America. According to the survey's director, Tom W. Smith, the GSS has been described as a "national resource" by the National Academy of Science and a "public utility for the community at large" by the National Science Foundation. The survey may not always show us a pretty picture of ourselves, but it is a more accurate picture than can be gleaned from scattershot surveys carried out by a multitude of organizations.

The sixth edition of *American Attitudes: Who Thinks What about the Issues that Shape Our Lives* brings you the results from the latest GSS, fielded in 2008. In five previous editions of *American Attitudes*, New Strategist Publications has coaxed GSS results out of the shadows of academia and placed them solidly in public view. This edition does even more with GSS results, not only examining changes in the public's attitudes over the past three decades, but also providing a demographic breakdown of those attitudes question by question. In hundreds of tables, the sixth edition of *American Attitudes* taps into the GSS gold mine, revealing what the public thinks about topics ranging from gay marriage to the American Dream, how Americans feel about their financial status, their hopes for their children, how often they socialize and with whom, their religious beliefs, political leanings, and working conditions. It shows those answers by the demographics that shape perspective—sex, age, race, Hispanic origin, and education. *American Attitudes* also compares attitudes in 2008 with 1998, 1988, and 1978 (if available), examining how opinions have or have not changed during those three decades.

Changing attitudes

On most issues, Americans have been surprisingly constant in their views. Over the decades of the GSS, the majority of Americans have consistently claimed to be at least "pretty happy," and most husbands and wives have described their marriage as "very happy." Religion remains highly important to the majority, although religious diversity has increased. Most support the death penalty. Most also support abortion, at least in some circumstances.

On some issues, however, there have been important shifts over time. Attitudes toward sexual behavior, sex roles, and race relations have changed profoundly as younger generations with different attitudes have replaced older ones. Overall, only 35 percent of Americans still favor traditional sex roles, for example. Among people aged 65 or older, however, the 54 percent majority thinks traditional roles are best—a relic of the era when most Americans subscribed to rigid boundaries between the sexes.

Between 1978 and 2008, there have been some important shifts in attitudes. One shift is the feeling that the federal government must do more about health care. The percentage of the public that believes the government spends too little on health care climbed from 57 to 77 percent between 1978 and 2008. The 54 percent majority of the public now believes the government should help people pay for medical care, up from 48 percent who felt that way in 1988. Other issues that have experienced significant attitudinal shifts in the past decade include a decline in the percentage of people who identify themselves as Protestant, a sharp drop in daily newspaper readership, a decline in the percentage of people who think two is the ideal number of children, and a drop in the percentage of people who believe their income is "average," falling from 53 percent in 1978 to 47 percent in 2008. The percentage of Americans who believe their income is below average relative to others has grown from 25 to 31 percent. Most disturbing, perhaps, is the loss of faith in the American Dream. The percentage of people who agree with the statement, "The way things are in America, people like me and my family have a good chance of improving our standard of living," has fallen from 75 percent in 1998 to 59 percent in 2008.

Differences by demographics

Demographics do not necessarily divide Americans. On many issues, men and women think alike, whites and blacks agree, young and old are on the same side, and college graduates are in accord with their less educated counterparts. Every demographic segment, for example, overwhelmingly supports gun control. Regardless of their demographics, few people have much confidence in Congress, television, or the press.

On some issues, however, there are large differences by demographic characteristic. Women are more likely than men to pray at least once a day (68 versus 46 percent). Whites are more likely than blacks to favor capital punishment (72 versus 46 percent). Young adults are more likely than older Americans to think gays and lesbians should have the right to marry (49 versus 22 percent). The college-educated are much more likely than those without a college degree to believe in evolution (63 versus 46 percent). Mix these diverse attitudes and values together, and you get the American perspective. That perspective is revealed in *American Attitudes*.

About the book

The sixth edition of *American Attitudes* is organized into nine topical chapters: Public Arena; Government and Politics; Science and Information; Religion; Work and Money; Family and Friends; Race; Personal Outlook; and Sexual Attitudes and Behavior.

Within chapters, a series of tables display the public's response to the survey's questions. The exact wording of the GSS question is shown above the table, minus instructional details. Each table shows the total response in 1998, 1988, and 1978 (when available) and in 2008. Each table also shows the 2008 response by sex, race and Hispanic origin (black, Hispanic, and white—the sample size is too small to allow for a breakout of Asian attitudes), broad age group (18 to 44, 45 to 64, 65 or older), and education (not a college graduate, and bachelor's degree or more). The chapters also include charts and text highlighting the findings and trends. Each chapter's introductory text examines what has—and has not—changed over the past decade.

About the General Social Survey

The GSS is fielded by the University of Chicago's National Opinion Research Center. NORC is the oldest nonprofit, university-affiliated national survey research facility in the nation. It conducts the GSS through face-to-face interviews with an independently drawn, nationally representative sample of approximately 3,000 to 4,000 people aged 18 or older living in households in the United States. NORC fielded the first GSS in 1972, conducted it annually through 1994 (except for the years 1979, 1981, and 1992), and has fielded the survey every two years since then.

Until recently, GSS data have not been readily available to the public. Although social scientists frequently use the GSS to study trends, the survey's results are not published comprehensively or regularly. Most GSS analysis appears in academic papers and journals, which are not readily available to the average person. A few years ago, the Computer-assisted Survey Methods Program of the University of California-Berkeley created a web-based tool for analyzing the GSS. The online tool allows users to create custom tables of GSS data. Using the tool, the researchers at New Strategist painstakingly produced *American Attitudes* line by line, extracting the results of the GSS like gold from a mine. With this volume, New Strategist Publications places the latest survey results into the hands of the public.

For more information

If you want more information about the GSS, visit the National Opinion Research Center site at http://www.norc.org/projects/general+social+survey.htm.

To explore the GSS extraction tool, visit the Computer-assisted Survey Methods Program site at http://sda.berkeley.edu/cgi-bin32/hsda?harcsda+gss08.

CHAPTER 1

The Public Arena

Public opinion on some issues has been remarkably stable over time. On other issues, changes in public opinion can—or should—raise alarm bells. Here is a synopsis of how attitudes regarding public institutions and public issues have changed—or not—over the past decade.

Little or no change

• **Little public confidence in institutions.** Confidence in most institutions has been abysmally low for decades. In 2008, the percentage of the public with a great deal of confidence in the nation's institutions was below 50 percent for all but the military. Confidence in banks and financial institutions has taken a hit recently because of their role in the economic downturn. Confidence is lowest in television and the press, with fewer than 10 percent of the public having a great deal of confidence in these institutions.

• **Americans want the courts to treat criminals more harshly.** Although the United States has more prisoners per capita than any other nation on earth, most Americans still think the courts in their area are not tough enough on criminals. Most also favor the death penalty.

• **Most support gun control.** Americans strongly support gun control. A shrinking share of the public owns a gun, the figure falling to 36 percent in 2008. Why are politicians unwilling to pass gun control laws? That is a question no one seems able to answer.

Big changes

• **Higher taxes for someone.** A shrinking share of the public believes its taxes are too high, perhaps paving the way for tax increases. But who will pay more? It might not be the rich because the plurality of Americans still believes taxes on the rich are too high.

• **Greater chance of a world war.** Americans feel secure in their homes and neighborhoods, but the world at large is a more dangerous place. Most believe the United States will be involved in another world war within 10 years.

• **Legalizing marijuana**. A growing share of the public favors legalizing marijuana. Adults under age 65 are far more likely to favor it than older Americans, boosting the chances that marijuana may one day be as acceptable as alcohol.

Public Confidence in Most Institutions Is Low

The public has little confidence in most institutions, including the press and television, the legislative and executive branches of the federal government, organized labor, and major companies. The public has the most confidence in the military, followed by the scientific and medical communities.

(percent of people aged 18 or older who say they have a great deal of confidence in selected institutions, 2008)

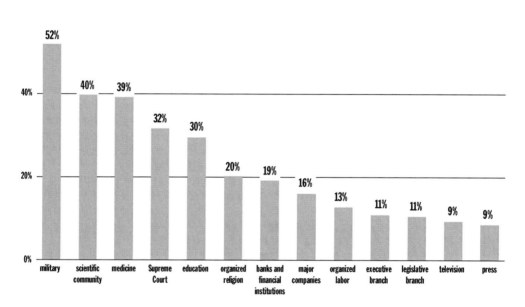

Source: General Social Surveys; calculations by New Strategist

Table 1.1 Confidence in Executive Branch of Federal Government, 1978 to 2008

"As far as the people running these institutions are concerned, would you say
you have a great deal of confidence, only some confidence, or hardly any
confidence at all in them: The executive branch of the federal government?"

*(percent of people aged 18 or older responding, 1978 to 2008; and percent responding by demographic charac-
teristic, 2008)*

	a great deal	only some	hardly any
TREND			
2008	10.9%	50.3%	38.9%
1998	13.7	49.7	36.6
1988	17.1	55.4	27.5
1978	12.0	61.9	26.2
2008 PROFILE			
Total people	**10.9**	**50.3**	**38.9**
Men	10.3	47.6	42.1
Women	11.4	52.7	36.0
Black	13.5	47.0	39.5
Hispanic	18.5	52.6	28.9
White	10.4	50.0	39.6
Aged 18 to 44	12.4	56.8	30.8
Aged 45 to 64	10.8	43.8	45.4
Aged 65 or older	6.5	44.0	49.5
Not a college graduate	10.9	52.3	36.7
Bachelor's degree or more	10.8	44.4	44.9

*Source: Survey Documentation and Analysis, Computer-assisted Survey Methods Program, University of California, Berkeley,
General Social Surveys, 1972–2008 Cumulative Data Files, Internet site http://sda.berkeley.edu/cgi-bin/hsda?harcsda+gss08;
calculations by New Strategist*

Table 1.2 Confidence in Legislative Branch of Federal Government, 1978 to 2008

"As far as the people running these institutions are concerned, would you say you have a great deal of confidence, only some confidence, or hardly any confidence at all in them: The legislative branch of the federal government?"

(percent of people aged 18 or older responding, 1978 to 2008; and percent responding by demographic characteristic, 2008)

	a great deal	only some	hardly any
TREND			
2008	10.5%	51.9%	37.6%
1998	10.7	58.1	31.3
1988	16.5	63.7	19.9
1978	12.8	66.1	21.2
2008 PROFILE			
Total people	**10.5**	**51.9**	**37.6**
Men	10.4	46.1	43.5
Women	10.6	57.1	32.3
Black	14.8	55.1	30.1
Hispanic	23.5	51.9	24.6
White	9.4	50.4	40.2
Aged 18 to 44	13.9	56.5	29.6
Aged 45 to 64	8.2	49.7	42.0
Aged 65 or older	4.9	42.7	52.4
Not a college graduate	11.7	51.3	37.0
Bachelor's degree or more	7.1	53.6	39.3

Source: Survey Documentation and Analysis, Computer-assisted Survey Methods Program, University of California, Berkeley, General Social Surveys, 1972–2008 Cumulative Data Files, Internet site http://sda.berkeley.edu/cgi-bin/hsda?harcsda+gss08; calculations by New Strategist

Table 1.3 Confidence in the United States Supreme Court, 1978 to 2008

"As far as the people running these institutions are concerned, would you say
you have a great deal of confidence, only some confidence, or hardly
any confidence at all in them: The United States Supreme Court?"

(percent of people aged 18 or older responding, 1978 to 2008; and percent responding by demographic characteristic, 2008)

	a great deal	only some	hardly any
TREND			
2008	31.6%	54.3%	14.2%
1998	32.7	52.7	14.6
1988	36.6	52.8	10.5
1978	30.9	54.6	14.5
2008 PROFILE			
Total people	**31.6**	**54.3**	**14.2**
Men	35.2	49.2	15.6
Women	28.3	58.8	13.0
Black	25.5	57.5	17.1
Hispanic	40.4	45.6	14.0
White	31.9	54.6	13.5
Aged 18 to 44	32.5	54.4	13.1
Aged 45 to 64	31.9	53.8	14.3
Aged 65 or older	27.6	54.6	17.7
Not a college graduate	29.7	54.9	15.4
Bachelor's degree or more	36.7	52.6	10.7

Source: Survey Documentation and Analysis, Computer-assisted Survey Methods Program, University of California, Berkeley, General Social Surveys, 1972–2008 Cumulative Data Files, Internet site http://sda.berkeley.edu/cgi-bin/hsda?harcsda+gss08; calculations by New Strategist

Table 1.4 Confidence in Banks and Financial Institutions, 1978 to 2008

"As far as the people running these institutions are concerned, would you say you have a great deal of confidence, only some confidence, or hardly any confidence at all in them: Banks and financial institutions?"

(percent of people aged 18 or older responding, 1978 to 2008; and percent responding by demographic characteristic, 2008)

	a great deal	only some	hardly any
TREND			
2008	19.2%	60.5%	20.3%
1998	26.6	57.1	16.3
1988	27.6	58.7	13.7
1978	31.1	57.0	12.0
2008 PROFILE			
Total people	**19.2**	**60.5**	**20.3**
Men	15.5	59.2	25.3
Women	22.5	61.7	15.8
Black	23.8	52.6	23.5
Hispanic	27.6	51.2	21.2
White	17.3	63.1	19.6
Aged 18 to 44	22.5	58.7	18.8
Aged 45 to 64	13.9	65.1	21.0
Aged 65 or older	21.6	55.0	23.4
Not a college graduate	20.7	59.3	20.0
Bachelor's degree or more	15.1	63.8	21.2

Source: Survey Documentation and Analysis, Computer-assisted Survey Methods Program, University of California, Berkeley, General Social Surveys, 1972–2008 Cumulative Data Files, Internet site http://sda.berkeley.edu/cgi-bin/hsda?harcsda+gss08; calculations by New Strategist

Table 1.5 Confidence in Major Companies, 1978 to 2008

"As far as the people running these institutions are concerned, would
you say you have a great deal of confidence, only some confidence,
or hardly any confidence at all in them: Major companies?"

*(percent of people aged 18 or older responding, 1978 to 2008; and percent responding by demographic charac-
teristic, 2008)*

	a great deal	only some	hardly any
TREND			
2008	16.0%	67.4%	16.6%
1998	26.6	57.1	16.3
1988	27.6	58.7	13.7
1978	31.1	57.0	12.0
2008 PROFILE			
Total people	**16.0**	**67.4**	**16.6**
Men	17.4	66.2	16.4
Women	14.8	68.4	16.8
Black	15.3	70.8	13.9
Hispanic	15.4	65.8	18.8
White	16.1	66.8	17.2
Aged 18 to 44	16.5	69.3	14.1
Aged 45 to 64	13.1	68.9	18.0
Aged 65 or older	21.6	57.7	20.7
Not a college graduate	14.4	67.5	18.1
Bachelor's degree or more	20.5	67.0	12.4

*Source: Survey Documentation and Analysis, Computer-assisted Survey Methods Program, University of California, Berkeley,
General Social Surveys, 1972–2008 Cumulative Data Files, Internet site http://sda.berkeley.edu/cgi-bin/hsda?harcsda+gss08;
calculations by New Strategist*

Table 1.6 Confidence in Organized Labor, 1978 to 2008

"As far as the people running these institutions are concerned, would
you say you have a great deal of confidence, only some confidence,
or hardly any confidence at all in them: Organized labor?"

(percent of people aged 18 or older responding, 1978 to 2008; and percent responding by demographic characteristic, 2008)

	a great deal	only some	hardly any
TREND			
2008	12.7%	59.1%	28.1%
1998	11.8	56.8	31.4
1988	11.4	52.9	35.7
1978	11.3	48.7	40.0
2008 PROFILE			
Total people	**12.7**	**59.1**	**28.1**
Men	13.7	51.5	34.8
Women	11.9	66.1	22.1
Black	15.1	62.7	22.2
Hispanic	19.8	62.4	17.8
White	11.9	58.1	30.0
Aged 18 to 44	15.0	63.4	21.7
Aged 45 to 64	10.8	56.4	32.8
Aged 65 or older	10.4	51.7	37.9
Not a college graduate	14.5	59.0	26.5
Bachelor's degree or more	7.8	59.4	32.8

Source: Survey Documentation and Analysis, Computer-assisted Survey Methods Program, University of California, Berkeley, General Social Surveys, 1972–2008 Cumulative Data Files, Internet site http://sda.berkeley.edu/cgi-bin/hsda?harcsda+gss08; calculations by New Strategist

Table 1.7 Confidence in the Scientific Community, 1978 to 2008

"As far as the people running these institutions are concerned, would you say you have a great deal of confidence, only some confidence, or hardly any confidence at all in them: The scientific community?"

(percent of people aged 18 or older responding, 1978 to 2008; and percent responding by demographic characteristic, 2008)

	a great deal	only some	hardly any
TREND			
2008	40.4%	53.8%	5.8%
1998	42.7	48.6	8.7
1988	42.5	51.8	5.7
1978	40.8	51.7	7.5
2008 PROFILE			
Total people	**40.4**	**53.8**	**5.8**
Men	43.5	51.7	4.9
Women	37.7	55.6	6.7
Black	29.3	62.3	8.3
Hispanic	46.7	45.9	7.4
White	42.2	52.6	5.3
Aged 18 to 44	44.6	50.2	5.2
Aged 45 to 64	38.5	55.3	6.2
Aged 65 or older	32.2	60.4	7.4
Not a college graduate	35.8	57.0	7.2
Bachelor's degree or more	52.7	45.1	2.2

Source: Survey Documentation and Analysis, Computer-assisted Survey Methods Program, University of California, Berkeley, General Social Surveys, 1972–2008 Cumulative Data Files, Internet site http://sda.berkeley.edu/cgi-bin/hsda?harcsda+gss08; calculations by New Strategist

Table 1.8 Confidence in Medicine, 1978 to 2008

"As far as the people running these institutions are concerned, would
you say you have a great deal of confidence, only some confidence,
or hardly any confidence at all in them: Medicine?"

(percent of people aged 18 or older responding, 1978 to 2008; and percent responding by demographic characteristic, 2008)

	a great deal	only some	hardly any
TREND			
2008	39.2%	50.3%	10.5%
1998	45.6	45.4	8.9
1988	53.2	40.9	5.9
1978	47.6	43.6	8.7
2008 PROFILE			
Total people	**39.2**	**50.3**	**10.5**
Men	39.9	48.7	11.4
Women	38.5	51.7	9.8
Black	33.9	50.9	15.3
Hispanic	50.0	41.8	8.2
White	39.1	50.6	10.3
Aged 18 to 44	43.2	46.5	10.3
Aged 45 to 64	32.3	56.4	11.3
Aged 65 or older	42.6	47.7	9.6
Not a college graduate	37.7	50.4	11.9
Bachelor's degree or more	43.1	50.1	6.8

Source: Survey Documentation and Analysis, Computer-assisted Survey Methods Program, University of California, Berkeley, General Social Surveys, 1972–2008 Cumulative Data Files, Internet site http://sda.berkeley.edu/cgi-bin/hsda?harcsda+gss08; calculations by New Strategist

Table 1.9 Confidence in Education, 1978 to 2008

"As far as the people running these institutions are concerned, would
you say you have a great deal of confidence, only some confidence,
or hardly any confidence at all in them: Education?"

*(percent of people aged 18 or older responding, 1978 to 2008; and percent responding by demographic charac-
teristic, 2008)*

	a great deal	only some	hardly any
TREND			
2008	29.5%	55.2%	15.2%
1998	27.2	55.7	17.1
1988	30.3	60.8	8.9
1978	28.5	56.9	14.6
2008 PROFILE			
Total people	**29.5**	**55.2**	**15.2**
Men	30.2	52.5	17.3
Women	28.9	57.7	13.4
Black	34.4	50.0	15.6
Hispanic	45.7	41.0	13.4
White	28.0	57.0	15.0
Aged 18 to 44	33.7	52.5	13.8
Aged 45 to 64	24.4	59.6	16.0
Aged 65 or older	28.4	53.6	18.0
Not a college graduate	31.6	54.9	13.5
Bachelor's degree or more	23.7	56.2	20.1

*Source: Survey Documentation and Analysis, Computer-assisted Survey Methods Program, University of California, Berkeley,
General Social Surveys, 1972–2008 Cumulative Data Files, Internet site http://sda.berkeley.edu/cgi-bin/hsda?harcsda+gss08;
calculations by New Strategist*

Table 1.10 Confidence in Organized Religion, 1978 to 2008

"As far as the people running these institutions are concerned, would
you say you have a great deal of confidence, only some confidence, or
hardly any confidence at all in them: Organized religion?"

(percent of people aged 18 or older responding, 1978 to 2008; and percent responding by demographic charac-teristic, 2008)

	a great deal	only some	hardly any
TREND			
2008	20.4%	54.1%	25.5%
1998	27.5	53.6	18.9
1988	21.2	49.1	29.8
1978	30.9	51.0	18.1
2008 PROFILE			
Total people	**20.4**	**54.1**	**25.5**
Men	17.2	52.7	30.1
Women	23.2	55.4	21.4
Black	24.9	60.7	14.4
Hispanic	21.2	51.4	27.4
White	18.9	53.9	27.2
Aged 18 to 44	19.3	54.0	26.7
Aged 45 to 64	20.3	52.8	26.9
Aged 65 or older	24.1	57.7	18.2
Not a college graduate	20.7	53.8	25.5
Bachelor's degree or more	19.2	55.4	25.4

Source: Survey Documentation and Analysis, Computer-assisted Survey Methods Program, University of California, Berkeley, General Social Surveys, 1972–2008 Cumulative Data Files, Internet site http://sda.berkeley.edu/cgi-bin/hsda?harcsda+gss08; calculations by New Strategist

Table 1.11 Confidence in the Military, 1978 to 2008

"As far as the people running these institutions are concerned, would you say you have a great deal of confidence, only some confidence, or hardly any confidence at all in them: The military?"

(percent of people aged 18 or older responding, 1978 to 2008; and percent responding by demographic characteristic, 2008)

	a great deal	only some	hardly any
TREND			
2008	51.9%	37.7%	10.4%
1998	37.2	49.8	13.0
1988	35.9	51.4	12.7
1978	31.2	55.5	13.2
2008 PROFILE			
Total people	**51.9**	**37.7**	**10.4**
Men	55.5	34.2	10.3
Women	48.6	40.8	10.5
Black	45.2	35.2	19.7
Hispanic	43.8	41.0	15.2
White	54.2	37.9	8.0
Aged 18 to 44	51.9	37.6	10.5
Aged 45 to 64	51.0	38.8	10.2
Aged 65 or older	53.8	35.9	10.3
Not a college graduate	53.6	36.5	10.0
Bachelor's degree or more	47.0	41.4	11.6

Source: Survey Documentation and Analysis, Computer-assisted Survey Methods Program, University of California, Berkeley, General Social Surveys, 1972–2008 Cumulative Data Files, Internet site http://sda.berkeley.edu/cgi-bin/hsda?harcsda+gss08; calculations by New Strategist

Table 1.12 Confidence in the Press, 1978 to 2008

"As far as the people running these institutions are concerned, would you say you have a great deal of confidence, only some confidence, or hardly any confidence at all in them: The press?"

(percent of people aged 18 or older responding, 1978 to 2008; and percent responding by demographic characteristic, 2008)

	a great deal	only some	hardly any
TREND			
2008	8.6%	46.3%	45.1%
1998	9.2	47.2	43.6
1988	19.5	55.1	25.4
1978	20.6	59.5	19.9
2008 PROFILE			
Total people	**8.6**	**46.3**	**45.1**
Men	7.6	45.3	47.1
Women	9.5	47.2	43.3
Black	10.9	43.7	45.4
Hispanic	16.3	48.1	35.6
White	7.5	45.9	46.6
Aged 18 to 44	9.9	46.0	44.1
Aged 45 to 64	8.1	46.7	45.2
Aged 65 or older	5.7	46.5	47.8
Not a college graduate	9.3	46.2	44.4
Bachelor's degree or more	6.6	46.3	47.1

Source: Survey Documentation and Analysis, Computer-assisted Survey Methods Program, University of California, Berkeley, General Social Surveys, 1972–2008 Cumulative Data Files, Internet site http://sda.berkeley.edu/cgi-bin/hsda?harcsda+gss08; calculations by New Strategist

Table 1.13 Confidence in Television, 1978 to 2008

"As far as the people running these institutions are concerned, would you say you have a great deal of confidence, only some confidence, or hardly any confidence at all in them: Television?"

(percent of people aged 18 or older responding, 1978 to 2008; and percent responding by demographic characteristic, 2008)

	a great deal	only some	hardly any
TREND			
2008	9.3%	51.9%	38.7%
1998	10.2	50.6	39.2
1988	14.3	59.3	26.4
1978	15.0	53.3	31.7
2008 PROFILE			
Total people	**9.3**	**51.9**	**38.7**
Men	9.2	49.2	41.7
Women	9.5	54.4	36.2
Black	15.9	49.5	34.6
Hispanic	14.3	57.5	28.2
White	8.0	51.8	40.2
Aged 18 to 44	9.2	50.2	40.6
Aged 45 to 64	10.0	53.0	37.0
Aged 65 or older	8.3	54.5	37.2
Not a college graduate	10.2	52.6	37.2
Bachelor's degree or more	6.8	50.0	43.2

Source: Survey Documentation and Analysis, Computer-assisted Survey Methods Program, University of California, Berkeley, General Social Surveys, 1972-2008 Cumulative Data Files, Internet site http://sda.berkeley.edu/cgi-bin/hsda?harcsda+gss08; calculations by New Strategist

Most Think Their Taxes Are Too High

The majority of Americans think their taxes are too high, but the percentage of people who feel that way fell from 67 to 57 percent between 1998 and 2008. Despite the financial crisis of 2008, Americans are still split on whether taxes on the rich are too high. The 40 percent plurality of the public thinks taxes on the rich are still too high, while a smaller 36 percent says taxes on the rich are too low. There is more agreement on other tax issues. The 60 percent majority of Americans believes the affluent should pay a higher share of their income in taxes. Most also agree that differences in income are too large in the United States.

(percent of people aged 18 or older who say their federal income tax is too high, 1988 to 2008)

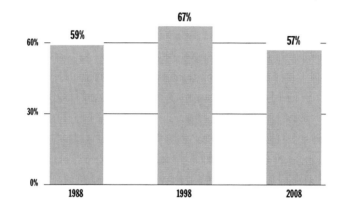

Table 1.14 Taxes Too High, 1988 to 2008

"Do you consider the amount of federal income tax which
you have to pay as too high, about right, or too low?"

(percent of taxpayers aged 18 or older responding, 1988 to 2008; and percent responding by demographic characteristic, 2008)

	too high	about right	too low
TREND			
2008	56.8%	41.8%	1.4%
1998	66.8	32.4	0.8
1988	58.9	40.0	1.2
2008 PROFILE			
Total people	**56.8**	**41.8**	**1.4**
Men	53.7	44.9	1.4
Women	59.6	39.1	1.4
Black	65.7	32.9	1.4
Hispanic	53.7	44.6	1.7
White	56.1	42.6	1.3
Aged 18 to 44	53.3	45.4	1.3
Aged 45 to 64	64.6	33.9	1.6
Aged 65 or older	48.9	50.1	1.0
Not a college graduate	58.8	40.1	1.1
Bachelor's degree or more	51.1	46.7	2.2

Source: Survey Documentation and Analysis, Computer-assisted Survey Methods Program, University of California, Berkeley, General Social Surveys, 1972–2008 Cumulative Data Files, Internet site http://sda.berkeley.edu/cgi-bin/hsda?harcsda+gss08; calculations by New Strategist

Table 1.15 Taxes on Rich, 2008

"Generally, how would you describe taxes in America today—we mean all taxes together, including Social Security, income tax, sales tax, and all the rest—for those with high incomes?"

(percent of people aged 18 or older responding by demographic characteristic, 2008)

	too high	about right	too low
Total people	**39.6%**	**24.4%**	**36.0%**
Men	37.8	26.7	35.5
Women	41.2	22.3	36.5
Black	51.0	21.5	27.5
Hispanic	41.7	25.4	32.9
White	37.1	24.4	38.5
Aged 18 to 44	41.4	28.2	30.4
Aged 45 to 64	39.3	18.0	42.7
Aged 65 or older	33.8	27.9	38.3
Not a college graduate	40.8	23.2	36.1
Bachelor's degree or more	36.2	27.8	35.9

Source: Survey Documentation and Analysis, Computer-assisted Survey Methods Program, University of California, Berkeley, General Social Survey, 2008 Cumulative Data Files, Internet site http://sda.berkeley.edu/cgi-bin/hsda?harcsda+gss08; calculations by New Strategist

Table 1.16 Rich Share of Taxes, 2008

"Do you think that people with high incomes should pay a larger share of their income in taxes than those with low incomes, the same share, or a smaller share?"

(percent of people aged 18 or older responding by demographic characteristic, 2008)

	larger	same	smaller
Total people	**60.2%**	**38.1%**	**1.6%**
Men	57.2	41.9	0.9
Women	63.1	34.7	2.3
Black	70.5	27.1	2.4
Hispanic	59.8	35.2	4.9
White	58.5	40.1	1.5
Aged 18 to 44	57.7	40.7	1.7
Aged 45 to 64	63.8	34.9	1.4
Aged 65 or older	60.1	37.7	2.2
Not a college graduate	59.5	39.0	1.5
Bachelor's degree or more	62.6	35.4	2.0

Source: Survey Documentation and Analysis, Computer-assisted Survey Methods Program, University of California, Berkeley, General Social Survey, 2008 Cumulative Data Files, Internet site http://sda.berkeley.edu/cgi-bin/hsda?harcsda+gss08; calculations by New Strategist

Table 1.17 Income Gap Too Big, 2008

"Do you agree or disagree: Differences in income in America are too large?"

(percent of people aged 18 or older responding by demographic characteristic, 2008)

	strongly agree	agree	neither	disagree	strongly disagree
Total people	**23.1%**	**39.1%**	**21.2%**	**13.2%**	**3.4%**
Men	22.5	37.2	20.4	14.6	5.2
Women	23.5	40.8	22.0	11.9	1.8
Black	27.3	38.2	15.3	13.9	5.3
Hispanic	25.7	44.3	23.2	6.4	0.3
White	22.7	39.4	21.6	12.8	3.5
Aged 18 to 44	22.5	39.6	23.3	11.4	3.3
Aged 45 to 64	22.6	39.0	19.8	16.6	2.1
Aged 65 or older	26.2	38.5	17.6	10.7	6.9
Not a college graduate	22.5	40.0	20.4	13.4	3.8
Bachelor's degree or more	24.6	36.8	23.6	12.6	2.3

Source: Survey Documentation and Analysis, Computer-assisted Survey Methods Program, University of California, Berkeley, General Social Survey, 2008 Cumulative Data Files, Internet site http://sda.berkeley.edu/cgi-bin/hsda?harcsda+gss08; calculations by New Strategist

Most Support the Death Penalty

Although the United States has more prisoners per capita than any other country in the world, fully 67 percent of Americans still think the courts in their area are not harsh enough on criminals. The figure is down from 90 percent in 1978, however. Sixty-eight percent of the public favors the death penalty for persons convicted of murder, the smallest proportion in the past 30 years.

(percent of people aged 18 or older who favor the death penalty for persons convicted of murder, 1978 to 2008)

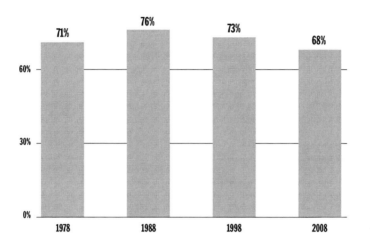

Table 1.18 Courts Deal Too Harshly with Criminals, 1978 to 2008

"In general, do you think the courts in this area deal too harshly
or not harshly enough with criminals?"

(percent of people aged 18 or older responding, 1978 to 2008; and percent responding by demographic characteristic, 2008)

	too harsh	not harsh enough	about right
TREND			
2008	11.9%	67.2%	20.8%
1998	6.5	79.9	13.7
1988	4.3	85.8	9.9
1978	2.8	90.2	7.0
2008 PROFILE			
Total people	**11.9**	**67.2**	**20.8**
Men	14.1	64.3	21.6
Women	10.0	69.9	20.2
Black	21.8	62.3	15.9
Hispanic	17.0	61.9	21.0
White	9.8	69.2	20.9
Aged 18 to 44	14.6	65.4	20.0
Aged 45 to 64	11.0	67.9	21.1
Aged 65 or older	6.1	70.3	23.6
Not a college graduate	12.0	70.4	17.6
Bachelor's degree or more	11.6	57.8	30.6

Source: Survey Documentation and Analysis, Computer-assisted Survey Methods Program, University of California, Berkeley, General Social Surveys, 1972–2008 Cumulative Data Files, Internet site http://sda.berkeley.edu/cgi-bin/hsda?harcsda+gss08; calculations by New Strategist

Table 1.19 Favor or Oppose Death Penalty for Murder, 1978 to 2008

"Do you favor or oppose the death penalty for persons convicted of murder?"

(percent of people aged 18 or older responding, 1978 to 2008; and percent responding by demographic characteristic, 2008)

	favor	oppose
TREND		
2008	67.6%	32.4%
1998	73.5	26.5
1988	76.3	23.7
1978	71.3	28.7
2008 PROFILE		
Total people	**67.6**	**32.4**
Men	71.5	28.5
Women	64.0	36.0
Black	46.0	54.0
Hispanic	56.3	43.7
White	72.5	27.5
Aged 18 to 44	66.8	33.2
Aged 45 to 64	68.3	31.7
Aged 65 or older	68.6	31.4
Not a college graduate	69.8	30.2
Bachelor's degree or more	61.1	38.9

Source: Survey Documentation and Analysis, Computer-assisted Survey Methods Program, University of California, Berkeley, General Social Surveys, 1972–2008 Cumulative Data Files, Internet site http://sda.berkeley.edu/cgi-bin/hsda?harcsda+gss08; calculations by New Strategist

The Public Believes Another World War Is Coming

Most Americans—even most women—feel safe in their neighborhood, but they do not feel as confident about their safety in the world. When asked whether they would be afraid to walk alone at night in the area around their house, 67 percent say no. But the 53 percent majority of the public believes the United States will become involved in a World War within 10 years. People aged 18 to 44 are much more likely than the oldest adults to feel this way.

(percent of people aged 18 or older who expect the United States to fight in another world war within 10 years, 1988 to 2008)

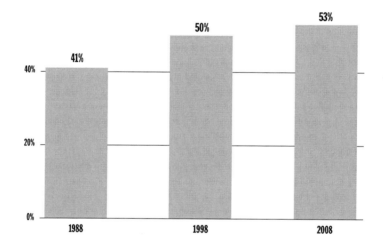

Table 1.20 Afraid to Walk in Neighborhood at Night, 1988 to 2008

"Is there any area right around here—that is, within a mile—
where you would be afraid to walk alone at night?"

*(percent of people aged 18 or older responding, 1988 to 2008; and percent responding by demographic charac-
teristic, 2008)*

	yes	no
TREND		
2008	32.7%	67.3%
1998	39.2	60.8
1988	38.0	62.0
2008 PROFILE		
Total people	**32.7**	**67.3**
Men	16.7	83.3
Women	46.4	53.6
Black	44.1	55.9
Hispanic	37.8	62.2
White	30.7	69.3
Aged 18 to 44	33.9	66.1
Aged 45 to 64	30.8	69.2
Aged 65 or older	33.5	66.5
Not a college graduate	33.4	66.6
Bachelor's degree or more	30.8	69.2

*Source: Survey Documentation and Analysis, Computer-assisted Survey Methods Program, University of California, Berkeley,
General Social Surveys, 1972–2008 Cumulative Data Files, Internet site http://sda.berkeley.edu/cgi-bin/hsda?harcsda+gss08;
calculations by New Strategist*

Table 1.21 Expect World War in 10 Years, 1988 to 2008

"Do you expect the United States to fight in another world war within the next 10 years?"

(percent of people aged 18 or older responding, 1988 to 2008; and percent responding by demographic characteristic, 2008)

	yes	no
TREND		
2008	52.7%	47.3%
1998	49.7	50.3
1988	40.7	59.3
2008 PROFILE		
Total people	**52.7**	**47.3**
Men	52.7	47.3
Women	52.6	47.4
Black	59.5	40.5
Hispanic	56.9	43.1
White	51.0	49.0
Aged 18 to 44	57.6	42.4
Aged 45 to 64	50.3	49.7
Aged 65 or older	43.6	56.4
Not a college graduate	57.3	42.7
Bachelor's degree or more	39.4	60.6

Source: Survey Documentation and Analysis, Computer-assisted Survey Methods Program, University of California, Berkeley, General Social Surveys, 1972–2008 Cumulative Data Files, Internet site http://sda.berkeley.edu/cgi-bin/hsda?harcsda+gss08; calculations by New Strategist

Americans Strongly Favor Gun Control

Nearly 80 percent of Americans think a police permit should be required before someone can buy a gun—a percentage that has not changed much over the decades. This level of support is surprising, considering how politically difficult it is to pass gun control laws. Only 36 percent of the public owned a gun in 2008, a figure that is down from 43 percent in 1988. Americans aged 65 or older are most likely to own a gun, with 54 percent owning at least one gun in 2008.

(percent of people aged 18 or older who favor a law that would require a police permit before a person could buy a gun, 1988 to 2008)

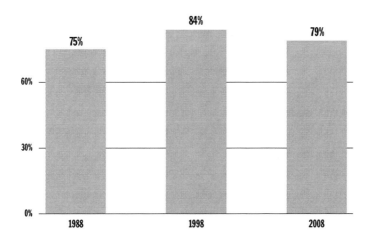

Table 1.22 Favor or Oppose Gun Permits, 1988 to 2008

"Would you favor or oppose a law which would require a person
to obtain a police permit before he or she could buy a gun?"

(percent of people aged 18 or older responding, 1988 to 2008; and percent responding by demographic characteristic, 2008)

	favor	oppose
TREND		
2008	79.1%	20.9%
1998	83.7	16.3
1988	75.4	24.6
2008 PROFILE		
Total people	**79.1**	**20.9**
Men	71.1	28.9
Women	85.9	14.1
Black	89.7	10.3
Hispanic	86.1	13.9
White	76.7	23.3
Aged 18 to 44	80.2	19.8
Aged 45 to 64	77.5	22.5
Aged 65 or older	78.9	21.1
Not a college graduate	77.6	22.4
Bachelor's degree or more	83.6	16.4

Source: Survey Documentation and Analysis, Computer-assisted Survey Methods Program, University of California, Berkeley, General Social Surveys, 1972–2008 Cumulative Data Files, Internet site http://sda.berkeley.edu/cgi-bin/hsda?harcsda+gss08; calculations by New Strategist

Table 1.23 Have Gun in Home, 1988 to 2008

"Do you happen to have in your home (or garage) any guns or revolvers?"

(percent of people aged 18 or older responding, 1988 to 2008; and percent responding by demographic characteristic, 2008)

	yes	no	refused
TREND			
2008	36.0%	63.0%	1.1%
1998	36.7	63.0	0.4
1988	43.4	55.8	0.9
2008 PROFILE			
Total people	**36.0**	**63.0**	**1.1**
Men	30.3	68.8	0.9
Women	42.7	56.1	1.3
Black	19.4	79.9	0.7
Hispanic	10.5	89.5	0.0
White	43.1	55.6	1.3
Aged 18 to 44	25.5	73.5	1.0
Aged 45 to 64	41.7	57.0	1.3
Aged 65 or older	54.0	45.2	0.8
Not a college graduate	38.3	60.6	1.1
Bachelor's degree or more	29.5	69.6	0.9

Source: Survey Documentation and Analysis, Computer-assisted Survey Methods Program, University of California, Berkeley, General Social Surveys, 1972–2008 Cumulative Data Files, Internet site http://sda.berkeley.edu/cgi-bin/hsda?harcsda+gss08; calculations by New Strategist

Table 1.24 Does Respondent or Spouse Hunt, 1988 to 2008

"Do you (or does your [husband/wife]) go hunting?"

(percent of people aged 18 or older responding, 1988 to 2008; and percent responding by demographic characteristic, 2008)

	respondent	spouse	both	neither
TREND				
2008	11.3%	4.8%	1.6%	82.3%
1998	11.5	6.0	1.8	80.7
1988	13.1	7.1	2.1	77.8
2008 PROFILE				
Total people	**11.3**	**4.8**	**1.6**	**82.3**
Men	21.9	0.3	1.2	76.6
Women	2.2	8.7	1.9	87.2
Black	5.6	2.3	0.0	92.0
Hispanic	2.3	2.5	0.0	95.2
White	13.5	5.9	2.0	78.6
Aged 18 to 44	11.0	4.3	1.4	83.3
Aged 45 to 64	12.4	5.2	2.6	79.8
Aged 65 or older	9.7	5.5	0.0	84.8
Not a college graduate	12.6	4.4	1.7	81.3
Bachelor's degree or more	7.4	5.9	1.2	85.4

Source: Survey Documentation and Analysis, Computer-assisted Survey Methods Program, University of California, Berkeley, General Social Surveys, 1972–2008 Cumulative Data Files, Internet site http://sda.berkeley.edu/cgi-bin/hsda?harcsda+gss08; calculations by New Strategist

More Support Legalizing Marijuana

The percentage of people who favor legalizing the use of marijuana is growing. Thirty-eight percent of the public supported legalizing marijuana in 2008, up from just 17 percent in 1988. Young and middle-aged adults are far more likely to favor the legalization of marijuana (41 percent) than those aged 65 or older (24 percent). As younger generations replace older Americans, the pressure for legalization is likely to grow.

(percent of people aged 18 or older who think marijuana should be legalized, 1978 to 2008)

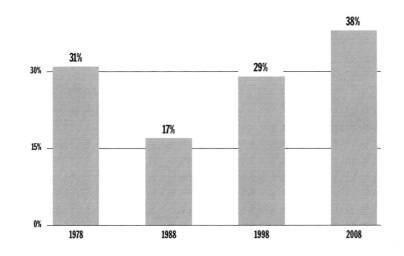

Table 1.25 Should Marijuana Be Made Legal, 1978 to 2008

"Do you think the use of marijuana should be made legal or not?"

(percent of people aged 18 or older responding, 1978 to 2008; and percent responding by demographic characteristic, 2008)

	legal	not legal
TREND		
2008	38.3%	61.7%
1998	29.1	70.9
1988	17.5	82.5
1978	31.3	68.7
2008 PROFILE		
Total people	**38.3**	**61.7**
Men	42.0	58.0
Women	35.0	65.0
Black	35.8	64.2
Hispanic	24.7	75.3
White	39.8	60.2
Aged 18 to 44	40.5	59.5
Aged 45 to 64	40.7	59.3
Aged 65 or older	24.1	75.9
Not a college graduate	36.8	63.2
Bachelor's degree or more	42.5	57.5

Source: Survey Documentation and Analysis, Computer-assisted Survey Methods Program, University of California, Berkeley, General Social Surveys, 1972–2008 Cumulative Data Files, Internet site http://sda.berkeley.edu/cgi-bin/hsda?harcsda+gss08; calculations by New Strategist

Physician-Assisted Suicide Is OK with Most Americans

Two of three Americans support physician-assisted suicide for the terminally ill. The majority of the public has favored physician-assisted suicide for decades. There is little difference in support by sex, age, or education. Blacks are least likely to support physician-assisted suicide, with half in favor and half opposed.

(percent of people aged 18 or older who think a doctor should be allowed to end the life of a patient with an incurable disease, 1978 to 2008)

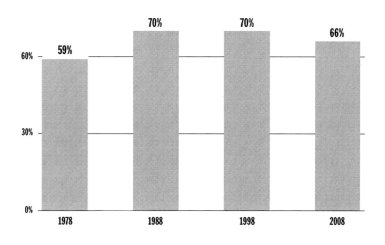

Table 1.26 Allow Patients with Incurable Disease to Die, 1978 to 2008

"When a person has a disease that cannot be cured, do you think doctors should be allowed by law to end the patient's life by some painless means if the patient and his family request it?"

(percent of people aged 18 or older responding, 1978 to 2008; and percent responding by demographic characteristic, 2008)

	yes	no
TREND		
2008	66.2%	33.8%
1998	70.7	29.3
1988	70.2	29.8
1978	59.3	40.7
2008 PROFILE		
Total people	**66.2**	**33.8**
Men	68.2	31.8
Women	64.4	35.6
Black	50.1	49.9
Hispanic	48.0	52.0
White	68.7	31.3
Aged 18 to 44	65.0	35.0
Aged 45 to 64	68.6	31.4
Aged 65 or older	63.4	36.6
Not a college graduate	66.6	33.4
Bachelor's degree or more	64.9	35.1

Source: Survey Documentation and Analysis, Computer-assisted Survey Methods Program, University of California, Berkeley, General Social Surveys, 1972–2008 Cumulative Data Files, Internet site http://sda.berkeley.edu/cgi-bin/hsda?harcsda+gss08; calculations by New Strategist

Most Would Permit a Racist to Give a Speech

The majority of the public thinks diverse viewpoints definitely or probably should be heard at public meetings, published in books, and included in public libraries. Most Americans would even allow people with diverse viewpoints to teach at a university. When asked whether revolutionaries, anti-religionists, racists, communists, militarists, or homosexuals should be allowed to speak, teach, or have their book published or included in a public library, most say yes. The only exception is allowing a racist to teach at a university. Fifty-four percent of the public says this should not be allowed.

(percent who say a racist should be permitted to express his views in selected ways, 2008)

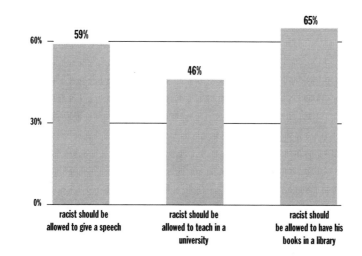

Table 1.27 Allow Anti-Religionist to Teach, 1988 to 2008

"There are always some people whose ideas are considered bad or dangerous by other people. For instance, somebody who is against churches and religion, should such a person be allowed to teach in a college or university, or not?"

(percent of people aged 18 or older responding, 1988 to 2008; and percent responding by demographic characteristic, 2008)

	allow	not allow
TREND		
2008	62.1%	37.9%
1998	60.9	39.1
1988	47.6	52.4
2008 PROFILE		
Total people	**62.1**	**37.9**
Men	61.1	38.9
Women	62.9	37.1
Black	54.5	45.5
Hispanic	52.1	47.9
White	63.9	36.1
Aged 18 to 44	65.6	34.4
Aged 45 to 64	64.2	35.8
Aged 65 or older	45.9	54.1
Not a college graduate	56.3	43.7
Bachelor's degree or more	78.4	21.6

Source: Survey Documentation and Analysis, Computer-assisted Survey Methods Program, University of California, Berkeley, General Social Surveys, 1972–2008 Cumulative Data Files, Internet site http://sda.berkeley.edu/cgi-bin/hsda?harcsda+gss08; calculations by New Strategist

Table 1.28 Allow Antireligious Book in Library, 1988 to 2008

"There are always some people whose ideas are considered bad or dangerous by other people. For instance, somebody who is against churches and religion: If some people in your community suggested a book he wrote against churches and religion should be taken out of your public library, would you favor removing this book or not?"

(percent of people aged 18 or older responding, 1988 to 2008; and percent responding by demographic characteristic, 2008)

	remove	not remove
TREND		
2008	27.1%	72.9%
1998	27.9	72.1
1988	34.6	65.4
2008 PROFILE		
Total people	**27.1**	**72.9**
Men	25.9	74.1
Women	28.1	71.9
Black	36.8	63.2
Hispanic	38.4	61.6
White	24.7	75.3
Aged 18 to 44	27.9	72.1
Aged 45 to 64	23.1	76.9
Aged 65 or older	33.8	66.2
Not a college graduate	32.3	67.7
Bachelor's degree or more	12.4	87.6

Source: Survey Documentation and Analysis, Computer-assisted Survey Methods Program, University of California, Berkeley, General Social Surveys, 1972–2008 Cumulative Data Files, Internet site http://sda.berkeley.edu/cgi-bin/hsda?harcsda+gss08; calculations by New Strategist

Table 1.29 Allow Racist to Speak, 1988 to 2008

"Consider a person who believes that blacks are genetically inferior.
If such a person wanted to make a speech in your community claiming that
blacks are inferior, should he be allowed to speak, or not?"

(percent of people aged 18 or older responding, 1988 to 2008; and percent responding by demographic charac-teristic, 2008)

	allow	not allow
TREND		
2008	59.4%	40.6%
1998	63.7	36.3
1988	63.1	37.9
2008 PROFILE		
Total people	**59.4**	**40.6**
Men	66.3	33.7
Women	53.5	46.5
Black	60.1	39.9
Hispanic	43.8	56.2
White	60.9	39.1
Aged 18 to 44	58.2	41.8
Aged 45 to 64	64.4	35.6
Aged 65 or older	51.9	48.1
Not a college graduate	55.2	44.8
Bachelor's degree or more	71.4	28.6

Source: Survey Documentation and Analysis, Computer-assisted Survey Methods Program, University of California, Berkeley, General Social Surveys, 1972–2008 Cumulative Data Files, Internet site http://sda.berkeley.edu/cgi-bin/hsda?harcsda+gss08; calculations by New Strategist

Table 1.30 Allow Racist to Teach, 1988 to 2008

"Consider a person who believes that blacks are genetically inferior. Should such a person be allowed to teach in a college or university or not?"

(percent of people aged 18 or older responding, 1988 to 2008; and percent responding by demographic characteristic, 2008)

	allow	not allow
TREND		
2008	46.3%	53.7%
1998	47.8	52.2
1988	42.3	57.7
2008 PROFILE		
Total people	**46.3**	**53.7**
Men	49.4	50.6
Women	43.6	56.4
Black	45.6	54.4
Hispanic	40.8	59.2
White	47.2	52.8
Aged 18 to 44	45.0	55.0
Aged 45 to 64	52.7	47.3
Aged 65 or older	35.0	65.0
Not a college graduate	43.3	56.7
Bachelor's degree or more	54.5	45.5

Source: Survey Documentation and Analysis, Computer-assisted Survey Methods Program, University of California, Berkeley, General Social Surveys, 1972–2008 Cumulative Data Files, Internet site http://sda.berkeley.edu/cgi-bin/hsda?harcsda+gss08; calculations by New Strategist

Table 1.31 Allow Racist's Book in Library, 1988 to 2008

"Consider a person who believes that blacks are genetically inferior. If some people in your community suggested that a book he wrote which said blacks are inferior should be taken out of your public library, would you favor removing this book or not?"

(percent of people aged 18 or older responding, 1988 to 2008; and percent responding by demographic characteristic, 2008)

	remove	not remove
TREND		
2008	34.9%	65.1%
1998	34.6	65.4
1988	36.9	63.1
2008 PROFILE		
Total people	**34.9**	**65.1**
Men	32.9	67.1
Women	36.7	63.3
Black	44.0	56.0
Hispanic	43.9	56.1
White	32.3	67.7
Aged 18 to 44	37.2	62.8
Aged 45 to 64	27.4	70.6
Aged 65 or older	40.7	59.3
Not a college graduate	39.3	60.7
Bachelor's degree or more	22.7	77.3

Source: Survey Documentation and Analysis, Computer-assisted Survey Methods Program, University of California, Berkeley, General Social Surveys, 1972–2008 Cumulative Data Files, Internet site http://sda.berkeley.edu/cgi-bin/hsda?harcsda+gss08; calculations by New Strategist

Table 1.32 Allow Communist to Speak, 1988 to 2008

"Suppose an admitted communist wanted to make a speech in your community.
Should he be allowed to speak, or not?"

(percent of people aged 18 or older responding, 1988 to 2008; and percent responding by demographic characteristic, 2008)

	allow	not allow
TREND		
2008	67.4%	32.6%
1998	68.1	31.9
1988	62.8	37.2
2008 PROFILE		
Total people	**67.4**	**32.6**
Men	71.9	28.1
Women	63.6	36.4
Black	61.3	38.7
Hispanic	57.5	42.5
White	68.7	31.3
Aged 18 to 44	68.6	31.4
Aged 45 to 64	70.2	29.8
Aged 65 or older	58.1	41.9
Not a college graduate	61.2	38.8
Bachelor's degree or more	85.2	14.8

Source: Survey Documentation and Analysis, Computer-assisted Survey Methods Program, University of California, Berkeley, General Social Surveys, 1972–2008 Cumulative Data Files, Internet site http://sda.berkeley.edu/cgi-bin/hsda?harcsda+gss08; calculations by New Strategist

Table 1.33 Should Communist Teacher Be Fired, 1988 to 2008

"What about a man who admits he is a communist.
Suppose he is teaching in a college. Should he be fired, or not?"

(percent of people aged 18 or older responding, 1988 to 2008; and percent responding by demographic characteristic, 2008)

	fired	not fired
TREND		
2008	38.8%	61.2%
1998	38.8	61.2
1988	48.7	51.3
2008 PROFILE		
Total people	**38.8**	**61.2**
Men	36.8	63.2
Women	40.5	59.5
Black	40.6	59.4
Hispanic	43.7	56.3
White	38.6	61.4
Aged 18 to 44	36.9	63.1
Aged 45 to 64	36.9	63.1
Aged 65 or older	48.6	51.4
Not a college graduate	44.3	55.7
Bachelor's degree or more	23.5	76.5

Source: Survey Documentation and Analysis, Computer-assisted Survey Methods Program, University of California, Berkeley, General Social Surveys, 1972–2008 Cumulative Data Files, Internet site http://sda.berkeley.edu/cgi-bin/hsda?harcsda+gss08; calculations by New Strategist

Table 1.34 Allow Communist's Book in Library, 1988 to 2008

"Suppose a man who admits he is a communist wrote a book which is in your public library. Somebody in your community suggests that the book should be removed from the library. Would you favor removing it, or not?"

(percent of people aged 18 or older responding, 1988 to 2008; and percent responding by demographic characteristic, 2008)

	remove	not remove
TREND		
2008	30.3%	69.7%
1998	30.0	70.0
1988	38.0	62.0
2008 PROFILE		
Total people	**30.3**	**69.7**
Men	28.6	71.4
Women	31.7	68.3
Black	39.9	60.1
Hispanic	40.0	60.0
White	29.1	70.9
Aged 18 to 44	28.5	71.5
Aged 45 to 64	28.1	71.9
Aged 65 or older	40.0	60.0
Not a college graduate	36.1	63.9
Bachelor's degree or more	13.8	86.2

Source: Survey Documentation and Analysis, Computer-assisted Survey Methods Program, University of California, Berkeley, General Social Surveys, 1972–2008 Cumulative Data Files, Internet site http://sda.berkeley.edu/cgi-bin/hsda?harcsda+gss08; calculations by New Strategist

Table 1.35 Allow Militarist to Speak, 1988 to 2008

"Consider a person who advocates doing away with elections and letting
the military run the country. If such a person wanted to make a speech
in your community, should he be allowed to speak, or not?"

(percent of people aged 18 or older responding, 1988 to 2008; and percent responding by demographic characteristic, 2008)

	allow	not allow
TREND		
2008	66.7%	33.3%
1998	68.1	31.9
1988	58.8	41.2
2008 PROFILE		
Total people	**66.7**	**33.3**
Men	67.8	32.2
Women	65.7	34.3
Black	57.2	42.8
Hispanic	59.2	40.8
White	69.8	30.2
Aged 18 to 44	70.3	29.7
Aged 45 to 64	70.6	29.4
Aged 65 or older	47.4	52.6
Not a college graduate	62.2	37.8
Bachelor's degree or more	79.6	20.4

Source: Survey Documentation and Analysis, Computer-assisted Survey Methods Program, University of California, Berkeley, General Social Surveys, 1972–2008 Cumulative Data Files, Internet site http://sda.berkeley.edu/cgi-bin/hsda?harcsda+gss08; calculations by New Strategist

Table 1.36 Allow Militarist to Teach, 1988 to 2008

"Consider a person who advocates doing away with elections and letting the military run the country. Should such a person be allowed to teach in a college or university, or not?"

(percent of people aged 18 or older responding, 1988 to 2008; and percent responding by demographic characteristic, 2008)

	allow	not allow
TREND		
2008	52.6%	47.4%
1998	53.8	46.2
1988	39.2	60.8
2008 PROFILE		
Total people	**52.6**	**47.4**
Men	53.0	47.0
Women	52.3	47.7
Black	46.4	53.6
Hispanic	44.4	55.6
White	54.0	46.0
Aged 18 to 44	58.4	41.6
Aged 45 to 64	54.9	45.1
Aged 65 or older	30.7	69.3
Not a college graduate	48.4	51.6
Bachelor's degree or more	64.8	35.2

Source: Survey Documentation and Analysis, Computer-assisted Survey Methods Program, University of California, Berkeley, General Social Surveys, 1972–2008 Cumulative Data Files, Internet site http://sda.berkeley.edu/cgi-bin/hsda?harcsda+gss08; calculations by New Strategist

Table 1.37 Allow Militarist's Book in Library, 1988 to 2008

"Consider a person who advocates doing away with elections and letting the military run the country. Suppose he wrote a book advocating doing away with elections and letting the military run the country. Somebody in your community suggests that the book should be removed from the library. Would you favor removing it, or not?"

(percent of people aged 18 or older responding, 1988 to 2008; and percent responding by demographic characteristic, 2008)

	remove	not remove
TREND		
2008	28.7%	71.3%
1998	30.0	70.0
1988	41.4	58.6
2008 PROFILE		
Total people	**28.7**	**71.3**
Men	29.1	70.9
Women	28.3	71.7
Black	41.0	59.0
Hispanic	35.9	64.1
White	26.5	73.5
Aged 18 to 44	27.4	72.6
Aged 45 to 64	24.7	75.3
Aged 65 or older	41.0	59.0
Not a college graduate	33.4	66.6
Bachelor's degree or more	15.3	84.7

Source: Survey Documentation and Analysis, Computer-assisted Survey Methods Program, University of California, Berkeley, General Social Surveys, 1972–2008 Cumulative Data Files, Internet site http://sda.berkeley.edu/cgi-bin/hsda?harcsda+gss08; calculations by New Strategist

Table 1.38 Allow Homosexual to Speak, 1988 to 2008

"What about a man who admits that he is a homosexual? Suppose this admitted
homosexual wanted to make a speech in your community.
Should he be allowed to speak, or not?"

*(percent of people aged 18 or older responding, 1988 to 2008; and percent responding by demographic charac-
teristic, 2008)*

	allow	not allow
TREND		
2008	83.1%	16.9%
1998	83.7	16.3
1988	72.7	27.3
2008 PROFILE		
Total people	**83.1**	**16.9**
Men	84.9	15.1
Women	81.6	18.4
Black	78.7	21.3
Hispanic	81.8	18.2
White	84.1	15.9
Aged 18 to 44	85.9	14.1
Aged 45 to 64	85.1	14.9
Aged 65 or older	70.1	29.9
Not a college graduate	79.6	20.4
Bachelor's degree or more	93.1	6.9

*Source: Survey Documentation and Analysis, Computer-assisted Survey Methods Program, University of California, Berkeley,
General Social Surveys, 1972–2008 Cumulative Data Files, Internet site http://sda.berkeley.edu/cgi-bin/hsda?harcsda+gss08;
calculations by New Strategist*

Table 1.39 Allow Homosexual to Teach, 1988 to 2008

"And what about a man who admits that he is a homosexual? Should such
a person be allowed to teach in a college or university, or not?"

(percent of people aged 18 or older responding, 1988 to 2008; and percent responding by demographic characteristic, 2008)

	allow	not allow
TREND		
2008	80.5%	19.5%
1998	77.7	22.3
1988	59.5	40.5
2008 PROFILE		
Total people	**80.5**	**19.5**
Men	79.5	20.5
Women	81.3	18.7
Black	79.0	21.0
Hispanic	75.8	24.2
White	81.0	19.0
Aged 18 to 44	83.0	17.0
Aged 45 to 64	83.7	16.3
Aged 65 or older	65.6	34.4
Not a college graduate	75.8	24.2
Bachelor's degree or more	93.8	6.2

Source: Survey Documentation and Analysis, Computer-assisted Survey Methods Program, University of California, Berkeley, General Social Surveys, 1972–2008 Cumulative Data Files, Internet site http://sda.berkeley.edu/cgi-bin/hsda?harcsda+gss08; calculations by New Strategist

Table 1.40 Allow Homosexual's Book in Library, 1988 to 2008

"What about a man who admits that he is a homosexual? If some people in your community suggested that a book he wrote in favor of homosexuality should be taken out of your public library, would you favor removing this book, or not?"

(percent of people aged 18 or older responding, 1988 to 2008; and percent responding by demographic characteristic, 2008)

	remove	not remove
TREND		
2008	22.7%	77.3%
1998	26.4	73.6
1988	37.0	63.0
2008 PROFILE		
Total people	**22.7**	**77.3**
Men	21.2	78.8
Women	23.9	76.1
Black	31.7	68.3
Hispanic	22.1	77.9
White	21.8	78.2
Aged 18 to 44	18.9	81.1
Aged 45 to 64	22.4	77.6
Aged 65 or older	35.0	65.0
Not a college graduate	26.5	73.5
Bachelor's degree or more	11.7	88.3

Source: Survey Documentation and Analysis, Computer-assisted Survey Methods Program, University of California, Berkeley, General Social Surveys, 1972–2008 Cumulative Data Files, Internet site http://sda.berkeley.edu/cgi-bin/hsda?harcsda+gss08; calculations by New Strategist

2

Government and Politics

The media talk about the growing partisan divide among Americans, but the General Social Survey finds Americans more alike than different. Our shared beliefs about government and politics have remained strikingly stable over the past few decades, despite the rancor of talk radio and the 24-hour news cycle. A few things have changed, however. Here's a synopsis of how attitudes regarding government and politics have changed or remained the same over the past few decades.

Little or no change

• **Political leanings have barely budged.** The lack of change in political perspectives is stunning considering the partisan bickering that has been center stage for the past decade. In 2008, 26 percent of Americans considered themselves liberal and 36 percent said they were conservative. In 1978 the figures were 27 and 33 percent, respectively.

• **Political affiliation is about the same.** As is true with political leanings, political party identification has barely moved over the decade. In 2008, 48 percent of Americans considered themselves Democrats and 34 percent said they were Republicans. In 1978 the figures were 51 and 33 percent, respectively.

Big changes

• **Americans want the government to help with health care.** The percentage of Americans who think it is the federal government's responsibility to help people pay for medical care has grown to encompass the 54 percent majority of Americans. Only 16 percent say people should fend for themselves. Interestingly, people aged 65 or older—who are covered by the government's Medicare program—are least likely to think the government should help out.

• **Americans want more spent on health care.** The percentage of the public that thinks the nation spends too little on protecting and improving the nation's health has grown from 57 percent in 1978 to 77 percent in 2008.

Moderates Outnumber Liberals or Conservatives

In a seeming contradiction, conservatives outnumber liberals in the United States, yet Democrats outnumber Republicans by a wide margin. When asked whether they are conservative or liberal, 26 percent of Americans say liberal and 36 percent say conservative—figures that have barely changed over the past three decades. But 48 percent of the public aligns with the Democratic Party and 34 percent with the Republican—again, numbers that have not changed much in decades.

(percent distribution of people aged 18 or older by political leaning and affiliation, 2008)

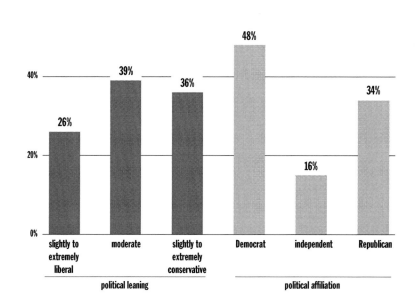

Table 2.1 Political Leanings, 1978 to 2008

"We hear a lot of talk these days about liberals and conservatives.
On a seven-point scale from extremely liberal (1) to
extremely conservative (7), where would you place yourself?"

(percent of people aged 18 or older responding, 1978 to 2008; and percent responding by demographic characteristic, 2008)

	1 extremely liberal	2 liberal	3 slightly liberal	4 moderate	5 slightly conservative	6 conservative	7 extremely conservative
TREND							
2008	2.9%	12.2%	10.6%	38.6%	15.1%	16.7%	3.9%
1998	2.4	12.2	12.7	37.7	15.9	15.7	3.4
1988	2.3	12.2	12.9	35.9	17.6	16.6	2.5
1978	1.4	10.4	15.5	40.0	18.9	11.5	2.2
2008 PROFILE							
Total people	**2.9**	**12.2**	**10.6**	**38.6**	**15.1**	**16.7**	**3.9**
Men	3.2	11.1	10.3	38.7	15.0	17.4	4.4
Women	2.6	13.3	10.8	38.5	15.2	16.2	3.4
Black	4.6	11.8	16.5	46.3	8.0	7.2	5.7
Hispanic	5.2	16.4	11.5	43.8	11.8	9.6	1.8
White	2.5	11.2	9.5	37.3	16.9	18.8	3.7
Aged 18 to 44	3.3	14.8	13.2	38.7	14.3	12.3	3.5
Aged 45 to 64	2.0	10.5	9.9	38.4	16.3	18.6	4.3
Aged 65 or older	3.6	8.7	4.6	37.8	15.4	25.8	4.1
Not a college graduate	2.5	10.6	9.5	42.1	14.6	16.5	4.1
Bachelor's degree or more	3.9	16.6	13.5	28.8	16.6	17.4	3.2

Source: Survey Documentation and Analysis, Computer-assisted Survey Methods Program, University of California, Berkeley, General Social Surveys, 1972–2008 Cumulative Data Files, Internet site http://sda.berkeley.edu/cgi-bin/hsda?harcsda+gss08; calculations by New Strategist

Table 2.2 Political Party Affiliation, 1978 to 2008

"Generally speaking, do you usually think of yourself as
a Republican, Democrat, Independent, or what?"

(percent of people aged 18 or older responding, 1978 to 2008; and percent responding by demographic characteristic, 2008)

	strong Democrat	not strong Democrat	independent, near Democrat	independent	independent, near Republican	not strong Republican	strong Republican	other party
TREND								
2008	18.9%	17.1%	12.1%	15.7%	8.1%	15.7%	10.5%	1.8%
1998	12.4	20.6	12.3	17.4	8.9	17.4	8.6	2.3
1988	15.2	21.3	12.1	12.6	9.5	18.7	10.2	0.2
1978	13.3	25.1	12.8	14.9	9.7	16.5	7.1	0.6
2008 PROFILE								
Total people	**18.9**	**17.1**	**12.1**	**15.7**	**8.1**	**15.7**	**10.5**	**1.8**
Men	16.6	17.3	12.6	14.7	10.6	15.2	10.3	2.7
Women	20.9	16.9	11.7	16.7	5.9	16.2	10.6	1.0
Black	47.5	26.1	10.1	10.1	2.4	0.5	2.5	0.8
Hispanic	17.3	27.9	13.5	22.8	7.1	9.3	1.8	0.3
White	14.6	14.5	11.8	15.8	9.4	19.2	12.5	2.2
Aged 18 to 44	17.1	19.1	12.9	18.1	6.9	15.9	7.6	2.3
Aged 45 to 64	18.4	16.8	11.1	15.0	9.7	16.3	11.5	1.3
Aged 65 or older	25.1	11.8	12.5	10.2	8.3	13.9	17.3	0.8
Not a college graduate	18.1	18.2	12.1	17.6	8.2	14.7	9.7	1.4
Bachelor's degree or more	21.0	14.0	12.4	10.3	8.0	18.9	12.7	2.8

Source: Survey Documentation and Analysis, Computer-assisted Survey Methods Program, University of California, Berkeley, General Social Surveys, 1972–2008 Cumulative Data Files, Internet site http://sda.berkeley.edu/cgi-bin/hsda?harcsda+gss08; calculations by New Strategist

Most Would Vote for a Woman for President

The election of Barack Obama proved that Americans are willing to vote for a black for president. Only 6 percent said they would not vote for a black person for president in 2008. The same proportion said they would not vote for a woman either. Both figures are down from the 14 to 18 percent who were resistant in 1978. A larger 26 percent of the public still thinks, however, that men are emotionally better suited than women for politics.

(percentage of people aged 18 or older who think most men are better suited emotionally for politics than women, 1978 to 2008)

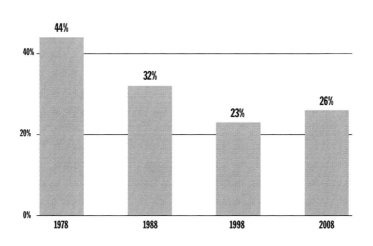

Table 2.3 Men Better Suited for Politics, 1978 to 2008

"Tell me if you agree or disagree with this statement: Most men are better suited emotionally for politics than are most women."

(percent of people aged 18 or older responding, 1978 to 2008; and percent responding by demographic characteristic, 2008)

	agree	disagree
TREND		
2008	25.9%	74.1%
1998	23.3	76.7
1988	32.4	67.6
1978	44.4	55.6
2008 PROFILE		
Total people	**25.9**	**74.1**
Men	27.3	72.7
Women	24.7	75.3
Black	24.1	75.9
Hispanic	29.8	70.2
White	24.8	75.2
Aged 18 to 44	25.7	74.3
Aged 45 to 64	22.9	77.1
Aged 65 or older	34.5	65.6
Not a college graduate	27.4	72.6
Bachelor's degree or more	21.6	78.4

Source: Survey Documentation and Analysis, Computer-assisted Survey Methods Program, University of California, Berkeley, General Social Surveys, 1972–2008 Cumulative Data Files, Internet site http://sda.berkeley.edu/cgi-bin/hsda?harcsda+gss08; calculations by New Strategist

Table 2.4 Vote for a Woman for President, 1978 to 2008

"If your party nominated a woman for President, would
you vote for her if she were qualified for the job?"

(percent of people aged 18 or older responding, 1978 to 2008; and percent responding by demographic charac-
teristic, 2008)

	yes	no
TREND		
2008	94.0%	6.0%
1998	93.7	6.3
1988	88.4	11.6
1978	82.2	17.8
2008 PROFILE		
Total people	**94.0**	**6.0**
Men	93.8	6.2
Women	94.1	5.9
Black	94.4	5.6
Hispanic	95.9	4.1
White	94.0	6.0
Aged 18 to 44	92.4	7.6
Aged 45 to 64	96.3	3.7
Aged 65 or older	93.4	6.6
Not a college graduate	92.9	7.1
Bachelor's degree or more	97.0	3.1

Source: Survey Documentation and Analysis, Computer-assisted Survey Methods Program, University of California, Berkeley,
General Social Surveys, 1972–2008 Cumulative Data Files, Internet site http://sda.berkeley.edu/cgi-bin/hsda?harcsda+gss08;
calculations by New Strategist

Table 2.5 Vote for a Black for President, 1978 to 2008

"If your party nominated a black/African American for President,
would you vote for him if he were qualified for the job?"

(percent of people aged 18 or older responding, 1978 to 2008; and percent responding by demographic characteristic, 2008)

	yes	no
TREND		
2008	94.5%	5.5%
1988	83.1	16.9
1978	85.9	14.1
2008 PROFILE		
Total people	**94.5**	**5.5**
Men	93.2	6.8
Women	95.7	4.3
Black	98.4	1.6
Hispanic	95.0	5.0
White	94.2	5.8
Aged 18 to 44	94.6	5.4
Aged 45 to 64	95.2	4.8
Aged 65 or older	92.1	7.9
Not a college graduate	92.8	7.2
Bachelor's degree or more	99.1	0.9

Note: The question was not asked in 1998.
Source: Survey Documentation and Analysis, Computer-assisted Survey Methods Program, University of California, Berkeley, General Social Surveys, 1972–2008 Cumulative Data Files, Internet site http://sda.berkeley.edu/cgi-bin/hsda?harcsda+gss08; calculations by New Strategist

Americans Can't Make Up Their Minds about Government

No wonder the country's politicians can't seem to get anything done. The citizens they represent are themselves torn about the role of government. When asked whether the federal government should do more or does too much, the public is almost evenly split. Thirty-one percent say it should do more and 28 percent say it does too much, while the other 41 percent say they feel both ways about it. On the issue of health care, however, the 54 percent majority now says the government needs to help.

(percent distribution of people aged 18 or older by whether they think the federal government is responsible for helping people pay for doctor and hospital bills, 2008)

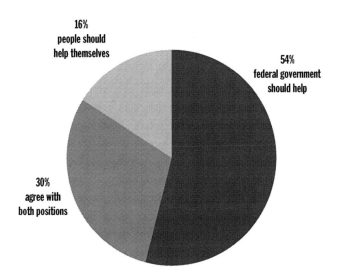

16%
people should
help themselves

54%
federal government
should help

30%
agree with
both positions

Table 2.6 Should Government Do More, 1988 to 2008

"Some people think that the government in Washington is trying to do too many things that should be left to individuals and private business; they are at point 5. Others disagree and think the government should do even more to solve our country's problems; they are at point 1. Where would you place yourself on the scale?"

(percent of people aged 18 or older responding, 1988 to 2008; and percent responding by demographic characteristic, 2008)

	1 government should do more	2	3 agree with both	4	5 government does too much
TREND					
2008	16.7%	14.5%	40.9%	13.1%	14.8%
1998	11.1	12.5	41.7	19.5	15.2
1988	14.0	14.8	42.1	15.7	13.3
2008 PROFILE					
Total people	**16.7**	**14.5**	**40.9**	**13.1**	**14.8**
Men	16.4	13.4	37.6	12.6	19.9
Women	16.9	15.4	43.9	13.5	10.3
Black	37.4	20.0	33.8	3.8	5.0
Hispanic	26.8	15.3	39.0	7.6	11.2
White	11.5	13.7	42.4	15.1	17.2
Aged 18 to 44	16.3	18.4	41.2	13.5	10.6
Aged 45 to 64	17.7	12.1	39.7	12.9	17.5
Aged 65 or older	16.1	6.9	42.4	12.0	22.6
Not a college graduate	19.0	13.8	41.1	10.7	15.5
Bachelor's degree or more	10.7	16.3	40.4	19.4	13.1

Source: Survey Documentation and Analysis, Computer-assisted Survey Methods Program, University of California, Berkeley, General Social Surveys, 1972–2008 Cumulative Data Files, Internet site http://sda.berkeley.edu/cgi-bin/hsda?harcsda+gss08; calculations by New Strategist

Table 2.7 Government Should Help Pay for Medical Care, 1988 and 2008

"In general, some people think that it is the responsibility of the government in Washington to see to it that people have help in paying for doctors and hospital bills; they are at point 1. Others think that these matters are not the responsibility of the federal government and that people should take care of these things themselves; they are at point 5. Where would you place yourself on the scale?"

(percent of people aged 18 or older responding, 1988 to 2008; and percent responding by demographic characteristic, 2008)

	1 government should help	2	3 agree with both	4	5 people should help themselves
TREND					
2008	34.9%	18.7%	30.0%	9.3%	7.1%
1998	25.5	23.3	32.9	10.1	8.3
1988	26.3	21.5	37.0	8.7	6.6
2008 PROFILE					
Total people	**34.9**	**18.7**	**30.0**	**9.3**	**7.1**
Men	33.6	19.2	27.9	11.0	8.4
Women	36.2	18.2	31.9	7.7	6.0
Black	54.2	18.1	23.8	1.0	2.8
Hispanic	41.6	15.7	32.1	3.5	7.0
White	31.5	18.5	31.3	11.3	7.4
Aged 18 to 44	36.4	21.4	28.9	7.7	5.7
Aged 45 to 64	35.4	17.7	27.5	11.2	8.2
Aged 65 or older	28.9	12.1	39.5	9.8	9.8
Not a college graduate	37.4	16.5	30.8	7.7	7.6
Bachelor's degree or more	28.0	24.6	27.8	13.6	6.0

Source: Survey Documentation and Analysis, Computer-assisted Survey Methods Program, University of California, Berkeley, General Social Surveys, 1972–2008 Cumulative Data Files, Internet site http://sda.berkeley.edu/cgi-bin/hsda?harcsda+gss08; calculations by New Strategist

Table 2.8 Government Should Improve Standard of Living, 1988 to 2008

"Some people think that the government in Washington should do everything possible to improve the standard of living of all poor Americans; they are at point 1. Other people think it is not the government's responsibility, and that each person should take care of himself; they are at point 5. Where would you place yourself on the scale?"

(percent of people aged 18 or older responding, 1988 to 2008; and percent responding by demographic characteristic, 2008)

	1 government should act	2	3 agree with both	4	5 people should help themselves
TREND					
2008	20.2%	12.9%	41.5%	14.8%	10.7%
1998	13.1	13.1	44.3	17.8	11.8
1988	16.6	12.2	46.1	13.0	12.0
2008 PROFILE					
Total people	**20.2**	**12.9**	**41.5**	**14.8**	**10.7**
Men	18.1	14.4	39.9	15.6	12.0
Women	22.0	11.6	42.8	14.0	9.6
Black	40.2	16.0	36.8	4.3	2.8
Hispanic	38.8	13.6	31.8	6.4	9.5
White	15.4	11.4	43.6	17.3	12.4
Aged 18 to 44	21.4	16.6	39.2	14.7	8.1
Aged 45 to 64	19.4	11.7	43.1	15.1	10.7
Aged 65 or older	17.8	4.4	44.4	14.1	19.3
Not a college graduate	22.5	11.7	42.8	12.1	10.8
Bachelor's degree or more	13.7	16.2	37.5	22.0	10.6

Source: Survey Documentation and Analysis, Computer-assisted Survey Methods Program, University of California, Berkeley, General Social Surveys, 1972–2008 Cumulative Data Files, Internet site http://sda.berkeley.edu/cgi-bin/hsda?harcsda+gss08; calculations by New Strategist

Table 2.9 Government Should Reduce Income Differences, 1978 and 2008

"On a scale from 1 to 7, think of a score of 1 as meaning that the government ought to reduce the income differences between rich and poor, and a score of 7 as meaning that the government should not concern itself with reducing income differences. What score between 1 and 7 comes closest to the way you feel?"

(percent of people aged 18 or older responding, 1978 to 2008; and percent responding by demographic characteristic, 2008)

	1 government should reduce	2	3	4	5	6	7 no government involvement
TREND							
2008	23.9%	8.0%	17.6%	18.7%	12.6%	7.1%	12.1%
1998	14.7	9.6	18.0	20.9	11.9	8.7	16.1
1988	19.4	8.9	18.8	20.7	12.4	8.1	11.7
1978	19.0	12.4	19.1	20.8	10.2	7.3	11.2
2008 PROFILE							
Total people	**23.9**	**8.0**	**17.6**	**18.7**	**12.6**	**7.1**	**12.1**
Men	22.3	6.5	17.3	19.9	11.7	8.6	13.7
Women	25.3	9.3	17.8	17.6	13.4	5.7	10.8
Black	38.3	10.5	18.5	19.4	6.5	1.5	5.3
Hispanic	34.1	11.4	15.5	19.9	11.6	4.8	2.7
White	21.2	7.4	17.4	18.3	13.5	8.1	14.0
Aged 18 to 44	25.0	8.8	19.0	18.1	11.8	7.8	9.4
Aged 45 to 64	23.5	7.8	19.9	16.3	12.5	7.6	12.4
Aged 65 or older	22.1	6.2	6.9	26.3	14.5	3.6	20.4
Not a college graduate	27.3	7.6	16.6	19.2	11.8	5.7	11.8
Bachelor's degree or more	14.6	9.2	20.3	17.2	14.8	10.7	13.2

Source: Survey Documentation and Analysis, Computer-assisted Survey Methods Program, University of California, Berkeley, General Social Surveys, 1972–2008 Cumulative Data Files, Internet site http://sda.berkeley.edu/cgi-bin/hsda?harcsda+gss08; calculations by New Strategist

Americans Want It Both Ways

The public may be about evenly split on whether the federal government should do more to solve the nation's problems, but when asked whether the nation spends too much or too little on specific problems, most think the nation spends too little on a range of issues. Few think the nation spends too much on anything. This attitude is a major obstacle to cutting government spending.

(percent of people aged 18 or older who think the nation spends too little on selected problems, 2008)

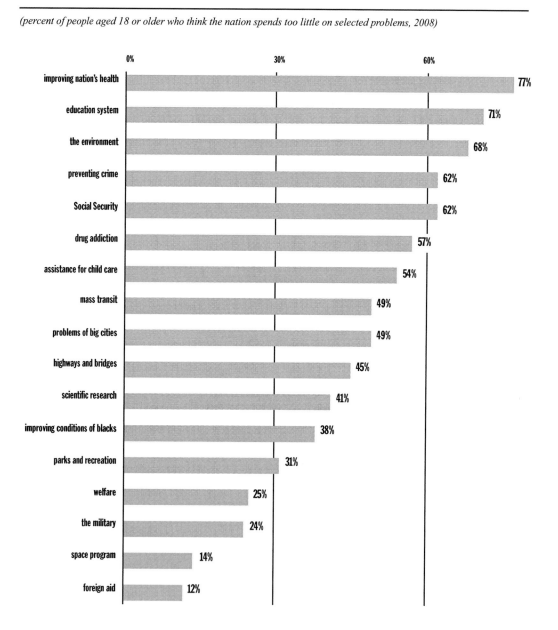

Table 2.10 Spending on Education, 1978 to 2008

"We are faced with many problems in this country, none of which can be solved easily or inexpensively. Do you think we're spending too much money, too little money, or about the right amount on the nation's education system?"

(percent of people aged 18 or older responding, 1978 to 2008; and percent responding by demographic characteristic, 2008)

	too little	about right	too much
TREND			
2008	70.8%	23.3%	5.8%
1998	71.3	21.8	6.9
1988	66.3	30.4	3.3
1978	53.9	33.7	12.4
2008 PROFILE			
Total people	**70.8**	**23.3**	**5.8**
Men	67.7	23.3	9.0
Women	73.5	23.3	3.1
Black	80.2	19.5	0.3
Hispanic	64.7	28.0	7.4
White	69.9	23.9	6.2
Aged 18 to 44	71.8	24.3	3.9
Aged 45 to 64	74.5	18.3	7.2
Aged 65 or older	59.9	31.6	8.5
Not a college graduate	68.2	25.5	5.3
Bachelor's degree or more	78.0	17.4	4.7

Source: Survey Documentation and Analysis, Computer-assisted Survey Methods Program, University of California, Berkeley, General Social Surveys, 1972–2008 Cumulative Data Files, Internet site http://sda.berkeley.edu/cgi-bin/hsda?harcsda+gss08; calculations by New Strategist

Table 2.11 Spending on the Environment, 1978 to 2008

"We are faced with many problems in this country, none of which can be solved easily or inexpensively. Do you think we're spending too much money, too little money, or about the right amount on improving and protecting the environment?"

(percent of people aged 18 or older responding, 1978 to 2008; and percent responding by demographic characteristic, 2008)

	too little	about right	too much
TREND			
2008	67.6%	24.5%	7.9%
1998	63.4	28.8	7.7
1988	67.7	27.9	4.4
1978	57.1	33.3	9.6
2008 PROFILE			
Total people	**67.6**	**24.5**	**7.9**
Men	66.4	24.9	8.7
Women	68.7	24.1	7.1
Black	70.2	23.3	6.5
Hispanic	70.8	18.0	11.2
White	67.6	24.8	7.6
Aged 18 to 44	72.5	21.4	6.2
Aged 45 to 64	67.7	23.8	8.5
Aged 65 or older	52.4	36.2	11.5
Not a college graduate	63.8	27.3	8.9
Bachelor's degree or more	78.0	17.0	5.0

Source: Survey Documentation and Analysis, Computer-assisted Survey Methods Program, University of California, Berkeley, General Social Surveys, 1972–2008 Cumulative Data Files, Internet site http://sda.berkeley.edu/cgi-bin/hsda?harcsda+gss08; calculations by New Strategist

Table 2.12 Spending on Drug Addiction, 1978 to 2008

"We are faced with many problems in this country, none of which can be solved easily or inexpensively. Do you think we're spending too much money, too little money, or about the right amount on dealing with drug addiction?"

(percent of people aged 18 or older responding, 1978 to 2008; and percent responding by demographic characteristic, 2008)

	too little	about right	too much
TREND			
2008	57.3%	32.6%	10.1%
1998	60.8	29.5	9.7
1988	70.9	25.0	4.1
1978	57.2	33.0	9.8
2008 PROFILE			
Total people	**57.3**	**32.6**	**10.1**
Men	52.5	32.4	15.1
Women	61.7	32.8	5.5
Black	75.1	19.3	5.6
Hispanic	52.8	37.9	9.3
White	54.3	34.8	10.9
Aged 18 to 44	54.9	36.8	8.4
Aged 45 to 64	60.0	29.0	11.0
Aged 65 or older	58.1	29.2	12.7
Not a college graduate	58.2	30.6	11.2
Bachelor's degree or more	54.8	38.1	7.0

Source: Survey Documentation and Analysis, Computer-assisted Survey Methods Program, University of California, Berkeley, General Social Surveys, 1972–2008 Cumulative Data Files, Internet site http://sda.berkeley.edu/cgi-bin/hsda?harcsda+gss08; calculations by New Strategist

Table 2.13 Spending on Preventing Crime, 1978 to 2008

"We are faced with many problems in this country, none of which can be solved easily or inexpensively. Do you think we're spending too much money, too little money, or about the right amount on halting the rising crime rate?"

(percent of people aged 18 or older responding, 1978 to 2008; and percent responding by demographic characteristic, 2008)

	too little	about right	too much
TREND			
2008	61.7%	31.5%	6.8%
1998	63.7	28.9	7.4
1988	72.4	23.4	4.2
1978	67.8	26.1	6.1
2008 PROFILE			
Total people	**61.7**	**31.5**	**6.8**
Men	53.5	36.0	10.4
Women	69.0	27.4	3.6
Black	79.3	17.4	3.3
Hispanic	58.7	33.2	8.1
White	58.5	34.6	6.8
Aged 18 to 44	58.4	33.9	7.6
Aged 45 to 64	63.3	32.2	4.5
Aged 65 or older	68.9	21.6	9.5
Not a college graduate	62.8	29.2	8.1
Bachelor's degree or more	58.9	37.8	3.3

Source: Survey Documentation and Analysis, Computer-assisted Survey Methods Program, University of California, Berkeley, General Social Surveys, 1972–2008 Cumulative Data Files, Internet site http://sda.berkeley.edu/cgi-bin/hsda?harcsda+gss08; calculations by New Strategist

Table 2.14 Spending on Solving the Problems of Big Cities, 1978 to 2008

"We are faced with many problems in this country, none of which can be solved easily or inexpensively. Do you think we're spending too much money, too little money, or about the right amount on solving the problems of big cities?"

(percent of people aged 18 or older responding, 1978 to 2008; and percent responding by demographic characteristic, 2008)

	too little	about right	too much
TREND			
2008	48.5%	38.6%	12.9%
1998	51.6	34.5	13.9
1988	54.7	34.4	10.9
1978	44.2	34.9	20.9
2008 PROFILE			
Total people	**48.5**	**38.6**	**12.9**
Men	44.5	39.1	16.4
Women	52.4	38.0	9.6
Black	62.8	27.3	9.9
Hispanic	43.0	35.9	21.1
White	45.0	42.0	13.0
Aged 18 to 44	51.1	38.6	10.3
Aged 45 to 64	47.2	39.6	13.2
Aged 65 or older	44.6	35.9	19.5
Not a college graduate	47.8	37.5	14.7
Bachelor's degree or more	50.6	41.3	8.1

Source: Survey Documentation and Analysis, Computer-assisted Survey Methods Program, University of California, Berkeley, General Social Surveys, 1972–2008 Cumulative Data Files, Internet site http://sda.berkeley.edu/cgi-bin/hsda?harcsda+gss08; calculations by New Strategist

Table 2.15 Spending on Improving the Nation's Health, 1978 to 2008

"We are faced with many problems in this country, none of which can be solved easily or inexpensively. Do you think we're spending too much money, too little money, or about the right amount on improving and protecting the nation's health?"

(percent of people aged 18 or older responding, 1978 to 2008; and percent responding by demographic characteristic, 2008)

	too little	about right	too much
TREND			
2008	77.1%	18.1%	4.8%
1998	68.5	25.3	6.3
1988	69.6	27.3	3.1
1978	57.4	35.7	6.9
2008 PROFILE			
Total people	**77.1**	**18.1**	**4.8**
Men	74.7	18.3	7.0
Women	79.2	17.9	2.8
Black	86.6	6.7	6.7
Hispanic	61.1	29.2	9.7
White	76.5	19.5	4.0
Aged 18 to 44	76.0	18.4	5.5
Aged 45 to 64	81.3	15.3	3.4
Aged 65 or older	69.9	23.7	6.4
Not a college graduate	75.5	19.5	5.0
Bachelor's degree or more	81.4	14.2	4.3

Source: Survey Documentation and Analysis, Computer-assisted Survey Methods Program, University of California, Berkeley, General Social Surveys, 1972–2008 Cumulative Data Files, Internet site http://sda.berkeley.edu/cgi-bin/hsda?harcsda+gss08; calculations by New Strategist

Table 2.16 Spending on Improving the Condition of Blacks, 1978 to 2008

"We are faced with many problems in this country, none of which can be solved easily or inexpensively. Do you think we're spending too much money, too little money, or about the right amount on improving the condition of blacks?"

(percent of people aged 18 or older responding, 1978 to 2008; and percent responding by demographic characteristic, 2008)

	too little	about right	too much
TREND			
2008	38.2%	47.7%	14.0%
1998	36.9	45.2	17.9
1988	38.0	45.3	16.6
1978	26.3	47.2	26.5
2008 PROFILE			
Total people	**38.2**	**47.7**	**14.0**
Men	34.9	48.2	16.9
Women	41.4	47.3	11.3
Black	80.4	18.9	0.7
Hispanic	44.9	36.0	19.1
White	30.7	53.0	16.3
Aged 18 to 44	35.7	49.9	14.4
Aged 45 to 64	41.9	44.2	13.9
Aged 65 or older	37.5	50.4	12.2
Not a college graduate	36.9	47.1	16.0
Bachelor's degree or more	41.7	49.4	8.9

Source: Survey Documentation and Analysis, Computer-assisted Survey Methods Program, University of California, Berkeley, General Social Surveys, 1972–2008 Cumulative Data Files, Internet site http://sda.berkeley.edu/cgi-bin/hsda?harcsda+gss08; calculations by New Strategist

Table 2.17 Spending on the Military, 1978 to 2008

"We are faced with many problems in this country, none of which can be solved easily or inexpensively. Do you think we're spending too much money, too little money, or about the right amount on military, armaments, and defense?"

(percent of people aged 18 or older responding, 1978 to 2008; and percent responding by demographic characteristic, 2008)

	too little	about right	too much
TREND			
2008	24.1%	33.3%	42.6%
1998	18.7	48.7	32.6
1988	16.5	42.4	41.1
1978	28.9	46.8	24.3
2008 PROFILE			
Total people	**24.1**	**33.3**	**42.6**
Men	22.1	30.7	47.2
Women	26.0	35.7	38.4
Black	21.4	30.0	48.6
Hispanic	24.0	18.8	57.2
White	25.3	34.7	40.0
Aged 18 to 44	17.4	34.9	47.7
Aged 45 to 64	30.8	34.3	34.9
Aged 65 or older	28.9	24.6	46.5
Not a college graduate	27.3	32.9	39.8
Bachelor's degree or more	15.6	34.3	50.1

Source: Survey Documentation and Analysis, Computer-assisted Survey Methods Program, University of California, Berkeley, General Social Surveys, 1972–2008 Cumulative Data Files, Internet site http://sda.berkeley.edu/cgi-bin/hsda?harcsda+gss08; calculations by New Strategist

Table 2.18 Spending on Foreign Aid, 1978 to 2008

"We are faced with many problems in this country, none of which can be solved easily or inexpensively. Do you think we're spending too much money, too little money, or about the right amount on foreign aid?"

(percent of people aged 18 or older responding, 1978 to 2008; and percent responding by demographic characteristic, 2008)

	too little	about right	too much
TREND			
2008	12.1%	28.8%	59.1%
1998	7.1	28.9	64.0
1988	5.0	24.4	70.6
1978	3.8	25.3	70.9
2008 PROFILE			
Total people	**12.1**	**28.8**	**59.1**
Men	14.3	24.4	61.3
Women	10.1	32.8	57.1
Black	22.3	23.5	54.2
Hispanic	21.3	45.2	33.6
White	8.6	29.4	62.0
Aged 18 to 44	15.2	32.8	51.9
Aged 45 to 64	10.3	22.9	66.9
Aged 65 or older	7.6	31.4	61.0
Not a college graduate	10.4	28.3	61.2
Bachelor's degree or more	16.4	30.1	53.5

Source: Survey Documentation and Analysis, Computer-assisted Survey Methods Program, University of California, Berkeley, General Social Surveys, 1972–2008 Cumulative Data Files, Internet site http://sda.berkeley.edu/cgi-bin/hsda?harcsda+gss08; calculations by New Strategist

Table 2.19 Spending on Welfare, 1978 to 2008

"We are faced with many problems in this country, none of which can be solved easily or inexpensively. Do you think we're spending too much money, too little money, or about the right amount on welfare?"

(percent of people aged 18 or older responding, 1978 to 2008; and percent responding by demographic characteristic, 2008)

	too little	about right	too much
TREND			
2008	25.4%	36.4%	38.2%
1998	16.0	37.7	46.3
1988	24.7	32.5	42.8
1978	13.6	24.1	62.3
2008 PROFILE			
Total people	**25.4**	**36.4**	**38.2**
Men	25.3	36.4	38.4
Women	25.5	36.4	38.1
Black	42.1	36.2	21.7
Hispanic	19.3	52.1	28.5
White	21.6	35.8	42.7
Aged 18 to 44	26.5	34.6	39.0
Aged 45 to 64	24.5	36.0	39.4
Aged 65 or older	24.7	42.6	32.7
Not a college graduate	25.5	34.9	39.7
Bachelor's degree or more	25.1	40.6	34.3

Source: Survey Documentation and Analysis, Computer-assisted Survey Methods Program, University of California, Berkeley, General Social Surveys, 1972–2008 Cumulative Data Files, Internet site http://sda.berkeley.edu/cgi-bin/hsda?harcsda+gss08; calculations by New Strategist

Table 2.20 Spending on the Space Program, 1978 to 2008

"We are faced with many problems in this country, none of which can be solved easily or inexpensively. Do you think we're spending too much money, too little money, or about the right amount on the space exploration program?"

(percent of people aged 18 or older responding, 1978 to 2008; and percent responding by demographic characteristic, 2008)

	too little	about right	too much
TREND			
2008	13.6%	50.9%	35.5%
1998	10.3	47.3	42.3
1988	18.4	45.0	36.6
1978	12.9	37.4	49.6
2008 PROFILE			
Total people	**13.6**	**50.9**	**35.5**
Men	18.0	51.2	30.9
Women	9.6	50.6	39.8
Black	7.3	35.9	56.8
Hispanic	16.6	44.6	38.8
White	14.7	54.7	30.6
Aged 18 to 44	13.1	54.6	32.3
Aged 45 to 64	16.3	47.4	36.3
Aged 65 or older	7.9	48.5	43.6
Not a college graduate	11.2	48.9	39.9
Bachelor's degree or more	19.9	56.0	24.1

Source: Survey Documentation and Analysis, Computer-assisted Survey Methods Program, University of California, Berkeley, General Social Surveys, 1972–2008 Cumulative Data Files, Internet site http://sda.berkeley.edu/cgi-bin/hsda?harcsda+gss08; calculations by New Strategist

Table 2.21 Spending on Mass Transportation, 1988 to 2008

"We are faced with many problems in this country, none of which can be solved easily or inexpensively. Do you think we're spending too much money, too little money, or about the right amount on mass transportation?"

(percent of people aged 18 or older responding, 1988 to 2008; and percent responding by demographic characteristic, 2008)

	too little	about right	too much
TREND			
2008	48.7%	43.4%	7.9%
1998	35.0	54.6	10.4
1988	31.7	57.2	11.1
2008 PROFILE			
Total people	**48.7**	**43.4**	**7.9**
Men	53.3	37.7	8.9
Women	44.4	48.6	7.0
Black	46.7	45.8	7.5
Hispanic	35.3	54.4	10.3
White	50.1	42.4	7.5
Aged 18 to 44	44.0	47.2	8.7
Aged 45 to 64	52.0	40.9	7.2
Aged 65 or older	56.2	37.6	6.3
Not a college graduate	44.5	46.8	8.7
Bachelor's degree or more	60.6	33.6	5.8

Source: Survey Documentation and Analysis, Computer-assisted Survey Methods Program, University of California, Berkeley, General Social Surveys, 1972–2008 Cumulative Data Files, Internet site http://sda.berkeley.edu/cgi-bin/hsda?harcsda+gss08; calculations by New Strategist

Table 2.22 Spending on Highways and Bridges, 1988 to 2008

"We are faced with many problems in this country, none of which can be solved
easily or inexpensively. Do you think we're spending too much money,
too little money, or about the right amount on highways and bridges?"

*(percent of people aged 18 or older responding, 1988 to 2008; and percent responding by demographic charac-
teristic, 2008)*

	too little	about right	too much
TREND			
2008	45.2%	44.9%	9.8%
1998	40.4	49.5	10.1
1988	37.4	54.7	7.9
2008 PROFILE			
Total people	**45.2**	**44.9**	**9.8**
Men	48.5	42.7	8.8
Women	42.3	47.0	10.8
Black	43.6	41.9	14.5
Hispanic	29.9	52.4	17.7
White	47.9	43.7	8.5
Aged 18 to 44	36.3	52.0	11.7
Aged 45 to 64	51.7	38.9	9.4
Aged 65 or older	57.9	36.9	5.1
Not a college graduate	44.4	44.4	11.2
Bachelor's degree or more	47.4	46.6	6.0

*Source: Survey Documentation and Analysis, Computer-assisted Survey Methods Program, University of California, Berkeley,
General Social Surveys, 1972–2008 Cumulative Data Files, Internet site http://sda.berkeley.edu/cgi-bin/hsda?harcsda+gss08;
calculations by New Strategist*

Table 2.23 Spending on Social Security, 1988 to 2008

"We are faced with many problems in this country, none of which can be solved easily or inexpensively. Do you think we're spending too much money, too little money, or about the right amount on Social Security?"

(percent of people aged 18 or older responding, 1988 to 2008; and percent responding by demographic characteristic, 2008)

	too little	about right	too much
TREND			
2008	61.6%	32.6%	5.8%
1998	59.9	33.2	6.9
1988	55.5	39.4	5.1
2008 PROFILE			
Total people	**61.6**	**32.6**	**5.8**
Men	59.1	32.9	8.0
Women	63.9	32.2	3.9
Black	83.4	15.0	1.6
Hispanic	50.7	40.2	9.1
White	58.8	35.1	6.1
Aged 18 to 44	62.0	29.7	8.3
Aged 45 to 64	66.4	29.9	3.7
Aged 65 or older	48.8	48.3	2.9
Not a college graduate	64.8	29.8	5.5
Bachelor's degree or more	52.5	40.6	6.8

Source: Survey Documentation and Analysis, Computer-assisted Survey Methods Program, University of California, Berkeley, General Social Surveys, 1972–2008 Cumulative Data Files, Internet site http://sda.berkeley.edu/cgi-bin/hsda?harcsda+gss08; calculations by New Strategist

Table 2.24 Spending on Parks and Recreation, 1988 to 2008

"We are faced with many problems in this country, none of which can be solved
easily or inexpensively. Do you think we're spending too much money,
too little money, or about the right amount on parks and recreation?"

(percent of people aged 18 or older responding, 1988 to 2008; and percent responding by demographic characteristic, 2008)

	too little	about right	too much
TREND			
2008	31.3%	63.3%	5.4%
1998	36.4	57.3	6.3
1988	31.3	63.2	5.5
2008 PROFILE			
Total people	**31.3**	**63.3**	**5.4**
Men	32.1	62.8	5.1
Women	30.6	63.8	5.7
Black	46.8	46.2	7.0
Hispanic	32.7	64.9	2.4
White	28.5	66.0	5.5
Aged 18 to 44	32.2	63.4	4.4
Aged 45 to 64	32.7	61.0	6.3
Aged 65 or older	25.6	68.3	6.0
Not a college graduate	30.8	63.5	5.7
Bachelor's degree or more	32.6	62.7	4.6

Source: Survey Documentation and Analysis, Computer-assisted Survey Methods Program, University of California, Berkeley, General Social Surveys, 1972–2008 Cumulative Data Files, Internet site http://sda.berkeley.edu/cgi-bin/hsda?harcsda+gss08; calculations by New Strategist

Table 2.25 Spending on Scientific Research, 2008

"We are faced with many problems in this country, none of which can be solved easily or inexpensively. Do you think we're spending too much money, too little money, or about the right amount on supporting scientific research?"

(percent of people aged 18 or older responding by demographic characteristic, 2008)

	too little	about right	too much
Total people	**40.6%**	**48.2%**	**11.2%**
Men	41.4	48.2	10.4
Women	39.9	48.1	12.0
Black	36.1	43.9	20.0
Hispanic	32.4	52.0	15.6
White	41.5	49.6	8.9
Aged 18 to 44	38.4	50.1	11.5
Aged 45 to 64	41.1	46.7	12.2
Aged 65 or older	45.8	46.4	7.8
Not a college graduate	36.7	50.1	13.2
Bachelor's degree or more	51.4	42.9	5.7

Source: Survey Documentation and Analysis, Computer-assisted Survey Methods Program, University of California, Berkeley, General Social Surveys, 1972–2008 Cumulative Data Files, Internet site http://sda.berkeley.edu/cgi-bin/hsda?harcsda+gss08; calculations by New Strategist

Table 2.26 Spending on Assistance for Child Care, 2008

"We are faced with many problems in this country, none of which can be solved easily or inexpensively. Do you think we're spending too much money, too little money, or about the right amount on assistance for child care?"

(percent of people aged 18 or older responding by demographic characteristic, 2008)

	too little	about right	too much
Total people	**54.4%**	**39.2%**	**6.5%**
Men	48.0	43.3	8.7
Women	59.9	35.6	4.5
Black	77.4	19.1	3.6
Hispanic	52.2	42.1	5.7
White	50.1	42.7	7.1
Aged 18 to 44	56.8	38.2	5.0
Aged 45 to 64	55.8	37.4	6.8
Aged 65 or older	44.0	46.5	9.5
Not a college graduate	55.7	37.2	7.1
Bachelor's degree or more	50.6	44.8	4.5

Source: Survey Documentation and Analysis, Computer-assisted Survey Methods Program, University of California, Berkeley, General Social Survey, 2008 Cumulative Data Files, Internet site http://sda.berkeley.edu/cgi-bin/hsda?harcsda+gss08; calculations by New Strategist

CHAPTER
3

Science

Most Americans support government funding of scientific research, have a general understanding of scientific study, and can answer basic questions about science correctly. The way people get their information about scientific issues is changing, however, and these changes have been well documented by the General Social Survey over the past 30 years.

Little or no change

• **Television is number one.** Television viewing has not changed much in three decades, most people watch TV at least two hours a day. The largest share of the public (48 percent) gets most of its news from television. When asked where they would seek information about scientific issues, however, the largest share of the public says the Internet.

• **Americans understand basic scientific concepts.** The great majority of Americans know the center of the Earth is very hot, that not all radioactivity is man-made, that electrons are smaller than atoms, and that the continents have been moving. The bare majority believes in evolution, however.

Big changes

• **Newspaper readership is down.** A paradigm shift is taking place in the news industry: The printed newspaper is rapidly losing readers. The percentage of people who read a newspaper every day fell from 58 percent in 1978 to 32 percent in 2008. When asked where they get most of their news, only 20 percent of the public says the newspaper—below the 22 percent who depend on the Internet.

• **The Internet is increasingly dominant.** Among people aged 18 to 44, a substantial 34 percent say they get most of their news from the Internet, not far behind the 42 percent who depend on television. Forty percent of 18-to-44-year-olds say they get most of their information about science and technology from the Internet, ahead of the 37 percent who get it from television. Sixty-seven percent of younger adults turn to the Internet to seek information about science. As younger generations age, the Internet is likely to become the number-one source for news.

Most Older Americans Read a Newspaper Every Day

Three out of four Americans say they have access to the Internet at home. The same proportion watch television at least two hours a day—a figure that has not changed in three decades. One thing that has changed is newspaper readership. Only 32 percent of adults read a newspaper every day, down from 58 percent in 1978. Just 19 percent of 18-to-44-year-olds are daily newspaper readers versus 65 percent of people aged 65 or older.

(percent of people aged 18 or older who read a newspaper every day, by age, 2008)

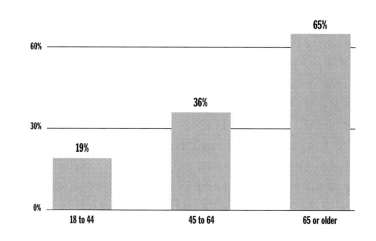

Table 3.1 Internet Access at Home, 2008

"Do you have access to the Internet in your home?"

(percent of people aged 18 or older responding by demographic characteristic, 2008)

	yes	no
Total people	**73.6%**	**26.4%**
Men	73.0	27.0
Women	74.1	25.9
Black	57.3	42.7
Hispanic	58.5	41.5
White	77.6	22.4
Aged 18 to 44	76.5	23.5
Aged 45 to 64	78.0	22.0
Aged 65 or older	53.5	46.5
Not a college graduate	67.1	32.9
Bachelor's degree or more	92.0	8.0

Source: Survey Documentation and Analysis, Computer-assisted Survey Methods Program, University of California, Berkeley, General Social Surveys, 1972–2008 Cumulative Data Files, Internet site http://sda.berkeley.edu/cgi-bin/hsda?harcsda+gss08; calculations by New Strategist

Table 3.2 Hours Watching TV, 1978 to 2008

"On the average day, about how many hours do you personally watch television?"

(percent responding, 1978 to 2008; and percent responding by demographic characteristic, 2008)

	0 hrs.	1 hr.	2 hrs.	3 hrs.	4 or more hrs.
TREND					
2008	6.2%	20.5%	29.8%	16.0%	27.5%
1998	4.6	21.7	27.3	17.5	28.9
1988	2.6	19.7	25.7	19.6	32.4
1978	5.1	21.0	27.2	19.9	26.8
2008 PROFILE					
Total people	**6.2**	**20.5**	**29.8**	**16.0**	**27.5**
Men	6.2	22.1	28.2	17.3	26.2
Women	6.1	19.0	31.2	14.8	28.8
Black	0.5	11.8	29.0	12.5	46.3
Hispanic	2.3	20.2	31.8	20.1	25.6
White	6.9	21.6	29.9	16.5	25.1
Aged 18 to 44	8.2	22.9	32.1	14.0	22.8
Aged 45 to 64	4.7	21.4	30.3	18.5	25.2
Aged 65 or older	3.7	11.3	20.6	16.5	47.9
Not a college graduate	5.2	17.5	27.5	17.1	32.8
Bachelor's degree or more	9.0	29.4	36.4	12.7	12.5

Source: Survey Documentation and Analysis, Computer-assisted Survey Methods Program, University of California, Berkeley, General Social Surveys, 1972–2008 Cumulative Data Files, Internet site http://sda.berkeley.edu/cgi-bin/hsda?harcsda+gss08; calculations by New Strategist

Table 3.3 Frequency of Reading the Newspaper, 1978 to 2008

"How often do you read the newspaper—every day,
a few times a week, less than once a week, or never?"

(percent of people aged 18 or older responding, 1978 to 2008; and percent responding by demographic characteristic, 2008)

	every day	a few times a week	once a week	less than once a week	never
TREND					
2008	32.2%	22.9%	17.3%	14.3%	13.2%
1998	43.0	22.7	16.4	10.4	7.5
1988	50.9	23.8	12.2	8.6	4.5
1978	58.0	20.5	9.3	7.3	4.9
2008 PROFILE					
Total people	**32.2**	**22.9**	**17.3**	**14.3**	**13.2**
Men	32.5	22.6	17.6	12.9	14.4
Women	32.0	23.1	17.1	15.7	12.1
Black	24.9	34.7	16.2	12.8	11.4
Hispanic	18.3	17.8	22.7	17.0	24.2
White	34.2	21.1	18.2	13.7	12.8
Aged 18 to 44	18.9	25.8	21.4	18.4	15.6
Aged 45 to 64	36.4	22.6	15.1	13.2	12.8
Aged 65 or older	64.8	14.0	10.5	4.7	6.1
Not a college graduate	28.9	22.9	18.5	15.8	14.0
Bachelor's degree or more	42.1	23.0	13.8	10.1	11.0

Source: Survey Documentation and Analysis, Computer-assisted Survey Methods Program, University of California, Berkeley, General Social Surveys, 1972–2008 Cumulative Data Files, Internet site http://sda.berkeley.edu/cgi-bin/hsda?harcsda+gss08; calculations by New Strategist

Young Adults Are Most Likely to Turn to the Internet for News

In 2008, television remained the most important medium for the news, with 48 percent of adults saying they get most of their information about current news events from TV. The Internet is second, at 22 percent. Newspapers are a close third at 20 percent. There are striking differences in the use of the Internet and newspapers by age. Thirty-four percent of people under age 45 get most of their news online versus only 4 percent of people aged 65 or older.

(percent of people aged 18 or older who say the Internet is their main source of information about current news events, by age, 2008)

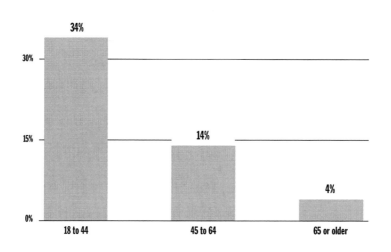

Table 3.4 Main Source of Information about Events in the News, 2008

"We are interested in how people get information about events in the news.
Where do you get most of your information about current news events?"

(percent of people aged 18 or older responding by demographic characteristic, 2008)

	television	Internet	newspapers	radio	family, friends, or colleagues	magazines, books, other
Total people	**47.5%**	**22.0%**	**19.6%**	**6.1%**	**2.8%**	**1.9%**
Men	45.1	25.4	18.6	7.2	1.6	2.1
Women	49.8	18.8	20.4	5.1	3.9	1.9
Black	63.7	11.4	17.9	1.2	3.9	1.9
Hispanic	60.0	16.4	13.8	4.7	1.2	4.0
White	44.8	22.9	20.3	6.9	2.9	2.1
Aged 18 to 44	42.0	34.0	12.3	5.9	4.4	1.5
Aged 45 to 64	52.3	14.0	22.8	7.4	1.5	2.2
Aged 65 or older	53.2	3.9	34.8	3.8	1.1	3.2
Not a college graduate	53.4	17.7	18.3	5.9	3.0	1.6
Bachelor's degree or more	30.9	34.1	23.1	6.6	2.0	3.2

Source: Survey Documentation and Analysis, Computer-assisted Survey Methods Program, University of California, Berkeley, General Social Survey, 2008 Cumulative Data Files, Internet site http://sda.berkeley.edu/cgi-bin/hsda?harcsda+gss08; calculations by New Strategist

For Young Adults, the Internet Is the Source of Science Information

Television is the number-one source of information about science and technology among the population as a whole, but among adults aged 18 to 44 the Internet is most important. Forty percent of people aged 18 to 44 say they get most of their science information from the Internet. An even larger 67 percent say they would turn to the Internet to get information about scientific issues.

(percent of people aged 18 or older who go to the Internet to get information about scientific issues, by age, 2008)

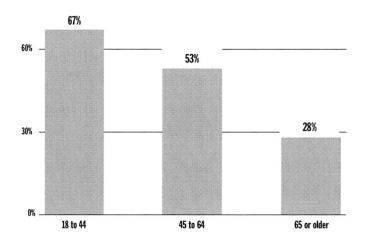

Table 3.5 Main Source of Information about Science and Technology, 2008

"We are interested in how people get information about science and technology.
Where do you get most of your information about science and technology?"

(percent of people aged 18 or older responding by demographic characteristic, 2008)

	television	Internet	newspapers	magazines	books and other printed material	family, friends, and colleagues	radio	other
Total people	**41.6%**	**28.1%**	**10.9%**	**10.9%**	**3.2%**	**3.1%**	**1.8%**	**0.5%**
Men	43.4	28.7	9.2	11.1	3.0	1.4	2.4	0.8
Women	39.8	27.6	12.4	10.7	3.4	4.6	1.3	0.3
Black	49.2	23.4	9.3	9.3	5.9	2.1	0.0	0.7
Hispanic	52.3	22.6	10.0	8.9	3.4	0.2	2.4	0.2
White	40.1	28.1	11.6	11.1	2.8	3.6	2.3	0.6
Aged 18 to 44	37.1	40.4	7.2	7.1	2.2	3.8	1.4	0.7
Aged 45 to 64	43.3	20.1	13.4	13.2	4.1	2.7	2.8	0.5
Aged 65 or older	51.6	9.1	16.3	16.6	4.2	1.8	0.4	
Not a college graduate	47.9	24.2	10.4	9.4	2.7	3.0	1.8	0.7
Bachelor's degree or more	23.9	39.0	12.2	15.1	4.8	3.3	1.8	0.0

Source: Survey Documentation and Analysis, Computer-assisted Survey Methods Program, University of California, Berkeley, General Social Survey, 2008 Cumulative Data Files, Internet site http://sda.berkeley.edu/cgi-bin/hsda?harcsda+gss08; calculations by New Strategist

Table 3.6 Where People Look for Information about Science and Technology, 2008

"If you wanted to learn about scientific issues such as global warming
or biotechnology, where would you get information?"

(percent of people aged 18 or older responding by demographic characteristic, 2008)

	television	Internet	newspapers	magazines	books and other printed material	family, friends, and colleagues	radio	other
Total people	**21.6%**	**55.7%**	**5.2%**	**4.9%**	**7.3%**	**2.5%**	**0.7%**	**2.0%**
Men	24.4	54.0	5.1	5.5	6.9	1.3	1.0	2.0
Women	19.1	57.3	5.4	4.4	7.7	3.6	0.5	2.2
Black	34.0	40.1	6.9	4.8	10.0	3.1	0.0	1.2
Hispanic	35.4	48.8	5.8	2.8	3.3	0.2	1.5	2.2
White	19.0	58.2	4.4	5.1	7.4	2.6	0.9	2.5
Aged 18 to 44	17.9	66.7	3.3	3.7	4.9	2.1	0.4	0.9
Aged 45 to 64	22.1	52.8	5.2	4.6	9.0	2.7	1.0	2.6
Aged 65 or older	33.4	27.7	11.5	9.2	10.5	3.2	0.8	4.7
Not a college graduate	24.8	52.9	5.4	4.5	7.2	2.1	0.6	2.5
Bachelor's degree or more	12.8	63.5	4.8	6.1	7.5	3.5	0.9	0.9

Source: Survey Documentation and Analysis, Computer-assisted Survey Methods Program, University of California, Berkeley, General Social Survey, 2008 Cumulative Data Files, Internet site http://sda.berkeley.edu/cgi-bin/hsda?harcsda+gss08; calculations by New Strategist

Many Think Science Makes Life Change Too Fast

Most of the public agrees that science and technology provide opportunity for younger generations, and most think the benefits of science outweigh any harmful results. But many do not feel comfortable with the speed of scientific progress. A substantial 48 percent of Americans agree that science makes our way of life change too fast. Among people aged 65 or older, the 53 percent majority say science makes things change too fast.

(percent distribution of people aged 18 or older by attitude toward the statement, "Science makes our way of life change too fast," 2008)

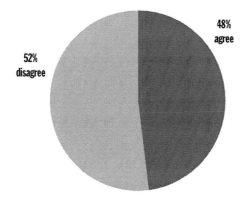

Table 3.7 Science and Technology Create Opportunity, 2008

"Because of science and technology, there will be
more opportunities for the next generation."

(percent of people aged 18 or older responding by demographic characteristic, 2008)

	strongly agree	agree	disagree	strongly disagree
Total people	**36.9%**	**54.6%**	**7.6%**	**0.9%**
Men	35.3	56.2	7.7	0.8
Women	38.4	53.2	7.5	0.9
Black	36.7	47.0	14.3	2.0
Hispanic	35.0	58.9	5.6	0.5
White	35.6	56.8	6.8	0.8
Aged 18 to 44	39.1	52.3	8.1	0.5
Aged 45 to 64	35.4	55.0	8.1	1.4
Aged 65 or older	33.5	61.0	4.9	0.6
Not a college graduate	34.7	55.2	9.0	1.0
Bachelor's degree or more	42.9	53.0	3.6	0.5

Source: Survey Documentation and Analysis, Computer-assisted Survey Methods Program, University of California, Berkeley, General Social Survey, 2008 Cumulative Data Files, Internet site http://sda.berkeley.edu/cgi-bin/hsda?harcsda+gss08; calculations by New Strategist

Table 3.8 Benefits of Science Outweigh Harmful Results, 2008

"People have frequently noted that scientific research has produced benefits and harmful results. Would you say that, on balance, the benefits of scientific research have outweighed the harmful results, or have the harmful results of scientific research been greater than its benefits?"

(percent of people aged 18 or older responding by demographic characteristic, 2008)

	benefits greater	about equal (volunteered)	harmful results greater
Total people	**72.8%**	**17.2%**	**10.0%**
Men	71.7	17.1	11.2
Women	73.9	17.2	8.9
Black	54.2	25.5	20.3
Hispanic	64.6	22.5	12.9
White	76.3	15.4	8.2
Aged 18 to 44	68.9	20.3	10.8
Aged 45 to 64	78.6	12.3	9.1
Aged 65 or older	70.7	19.2	10.1
Not a college graduate	67.7	19.7	12.6
Bachelor's degree or more	86.4	10.3	3.3

Source: Survey Documentation and Analysis, Computer-assisted Survey Methods Program, University of California, Berkeley, General Social Survey, 2008 Cumulative Data Files, Internet site http://sda.berkeley.edu/cgi-bin/hsda?harcsda+gss08; calculations by New Strategist

Table 3.9 Science Makes Our Way of Life Change Too Fast, 2008

"Science makes our way of life change too fast."

(percent of people aged 18 or older responding by demographic characteristic, 2008)

	strongly agree	agree	disagree	strongly disagree
Total people	**9.0%**	**38.8%**	**43.9%**	**8.3%**
Men	8.4	38.0	45.0	8.6
Women	9.5	39.6	42.9	8.0
Black	14.6	42.6	37.3	5.5
Hispanic				
White	7.2	36.9	47.1	8.9
Aged 18 to 44	8.7	37.9	45.1	8.3
Aged 45 to 64	9.6	37.6	43.6	9.2
Aged 65 or older	8.2	44.8	40.9	6.2
Not a college graduate	9.9	41.6	42.3	6.2
Bachelor's degree or more	6.3	31.1	48.4	14.1

Source: Survey Documentation and Analysis, Computer-assisted Survey Methods Program, University of California, Berkeley, General Social Survey, 2008 Cumulative Data Files, Internet site http://sda.berkeley.edu/cgi-bin/hsda?harcsda+gss08; calculations by New Strategist

Table 3.10 Science Does More Harm than Good, 1998 and 2008

"How much do you agree or disagree? Overall,
modern science does more harm than good."

(percent of people aged 18 or older responding, 1998 and 2008; and percent responding by demographic characteristic, 2008)

	strongly agree	agree	neither agree nor disagree	disagree	strongly disagree
TREND					
2008	2.5%	10.6%	22.1%	46.8%	18.0%
1998	4.0	10.2	27.1	40.1	18.6
2008 PROFILE					
Total people	**2.5**	**10.6**	**22.1**	**46.8**	**18.0**
Men	2.7	9.7	19.9	48.2	19.5
Women	2.4	11.3	24.1	45.6	16.6
Black	6.2	17.2	28.6	35.0	13.0
Hispanic	4.5	20.8	24.2	33.9	16.6
White	2.0	9.4	21.3	49.0	18.3
Aged 18 to 44	1.9	10.3	24.1	43.4	20.3
Aged 45 to 64	3.4	9.1	19.0	51.8	16.8
Aged 65 or older	2.6	15.3	23.4	45.3	13.4
Not a college graduate	3.1	12.6	26.2	44.2	13.8
Bachelor's degree or more	1.0	4.7	11.0	54.1	29.2

Source: Survey Documentation and Analysis, Computer-assisted Survey Methods Program, University of California, Berkeley, General Social Surveys, 1972–2008 Cumulative Data Files, Internet site http://sda.berkeley.edu/cgi-bin/hsda?harcsda+gss08; calculations by New Strategist

The Public Supports Federal Funding of Scientific Research

Three out of four Americans think the quality of science and math education is inadequate. Nearly nine out of ten think the federal government should support scientific research. The 61 percent majority do not think scientists should be allowed to do scientific research that causes pain and injury to animals, however. Only 48 percent of men are against research using animals compared with 73 percent of women.

(percent distribution of people aged 18 or older by attitude toward federal funding of scientific research, 2008)

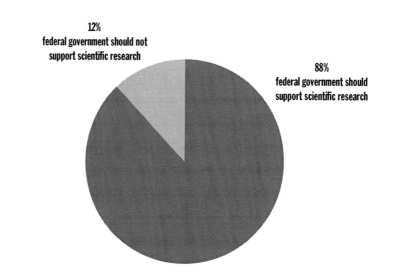

12%
federal government should not
support scientific research

88%
federal government should
support scientific research

Table 3.11 Quality of Science and Math Education Is Inadequate, 2008

"The quality of science and mathematics education in American schools is inadequate.
Do you strongly agree, agree, disagree, or strongly disagree?"

(percent of people aged 18 or older responding by demographic characteristic, 2008)

	strongly agree	agree	disagree	strongly disagree
Total people	**22.7%**	**52.3%**	**23.3%**	**1.7%**
Men	21.1	54.3	23.1	1.5
Women	24.3	50.5	23.4	1.8
Black	18.0	49.7	28.8	3.5
Hispanic				
White	23.6	52.8	22.2	1.4
Aged 18 to 44	17.0	53.1	28.0	1.8
Aged 45 to 64	27.8	49.8	20.6	1.8
Aged 65 or older	29.0	56.6	13.6	0.8
Not a college graduate	20.4	51.5	26.3	1.8
Bachelor's degree or more	29.2	54.8	14.9	1.2

Source: Survey Documentation and Analysis, Computer-assisted Survey Methods Program, University of California, Berkeley, General Social Survey, 2008 Cumulative Data Files, Internet site http://sda.berkeley.edu/cgi-bin/hsda?harcsda+gss08; calculations by New Strategist

Table 3.12 Science Research Should Be Supported by Federal Government, 2008

"Even if it brings no immediate benefits, scientific research that advances the frontiers of knowledge is necessary and should be supported by the federal government."

(percent of people aged 18 or older responding by demographic characteristic, 2008)

	strongly agree	agree	disagree	strongly disagree
Total people	**26.0%**	**62.0%**	**11.4%**	**0.7%**
Men	27.3	60.4	11.7	0.7
Women	24.7	63.5	11.1	0.7
Black	13.9	68.0	18.1	0.0
Hispanic	24.4	65.2	9.2	1.2
White	28.2	60.3	10.7	0.8
Aged 18 to 44	23.6	64.6	11.2	0.6
Aged 45 to 64	28.2	59.9	10.9	1.1
Aged 65 or older	27.5	58.8	13.7	0.0
Not a college graduate	23.5	62.0	13.8	0.7
Bachelor's degree or more	32.7	61.8	4.9	0.7

Source: Survey Documentation and Analysis, Computer-assisted Survey Methods Program, University of California, Berkeley, General Social Survey, 2008 Cumulative Data Files, Internet site http://sda.berkeley.edu/cgi-bin/hsda?harcsda+gss08; calculations by New Strategist

Table 3.13 Scientists Should Be Allowed to Do Research That Causes Pain to Animals, 2008

"Scientists should be allowed to do research that causes pain and injury to animals like dogs and chimpanzees if it produces new information about human health problems. Do you strongly agree, agree, disagree, or strongly disagree?"

(percent of people aged 18 or older responding by demographic characteristic, 2008)

	strongly agree	agree	disagree	strongly disagree
Total people	**6.3%**	**33.1%**	**37.8%**	**22.8%**
Men	8.4	43.9	33.9	13.9
Women	4.3	23.0	41.5	31.2
Black	7.3	40.6	35.6	16.5
Hispanic	8.1	39.6	31.6	20.7
White	5.7	31.0	39.2	24.1
Aged 18 to 44	3.6	34.7	38.8	22.8
Aged 45 to 64	9.3	31.0	36.1	23.6
Aged 65 or older	7.2	33.3	39.2	20.3
Not a college graduate	6.1	32.0	37.7	24.2
Bachelor's degree or more	6.8	36.1	38.2	19.0

Source: Survey Documentation and Analysis, Computer-assisted Survey Methods Program, University of California, Berkeley, General Social Survey, 2008 Cumulative Data Files, Internet site http://sda.berkeley.edu/cgi-bin/hsda?harcsda+gss08; calculations by New Strategist

Most Do Not Think Astrology Is Scientific

Although horoscopes appear in many daily newspapers, they are not taken seriously by the majority of the public. Two out of three adults say astrology is not at all scientific. The proportion reaches 80 percent among college graduates.

(percent distribution of people aged 18 or older by attitude toward astrology, 2008)

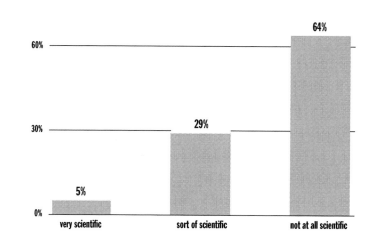

Table 3.14 Astrology Is Scientific, 2008

"Would you say that astrology is very scientific, sort of scientific, or not at all scientific?"

(percent of people aged 18 or older responding by demographic characteristic, 2008)

	very scientific	sort of scientific	not at all scientific
Total people	**5.1%**	**29.5%**	**64.5%**
Men	4.3	29.1	66.7
Women	5.8	29.8	64.4
Black	7.7	40.6	51.7
Hispanic	7.1	42.0	50.8
White	4.2	26.4	69.4
Aged 18 to 44	5.6	34.0	60.4
Aged 45 to 64	4.5	25.4	70.1
Aged 65 or older	4.1	25.5	70.4
Not a college graduate	6.2	33.6	60.2
Bachelor's degree or more	2.0	18.2	79.8

Source: Survey Documentation and Analysis, Computer-assisted Survey Methods Program, University of California, Berkeley, General Social Survey, 2008 Cumulative Data Files, Internet site http://sda.berkeley.edu/cgi-bin/hsda?harcsda+gss08; calculations by New Strategist

Many Do Not Believe in Evolution

When asked how well they understand the concept of scientific study, 78 percent of Americans say they have at least a general sense of what it means. When quizzed on basic scientific concepts, the great majority answers correctly—with a few exceptions. A substantial 42 percent of the public thinks antibiotics kill viruses as well as bacteria. Forty-five percent do not believe that the universe started with a big bang. And nearly half—49 percent—do not think that humans developed from earlier species of animals.

(percent distribution of people aged 18 or older by whether they think the statement, "Human beings developed from earlier species of animals" is true or false, 2008)

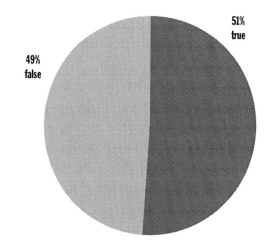

51%
true

49%
false

Table 3.15 Understanding of Scientific Study, 2008

"When you read or hear the term scientific study, do you have
a clear understanding of what it means, a general sense of what it means,
or little understanding of what it means?"

(percent of people aged 18 or older responding by demographic characteristic, 2008)

	clear understanding	general sense	little understanding
Total people	**27.7%**	**50.5%**	**21.8%**
Men	30.4	51.2	18.4
Women	25.1	49.8	25.1
Black	19.5	47.0	33.5
Hispanic	21.6	38.1	40.3
White	29.3	52.7	18.0
Aged 18 to 44	30.8	48.3	20.9
Aged 45 to 64	28.7	53.0	18.3
Aged 65 or older	14.9	51.2	33.9
Not a college graduate	22.0	51.2	26.8
Bachelor's degree or more	43.9	48.5	7.5

Source: Survey Documentation and Analysis, Computer-assisted Survey Methods Program, University of California, Berkeley, General Social Survey, 2008 Cumulative Data Files, Internet site http://sda.berkeley.edu/cgi-bin/hsda?harcsda+gss08; calculations by New Strategist

Table 3.16 Scientific Knowledge: The Center of Earth Is Very Hot, 2008

"The center of the Earth is very hot. Is that true or false?"

(percent of people aged 18 or older responding by demographic characteristic, 2008)

	true	false
Total people	**93.8%**	**6.2%**
Men	95.4	4.6
Women	92.3	7.7
Black	89.6	10.4
Hispanic	89.3	10.7
White	95.3	4.7
Aged 18 to 44	93.1	6.9
Aged 45 to 64	94.1	5.9
Aged 65 or older	95.3	4.7
Not a college graduate	93.1	6.9
Bachelor's degree or more	95.6	4.4

Source: Survey Documentation and Analysis, Computer-assisted Survey Methods Program, University of California, Berkeley, General Social Survey, 2008 Cumulative Data Files, Internet site http://sda.berkeley.edu/cgi-bin/hsda?harcsda+gss08; calculations by New Strategist

Table 3.17 Scientific Knowledge: All Radioactivity Is Man-Made, 2008

"All radioactivity is man-made. Is that true or false?"

(percent of people aged 18 or older responding by demographic characteristic, 2008)

	true	false
Total people	**20.5%**	**79.5%**
Men	20.6	79.4
Women	20.3	79.7
Black	33.1	66.9
Hispanic	45.2	54.8
White	16.5	83.5
Aged 18 to 44	24.2	75.8
Aged 45 to 64	16.0	84.0
Aged 65 or older	20.1	79.9
Not a college graduate	24.6	75.4
Bachelor's degree or more	9.3	90.7

Source: Survey Documentation and Analysis, Computer-assisted Survey Methods Program, University of California, Berkeley, General Social Survey, 2008 Cumulative Data Files, Internet site http://sda.berkeley.edu/cgi-bin/hsda?harcsda+gss08; calculations by New Strategist

Table 3.18 Scientific Knowledge: Father's Gene Decides Sex of Baby, 2008

"It is the father's gene that decides whether the baby is a boy or a girl.
Is that true or false?"

(percent of people aged 18 or older responding by demographic characteristic, 2008)

	true	false
Total people	**71.1%**	**28.9%**
Men	62.6	37.4
Women	78.5	21.5
Black	56.4	43.6
Hispanic	63.5	36.5
White	74.4	25.6
Aged 18 to 44	71.9	28.1
Aged 45 to 64	69.2	30.8
Aged 65 or older	73.1	26.9
Not a college graduate	69.4	30.7
Bachelor's degree or more	76.2	23.8

Source: Survey Documentation and Analysis, Computer-assisted Survey Methods Program, University of California, Berkeley, General Social Survey, 2008 Cumulative Data Files, Internet site http://sda.berkeley.edu/cgi-bin/hsda?harcsda+gss08; calculations by New Strategist

Table 3.19 Scientific Knowledge: Mother's Gene Decides Sex of Baby, 2008

"Does mom's gene decide baby's sex?"

(percent of people aged 18 or older responding by demographic characteristic, 2008)

	yes	no
Total people	**19.0%**	**81.0%**
Men	24.7	75.3
Women	13.6	86.4
Black	21.0	79.0
Hispanic	30.4	69.6
White	15.6	84.4
Aged 18 to 44	18.7	81.3
Aged 45 to 64	22.7	77.3
Aged 65 or older	8.8	91.2
Not a college graduate	25.0	75.0
Bachelor's degree or more	4.3	95.7

Source: Survey Documentation and Analysis, Computer-assisted Survey Methods Program, University of California, Berkeley, General Social Survey, 2008 Cumulative Data Files, Internet site http://sda.berkeley.edu/cgi-bin/hsda?harcsda+gss08; calculations by New Strategist

Table 3.20 Scientific Knowledge: Lasers Work by Focusing Sound Waves, 2008

"Lasers work by focusing sound waves. Is that true or false?"

(percent of people aged 18 or older responding by demographic characteristic, 2008)

	true	false
Total people	**33.1%**	**66.9%**
Men	22.1	77.9
Women	46.4	53.6
Black	50.7	49.3
Hispanic	49.9	50.1
White	29.6	70.4
Aged 18 to 44	30.7	69.3
Aged 45 to 64	30.7	69.3
Aged 65 or older	49.0	51.0
Not a college graduate	39.0	61.0
Bachelor's degree or more	17.8	82.2

Source: Survey Documentation and Analysis, Computer-assisted Survey Methods Program, University of California, Berkeley, General Social Survey, 2008 Cumulative Data Files, Internet site http://sda.berkeley.edu/cgi-bin/hsda?harcsda+gss08; calculations by New Strategist

Table 3.21 Scientific Knowledge: Electrons Are Smaller than Atoms, 2008

"Electrons are smaller than atoms. Is that true or false?"

(percent of people aged 18 or older responding by demographic characteristic, 2008)

	true	false
Total people	**69.6%**	**30.4%**
Men	71.2	28.8
Women	67.8	32.2
Black	59.8	40.2
Hispanic	59.3	40.7
White	72.1	27.9
Aged 18 to 44	69.1	30.9
Aged 45 to 64	69.8	30.2
Aged 65 or older	71.1	28.9
Not a college graduate	65.9	34.1
Bachelor's degree or more	78.1	21.9

Source: Survey Documentation and Analysis, Computer-assisted Survey Methods Program, University of California, Berkeley, General Social Survey, 2008 Cumulative Data Files, Internet site http://sda.berkeley.edu/cgi-bin/hsda?harcsda+gss08; calculations by New Strategist

Table 3.22 Scientific Knowledge: Antibiotics Kill Viruses As Well As Bacteria, 2008

"Antibiotics kill viruses as well as bacteria. Is that true or false?"

(percent of people aged 18 or older responding by demographic characteristic, 2008)

	true	false
Total people	**42.1%**	**57.9%**
Men	48.6	51.4
Women	36.2	63.8
Black	73.5	26.5
Hispanic	66.0	34.0
White	35.3	64.7
Aged 18 to 44	48.3	51.7
Aged 45 to 64	34.7	65.3
Aged 65 or older	41.8	58.2
Not a college graduate	49.7	50.3
Bachelor's degree or more	21.4	78.6

Source: Survey Documentation and Analysis, Computer-assisted Survey Methods Program, University of California, Berkeley, General Social Survey, 2008 Cumulative Data Files, Internet site http://sda.berkeley.edu/cgi-bin/hsda?harcsda+gss08; calculations by New Strategist

Table 3.23 Scientific Knowledge: The Universe Began with a Huge Explosion, 2008

"The universe began with a huge explosion. Is that true or false?"

(percent of people aged 18 or older responding by demographic characteristic, 2008)

	true	false
Total people	**45.1%**	**54.9%**
Men	55.9	44.1
Women	35.3	64.7
Black	23.9	76.1
Hispanic	47.9	52.1
White	47.5	52.5
Aged 18 to 44	49.8	50.2
Aged 45 to 64	40.2	59.8
Aged 65 or older	42.0	58.0
Not a college graduate	38.9	61.1
Bachelor's degree or more	62.2	37.8

Source: Survey Documentation and Analysis, Computer-assisted Survey Methods Program, University of California, Berkeley, General Social Survey, 2008 Cumulative Data Files, Internet site http://sda.berkeley.edu/cgi-bin/hsda?harcsda+gss08; calculations by New Strategist

Table 3.24 Scientific Knowledge: The Continents Have Been Moving, 2008

"The continents on which we live have been moving their locations for millions of years and will continue to move in the future. Is that true or false?"

(percent of people aged 18 or older responding by demographic characteristic, 2008)

	true	false
Total people	**88.3%**	**11.7%**
Men	90.9	9.4
Women	85.9	14.1
Black	77.9	22.1
Hispanic	83.3	16.7
White	90.0	10.0
Aged 18 to 44	90.3	9.7
Aged 45 to 64	87.8	12.2
Aged 65 or older	82.5	17.5
Not a college graduate	86.7	13.3
Bachelor's degree or more	92.2	7.8

Source: Survey Documentation and Analysis, Computer-assisted Survey Methods Program, University of California, Berkeley, General Social Survey, 2008 Cumulative Data Files, Internet site http://sda.berkeley.edu/cgi-bin/hsda?harcsda+gss08; calculations by New Strategist

Table 3.25 Scientific Knowledge: Human Beings Developed from Animals, 2008

"Human beings, as we know them today, developed from
earlier species of animals. Is that true or false?"

(percent of people aged 18 or older responding by demographic characteristic, 2008)

	true	false
Total people	**50.9%**	**49.1%**
Men	58.6	41.4
Women	43.6	56.4
Black	40.5	59.5
Hispanic	46.3	53.7
White	52.2	47.8
Aged 18 to 44	56.3	43.7
Aged 45 to 64	47.6	52.4
Aged 65 or older	41.2	58.8
Not a college graduate	46.2	53.8
Bachelor's degree or more	63.3	36.7

Source: Survey Documentation and Analysis, Computer-assisted Survey Methods Program, University of California, Berkeley, General Social Survey, 2008 Cumulative Data Files, Internet site http://sda.berkeley.edu/cgi-bin/hsda?harcsda+gss08; calculations by New Strategist

Table 3.26 Scientific Knowledge: The Earth Goes around the Sun, 2008

"Does the Earth go around the Sun, or does the Sun go around the Earth?"

(percent of people aged 18 or older responding by demographic characteristic, 2008)

	Earth around Sun	Sun around Earth
Total people	**77.5%**	**22.5%**
Men	83.3	16.7
Women	71.8	28.2
Black	58.8	41.2
Hispanic	75.4	24.6
White	80.0	20.0
Aged 18 to 44	78.9	21.1
Aged 45 to 64	77.9	22.1
Aged 65 or older	71.2	28.8
Not a college graduate	72.9	27.1
Bachelor's degree or more	89.5	10.5

Source: Survey Documentation and Analysis, Computer-assisted Survey Methods Program, University of California, Berkeley, General Social Survey, 2008 Cumulative Data Files, Internet site http://sda.berkeley.edu/cgi-bin/hsda?harcsda+gss08; calculations by New Strategist

Table 3.27 Scientific Knowledge: How Long the Earth Goes around the Sun, 2008

"How long does it take for the Earth to go around the Sun:
one day, one month, or one year?"

(percent of people aged 18 or older responding by demographic characteristic, 2008)

	one day	one month	one year
Total people	**20.5%**	**3.2%**	**76.2%**
Men	19.2	3.3	77.4
Women	22.0	3.2	74.9
Black	28.2	2.4	69.4
Hispanic	30.9	6.8	62.3
White	18.7	3.5	77.7
Aged 18 to 44	18.7	3.9	77.2
Aged 45 to 64	18.2	2.5	79.3
Aged 65 or older	34.6	2.8	62.5
Not a college graduate	26.6	4.2	69.1
Bachelor's degree or more	8.0	1.3	90.7

Note: Numbers may not add to total because "other time period if volunteered" is not shown.
Source: Survey Documentation and Analysis, Computer-assisted Survey Methods Program, University of California, Berkeley, General Social Survey, 2008 Cumulative Data Files, Internet site http://sda.berkeley.edu/cgi-bin/hsda?harcsda+gss08; calculations by New Strategist

Medical Discoveries Receive the Most Attention

When Americans are asked how interested they are in a variety of topics, medical discoveries are number one. Sixty-one percent say they are very interested in medical discoveries. The only other topic that captures the attention of at least half the public is the environment. Economic issues interest only 49 percent. Local school issues are close behind at 48 percent. Among blacks, however, a much larger 68 percent are very interested in local school issues.

(percent of people aged 18 or older who are very interested in selected topics, 2008)

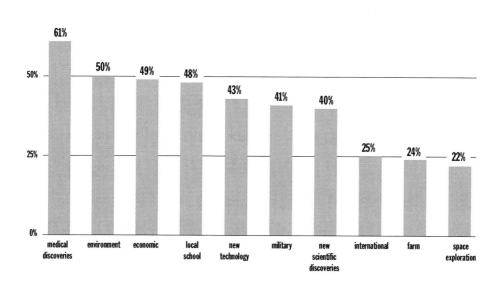

Table 3.28 Interest in International Issues, 2008

"There are a lot of issues in the news, and it is hard to keep up
with every area. Are you very interested, moderately interested,
or not at all interested in international and foreign policy issues?"

(percent of people aged 18 or older responding by demographic characteristic, 2008)

	very interested	moderately interested	not at all interested
Total people	**24.5%**	**47.7%**	**27.8%**
Men	31.1	45.6	23.2
Women	18.3	49.7	32.0
Black	18.6	42.7	38.7
Hispanic	22.0	38.1	39.9
White	25.6	49.3	25.0
Aged 18 to 44	18.8	48.3	32.9
Aged 45 to 64	28.8	46.6	24.6
Aged 65 or older	31.9	48.3	19.8
Not a college graduate	19.0	46.4	34.7
Bachelor's degree or more	40.3	51.6	8.0

Source: Survey Documentation and Analysis, Computer-assisted Survey Methods Program, University of California, Berkeley, General Social Survey, 2008 Cumulative Data Files, Internet site http://sda.berkeley.edu/cgi-bin/hsda?harcsda+gss08; calculations by New Strategist

Table 3.29 Interest in Farm Issues, 2008

"There are a lot of issues in the news, and it is hard to keep up
with every area. Are you very interested, moderately interested,
or not at all interested in agricultural and farm issues?"

(percent of people aged 18 or older responding by demographic characteristic, 2008)

	very interested	moderately interested	not at all interested
Total people	**24.1%**	**52.1%**	**23.9%**
Men	29.3	53.0	17.7
Women	19.2	51.2	29.6
Black	21.4	40.2	38.4
Hispanic	21.9	50.8	27.3
White	24.9	54.4	20.8
Aged 18 to 44	19.3	50.6	30.1
Aged 45 to 64	27.5	53.5	19.0
Aged 65 or older	31.1	52.5	16.4
Not a college graduate	24.4	51.3	24.3
Bachelor's degree or more	23.2	54.2	22.6

Source: Survey Documentation and Analysis, Computer-assisted Survey Methods Program, University of California, Berkeley, General Social Survey, 2008 Cumulative Data Files, Internet site http://sda.berkeley.edu/cgi-bin/hsda?harcsda+gss08; calculations by New Strategist

Table 3.30 Interest in Local School Issues, 2008

"There are a lot of issues in the news, and it is hard to keep up
with every area. Are you very interested, moderately interested,
or not at all interested in local school issues?"

(percent of people aged 18 or older responding by demographic characteristic, 2008)

	very interested	moderately interested	not at all interested
Total people	**48.0%**	**39.0%**	**13.1%**
Men	43.5	42.2	14.2
Women	52.1	35.9	12.0
Black	67.8	23.9	8.3
Hispanic	53.2	35.9	10.9
White	43.9	42.2	13.9
Aged 18 to 44	53.9	33.9	12.1
Aged 45 to 64	44.6	42.7	12.7
Aged 65 or older	37.6	46.0	16.4
Not a college graduate	45.4	41.2	13.4
Bachelor's degree or more	55.3	32.5	12.1

Source: Survey Documentation and Analysis, Computer-assisted Survey Methods Program, University of California, Berkeley, General Social Survey, 2008 Cumulative Data Files, Internet site http://sda.berkeley.edu/cgi-bin/hsda?harcsda+gss08; calculations by New Strategist

Table 3.31 Interest in New Scientific Discoveries, 2008

"There are a lot of issues in the news, and it is hard to keep up
with every area. Are you very interested, moderately interested,
or not at all interested in new scientific discoveries?"

(percent of people aged 18 or older responding by demographic characteristic, 2008)

	very interested	moderately interested	not at all interested
Total people	**40.0%**	**45.5%**	**14.5%**
Men	43.9	43.7	12.4
Women	36.5	47.1	16.4
Black	31.3	45.9	22.8
Hispanic	35.7	44.5	19.8
White	41.2	45.7	13.2
Aged 18 to 44	38.4	46.4	15.2
Aged 45 to 64	39.5	46.4	14.1
Aged 65 or older	46.1	40.7	13.1
Not a college graduate	35.8	46.4	17.8
Bachelor's degree or more	52.2	42.9	4.9

Source: Survey Documentation and Analysis, Computer-assisted Survey Methods Program, University of California, Berkeley, General Social Survey, 2008 Cumulative Data Files, Internet site http://sda.berkeley.edu/cgi-bin/hsda?harcsda+gss08; calculations by New Strategist

Table 3.32 Interest in Economic Issues, 2008

"There are a lot of issues in the news, and it is hard to keep up
with every area. Are you very interested, moderately interested,
or not at all interested in economic issues and business conditions?"

(percent of people aged 18 or older responding by demographic characteristic, 2008)

	very interested	moderately interested	not at all interested
Total people	**49.2%**	**41.1%**	**9.8%**
Men	53.4	37.6	9.0
Women	45.2	44.3	10.5
Black	58.6	26.8	14.6
Hispanic	41.3	45.2	13.5
White	47.7	43.5	8.8
Aged 18 to 44	47.2	41.6	11.2
Aged 45 to 64	52.6	40.0	7.3
Aged 65 or older	47.1	41.6	11.2
Not a college graduate	46.4	41.8	11.7
Bachelor's degree or more	57.1	38.8	4.1

Source: Survey Documentation and Analysis, Computer-assisted Survey Methods Program, University of California, Berkeley, General Social Survey, 2008 Cumulative Data Files, Internet site http://sda.berkeley.edu/cgi-bin/hsda?harcsda+gss08; calculations by New Strategist

Table 3.33 Interest in Technology, 2008

"There are a lot of issues in the news, and it is hard to keep up with every area. Are you very interested, moderately interested, or not at all interested in issues about the use of new inventions and technologies?"

(percent of people aged 18 or older responding by demographic characteristic, 2008)

	very interested	moderately interested	not at all interested
Total people	**43.0%**	**44.7%**	**12.2%**
Men	52.2	39.1	8.7
Women	34.5	49.9	15.6
Black	37.6	41.2	21.2
Hispanic	41.5	41.5	17.1
White	43.5	45.7	10.8
Aged 18 to 44	43.8	43.7	12.5
Aged 45 to 64	42.5	45.3	12.2
Aged 65 or older	41.1	47.3	11.6
Not a college graduate	41.3	45.2	13.6
Bachelor's degree or more	48.1	43.4	8.5

Source: Survey Documentation and Analysis, Computer-assisted Survey Methods Program, University of California, Berkeley, General Social Survey, 2008 Cumulative Data Files, Internet site http://sda.berkeley.edu/cgi-bin/hsda?harcsda+gss08; calculations by New Strategist

Table 3.34 Interest in Medical Discoveries, 2008

"There are a lot of issues in the news, and it is hard to keep up
with every area. Are you very interested, moderately interested,
or not at all interested in issues about new medical discoveries?"

(percent of people aged 18 or older responding by demographic characteristic, 2008)

	very interested	moderately interested	not at all interested
Total people	**60.7%**	**33.0%**	**6.4%**
Men	57.6	35.0	7.4
Women	63.5	31.1	5.4
Black	65.9	23.7	10.4
Hispanic	59.1	27.7	13.1
White	59.1	35.5	5.4
Aged 18 to 44	56.8	35.1	8.1
Aged 45 to 64	62.6	31.8	5.5
Aged 65 or older	67.8	29.2	3.0
Not a college graduate	60.2	32.2	7.6
Bachelor's degree or more	61.9	35.2	2.9

Source: Survey Documentation and Analysis, Computer-assisted Survey Methods Program, University of California, Berkeley, General Social Survey, 2008 Cumulative Data Files, Internet site http://sda.berkeley.edu/cgi-bin/hsda?harcsda+gss08; calculations by New Strategist

Table 3.35 Interest in Space Exploration, 2008

"There are a lot of issues in the news, and it is hard to keep up
with every area. Are you very interested, moderately interested,
or not at all interested in issues about space exploration?"

(percent of people aged 18 or older responding by demographic characteristic, 2008)

	very interested	moderately interested	not at all interested
Total people	**21.6%**	**44.6%**	**33.7%**
Men	29.5	43.4	27.2
Women	14.4	45.8	39.9
Black	11.5	37.0	51.4
Hispanic	24.1	43.8	32.1
White	22.8	46.2	31.1
Aged 18 to 44	20.8	44.5	34.7
Aged 45 to 64	22.7	44.2	33.0
Aged 65 or older	21.4	46.6	32.0
Not a college graduate	19.4	42.9	37.7
Bachelor's degree or more	28.1	49.6	22.3

Source: Survey Documentation and Analysis, Computer-assisted Survey Methods Program, University of California, Berkeley, General Social Survey, 2008 Cumulative Data Files, Internet site http://sda.berkeley.edu/cgi-bin/hsda?harcsda+gss08; calculations by New Strategist

Table 3.36 Interest in Environmental Issues, 2008

"There are a lot of issues in the news, and it is hard to keep up with every area. Are you very interested, moderately interested, or not at all interested in issues about environmental pollution?"

(percent of people aged 18 or older responding by demographic characteristic, 2008)

	very interested	moderately interested	not at all interested
Total people	**49.9%**	**40.1%**	**10.0%**
Men	48.2	40.8	11.0
Women	51.5	39.4	9.0
Black	48.1	37.1	14.8
Hispanic	51.3	35.2	13.6
White	49.7	41.1	9.2
Aged 18 to 44	45.2	43.2	11.6
Aged 45 to 64	54.0	37.7	8.3
Aged 65 or older	54.1	36.8	9.1
Not a college graduate	47.9	39.8	12.3
Bachelor's degree or more	55.6	41.0	3.4

Source: Survey Documentation and Analysis, Computer-assisted Survey Methods Program, University of California, Berkeley, General Social Survey, 2008 Cumulative Data Files, Internet site http://sda.berkeley.edu/cgi-bin/hsda?harcsda+gss08; calculations by New Strategist

Table 3.37 Interest in Military Policy, 2008

"There are a lot of issues in the news, and it is hard to keep up with every area. Are you very interested, moderately interested, or not at all interested in issues about military and defense policy?"

(percent of people aged 18 or older responding by demographic characteristic, 2008)

	very interested	moderately interested	not at all interested
Total people	**40.7%**	**45.3%**	**14.1%**
Men	46.1	42.3	11.6
Women	35.5	48.1	16.4
Black	42.3	33.2	24.4
Hispanic	31.8	42.0	26.3
White	41.6	47.4	11.0
Aged 18 to 44	33.7	49.1	17.2
Aged 45 to 64	45.2	43.5	11.3
Aged 65 or older	52.0	37.6	10.5
Not a college graduate	40.0	44.9	15.1
Bachelor's degree or more	42.6	46.4	11.0

Source: Survey Documentation and Analysis, Computer-assisted Survey Methods Program, University of California, Berkeley, General Social Survey, 2008 Cumulative Data Files, Internet site http://sda.berkeley.edu/cgi-bin/hsda?harcsda+gss08; calculations by New Strategist

4

Religion

Religion has held center stage in the political arena for some years. Religious commitments and beliefs have been discussed, dissected, and challenged. Despite the attention to religion, Americans' beliefs and behavior have shifted surprisingly little. But the terrorist attacks have given the public a new perspective on religious intolerance. Here is a look at trends in religion over the past few decades.

Little or no change

• **Belief in God.** Sixty-three percent of people aged 18 or older know God exists and have no doubt about it. Belief in God has not changed over the past 20 years.

• **Frequent prayer.** In 2008, the 57 percent majority of Americans said they prayed at least once a day, a proportion that is slightly higher than the 53 percent of 1988.

• **Bible is inspired word of God.** The largest share of Americans continues to believe that the Bible is the inspired word of God and is not to be taken literally—a percentage that has not changed significantly in the past two decades.

Big changes

• **Attendance at religious services.** The gap is growing between the percentage of Americans who attend church once a year or less often (42 percent in 2008) and the number attending nearly once a week or more often (30 percent in 2008). In 1978, the numbers were even at 36 percent each.

• **Fewer Protestants.** Protestant dominance is on the wane. The percentage of Americans who identify themselves as Protestant has declined over the past three decades. Currently, just under half of adults identify themselves as Protestants, down from 63 percent in 1978.

• **9/11 brings second thoughts.** The terrorist attacks of September 11, 2001, have given many a different perspective on religion. In 1998, only 34 percent of Americans agreed that religion brings more conflict than peace. By 2008, the figure had climbed to 61 percent.

Many Americans Rarely Attend Church

More than 40 percent of the public attends church only once a year or less. The percentage of Americans who say they are Protestant fell from 63 to just under 50 percent during the past 30 years. At the same time, the percentage with no religion has grown from 8 to 17 percent.

(percent distribution of people aged 18 or older by frequency of attendance at religious services, 2008)

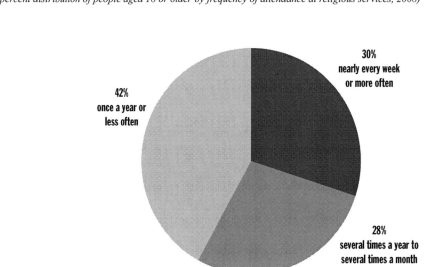

30%
nearly every week
or more often

42%
once a year or
less often

28%
several times a year to
several times a month

Table 4.1 Religious Background, 1978 to 2008

"In what religion were you raised?"

(percent of people aged 18 or older responding, 1978 to 2008; and percent responding by demographic characteristic, 2008)

	Protestant	Catholic	Jewish	Buddhism	Hinduism	Moslem/ Islam	other	none
TREND								
2008	52.9%	33.2%	1.8%	0.3%	0.6%	0.5%	2.0%	8.7%
1998	57.9	31.2	1.8	0.2	0.2	0.6	2.2	5.9
1988	62.9	29.4	2.1	–	–	–	2.1	3.6
1978	66.0	28.2	1.8	–	–	–	0.8	3.2
2008 PROFILE								
Total people	**52.9**	**33.2**	**1.8**	**0.3**	**0.6**	**0.5**	**2.0**	**8.7**
Men	52.8	33.1	1.2	0.5	0.8	0.1	2.0	9.5
Women	53.1	33.3	2.3	0.1	0.4	0.9	1.9	8.0
Black	81.8	6.8	0.0	0.0	0.0	1.2	3.0	7.2
Hispanic	13.1	79.0	0.0	0.0	0.0	0.0	2.4	5.5
White	52.5	34.4	2.4	0.0	0.0	0.0	1.9	8.8
Aged 18 to 44	42.8	37.4	2.5	0.3	1.1	1.1	2.6	12.2
Aged 45 to 64	62.8	29.3	1.1	0.2	0.1	0.0	1.0	5.5
Aged 65 or older	60.2	29.6	1.5	0.4	0.1	0.0	2.5	5.7
Not a college graduate	52.5	35.1	0.9	0.1	0.1	0.0	1.8	9.5
Bachelor's degree or more	54.1	28.1	4.5	0.6	2.2	1.9	2.1	6.5

Note: "–" means data are not available.
Source: Survey Documentation and Analysis, Computer-assisted Survey Methods Program, University of California, Berkeley, General Social Surveys, 1972–2008 Cumulative Data Files, Internet site http://sda.berkeley.edu/cgi-bin/hsda?harcsda+gss08; calculations by New Strategist

Table 4.2 Religious Preference, 1978 to 2008

"What is your religious preference?"

(percent of people aged 18 or older responding, 1978 to 2008; and percent responding by demographic characteristic, 2008)

	Protestant	Catholic	Jewish	Buddhism	Hinduism	Moslem/ Islam	other	none
TREND								
2008	49.8%	25.1%	1.7%	0.6%	0.4%	0.7%	4.9%	16.8%
1998	53.7	26.2	1.8	0.3	0.3	0.5	3.5	13.7
1988	60.4	27.1	2.0	–	–	–	2.8	7.7
1978	63.0	25.8	1.6	–	–	–	1.1	8.4
2008 PROFILE								
Total people	**49.8**	**25.1**	**1.7**	**0.6**	**0.4**	**0.7**	**4.9**	**16.8**
Men	46.1	24.0	1.5	1.1	0.7	0.2	3.7	22.7
Women	53.1	26.1	1.9	0.2	0.2	1.2	5.7	11.6
Black	72.9	5.1	0.3	0.2	0.0	2.4	5.4	13.7
Hispanic	22.0	61.1	0.2	0.0	0.0	0.0	4.1	12.6
White	49.3	26.2	2.1	0.4	0.0	0.0	4.8	17.2
Aged 18 to 44	39.3	27.8	1.9	0.7	0.8	1.2	6.1	22.2
Aged 45 to 64	59.2	20.4	1.1	0.7	0.1	0.5	4.2	13.8
Aged 65 or older	60.0	26.8	2.5	0.4	0.0	0.0	2.6	7.7
Not a college graduate	51.2	26.0	0.8	0.2	0.1	0.5	4.8	16.4
Bachelor's degree or more	45.9	22.5	4.3	1.8	1.5	1.3	4.6	18.1

Note: "–" means data are not available.
Source: Survey Documentation and Analysis, Computer-assisted Survey Methods Program, University of California, Berkeley, General Social Surveys, 1972–2008 Cumulative Data Files, Internet site http://sda.berkeley.edu/cgi-bin/hsda?harcsda+gss08; calculations by New Strategist

Table 4.3 Attendance at Religious Services, 1978 to 2008

"How often do you attend religious services?"

(percent of people aged 18 or older responding, 1978 to 2008; and percent responding by demographic characteristic, 2008)

	more than once a week	every week	nearly every week	two or three times a month	once a month	several times a year	once a year	less than once a year	never
TREND									
2008	7.8%	17.6%	4.6%	9.1%	7.5%	11.1%	13.5%	6.9%	21.8%
1998	8.0	18.6	6.6	8.6	7.2	11.1	10.4	10.6	18.9
1988	7.4	19.6	7.2	10.1	7.7	12.4	12.1	6.9	16.6
1978	7.7	20.9	7.0	9.3	6.1	12.7	13.7	8.1	14.5
2008 PROFILE									
Total people	**7.8**	**17.6**	**4.6**	**9.1**	**7.5**	**11.1**	**13.5**	**6.9**	**21.8**
Men	6.2	14.6	4.5	9.0	8.1	9.9	15.6	8.1	24.0
Women	9.2	20.4	4.7	9.1	7.0	12.2	11.7	5.9	19.9
Black	12.4	17.2	7.4	15.6	4.3	10.2	13.5	6.6	12.7
Hispanic	8.9	15.6	5.0	11.7	8.5	8.9	18.7	6.1	16.7
White	7.2	17.7	4.3	8.0	8.1	10.9	13.3	7.1	23.4
Aged 18 to 44	5.5	13.4	3.9	10.7	7.8	11.2	15.1	6.5	25.8
Aged 45 to 64	8.2	18.6	5.5	7.6	8.0	12.2	13.7	7.9	18.3
Aged 65 or older	14.0	28.3	4.2	7.2	5.7	8.4	7.8	6.2	18.0
Not a college graduate	8.5	16.1	4.1	9.0	7.9	11.2	13.5	6.7	23.0
Bachelor's degree or more	5.7	22.0	5.9	9.3	6.3	11.0	13.5	7.6	18.6

Source: Survey Documentation and Analysis, Computer-assisted Survey Methods Program, University of California, Berkeley, General Social Surveys, 1972–2008 Cumulative Data Files, Internet site http://sda.berkeley.edu/cgi-bin/hsda?harcsda+gss08; calculations by New Strategist

Table 4.4 Frequency of Prayer, 1988 to 2008

"About how often do you pray?"

(percent of people aged 18 or older responding, 1988 to 2008; and percent responding by demographic charac-teristic, 2008)

	several times a day	once a day	several times a week	once a week	less than once a week	never
TREND						
2008	27.4%	29.9%	11.0%	6.2%	13.5%	11.9%
1998	24.0	29.5	14.9	7.4	22.6	1.6
1988	22.0	30.8	16.1	8.5	22.4	0.3
2008 PROFILE						
Total people	**27.4**	**29.9**	**11.0**	**6.2**	**13.5**	**11.9**
Men	20.9	24.7	10.5	7.5	18.4	18.0
Women	33.2	34.5	11.4	5.1	9.2	6.6
Black	43.0	31.6	8.5	5.5	5.5	5.8
Hispanic	18.8	35.1	13.1	9.7	16.5	6.9
White	25.6	29.3	11.5	6.1	14.7	12.9
Aged 18 to 44	20.3	27.6	13.8	7.3	16.5	14.4
Aged 45 to 64	33.2	30.6	8.5	5.9	11.5	10.3
Aged 65 or older	36.3	34.7	7.9	3.8	9.2	8.1
Not a college graduate	28.9	30.0	11.3	6.8	12.2	10.8
Bachelor's degree or more	23.1	29.9	10.0	4.5	17.3	15.2

Source: Survey Documentation and Analysis, Computer-assisted Survey Methods Program, University of California, Berkeley, General Social Surveys, 1972–2008 Cumulative Data Files, Internet site http://sda.berkeley.edu/cgi-bin/hsda?harcsda+gss08; calculations by New Strategist

Americans Believe in God

The 62 percent majority of people aged 18 or older say they know God exists and have no doubt about it. Most believe in life after death (81 percent), heaven (64 percent), and hell (52 percent). Fifty-five percent of the American public also believes in religious miracles.

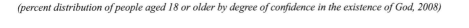

(percent distribution of people aged 18 or older by degree of confidence in the existence of God, 2008)

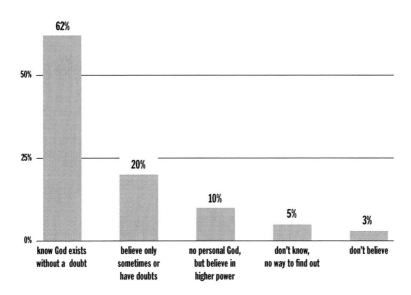

Table 4.5 Confidence in the Existence of God, 1988 to 2008

"Which statement comes closest to expressing what you believe about God?
1) I don't believe in God. 2) I don't know whether there is a God and I don't believe
there is any way to find out. 3) I don't believe in a personal God, but I do believe
in a Higher Power of some kind. 4) I find myself believing in God some of the time,
but not at others. 5) While I have doubts, I feel that I do believe in God.
6) I know God really exists and I have no doubts about it."

(percent of people aged 18 or older responding, 1988 to 2008; and percent responding by demographic characteristic, 2008)

	1 don't believe	2 no way to find out	3 higher power	4 believe sometimes	5 believe but doubts	6 know God exists
TREND						
2008	3.1%	4.9%	10.1%	3.4%	16.9%	61.6%
1998	3.2	5.1	10.0	4.6	13.8	63.3
1988	1.5	3.6	7.4	5.1	19.0	63.3
2008 PROFILE						
Total people	**3.1**	**4.9**	**10.1**	**3.4**	**16.9**	**61.6**
Men	5.4	7.8	13.0	4.1	18.6	51.2
Women	1.0	2.4	7.5	2.8	15.4	70.8
Black	2.3	0.7	3.9	1.3	12.8	79.0
Hispanic	0.7	3.8	6.0	5.1	11.0	73.4
White	3.2	5.3	10.8	3.3	18.3	59.0
Aged 18 to 44	3.2	6.1	12.6	4.0	16.6	57.5
Aged 45 to 64	3.3	3.5	9.1	2.0	18.9	63.2
Aged 65 or older	1.8	4.7	5.1	5.1	13.5	69.8
Not a college graduate	2.6	3.7	8.5	3.5	16.5	65.3
Bachelor's degree or more	4.4	8.5	14.6	3.1	18.2	51.1

Source: Survey Documentation and Analysis, Computer-assisted Survey Methods Program, University of California, Berkeley, General Social Surveys, 1972–2008 Cumulative Data Files, Internet site http://sda.berkeley.edu/cgi-bin/hsda?harcsda+gss08; calculations by New Strategist

Table 4.6 Beliefs about God, 1998 and 2008

"Which best describes your beliefs about God?"

(percent of people aged 18 or older responding, 1998 and 2008; and percent responding by demographic characteristic, 2008)

	don't believe now, never have	don't believe now, used to	believe now, didn't used to	believe now, always have
TREND				
2008	4.6%	5.3%	6.7%	83.4%
1998	3.2	5.5	6.1	85.1
2008 PROFILE				
Total people	**4.6**	**5.3**	**6.7**	**83.4**
Men	7.6	8.7	8.5	75.2
Women	1.9	2.3	5.2	90.6
Black	0.8	2.3	8.9	88.0
Hispanic	1.3	3.9	4.3	90.5
White	5.0	5.8	6.6	82.6
Aged 18 to 44	6.7	6.0	6.8	80.5
Aged 45 to 64	2.9	4.8	6.5	85.8
Aged 65 or older	1.6	4.1	7.5	86.8
Not a college graduate	3.5	3.7	7.2	85.6
Bachelor's degree or more	7.4	9.6	5.6	77.4

Source: Survey Documentation and Analysis, Computer-assisted Survey Methods Program, University of California, Berkeley, General Social Surveys, 1972–2008 Cumulative Data Files, Internet site http://sda.berkeley.edu/cgi-bin/hsda?harcsda+gss08; calculations by New Strategist

Table 4.7 Life Meaningful Because God Exists, 1998 and 2008

"Do you agree or disagree: To me, life is meaningful only because God exists?"

(percent of people aged 18 or older responding, 1998 and 2008; and percent responding by demographic characteristic, 2008)

	strongly agree	agree	neither agree nor disagree	disagree	strongly disagree
TREND					
2008	19.3%	25.6%	21.0%	22.4%	11.8%
1998	21.1	23.1	25.0	20.4	10.4
2008 PROFILE					
Total people	**19.3**	**25.6**	**21.0**	**22.4**	**11.8**
Men	15.3	23.7	20.2	24.6	16.1
Women	22.7	27.2	21.7	20.4	8.0
Black	30.8	30.3	20.9	14.1	3.9
Hispanic	18.4	37.2	18.9	19.0	6.5
White	17.4	24.7	21.3	23.6	13.0
Aged 18 to 44	15.8	21.0	23.4	24.2	15.7
Aged 45 to 64	21.2	29.4	19.1	21.4	8.9
Aged 65 or older	25.6	30.5	17.8	19.6	6.5
Not a college graduate	20.9	27.8	20.3	22.1	8.9
Bachelor's degree or more	14.9	19.5	22.7	23.1	19.8

Source: Survey Documentation and Analysis, Computer-assisted Survey Methods Program, University of California, Berkeley, General Social Surveys, 1972–2008 Cumulative Data Files, Internet site http://sda.berkeley.edu/cgi-bin/hsda?harcsda+gss08; calculations by New Strategist

Table 4.8 Belief in Life after Death, 1988 to 2008

"Do you believe there is a life after death?"

(percent of people aged 18 or older responding, 1988 to 2008; and percent responding by demographic characteristic, 2008)

	yes	no
TREND		
2008	81.3%	18.7%
1998	81.8	18.2
1988	78.9	21.1
2008 PROFILE		
Total people	**81.3**	**18.7**
Men	77.1	22.9
Women	85.0	15.0
Black	82.5	17.5
Hispanic	75.2	24.8
White	81.7	18.3
Aged 18 to 44	79.2	20.8
Aged 45 to 64	83.6	16.4
Aged 65 or older	82.3	17.7
Not a college graduate	81.8	18.2
Bachelor's degree or more	80.1	19.9

Source: Survey Documentation and Analysis, Computer-assisted Survey Methods Program, University of California, Berkeley, General Social Surveys, 1972–2008 Cumulative Data Files, Internet site http://sda.berkeley.edu/cgi-bin/hsda?harcsda+gss08; calculations by New Strategist

Table 4.9 Belief in Heaven, 1998 and 2008

"Do you believe in heaven?"

(percent of people aged 18 or older responding, 1998 and 2008; and percent responding by demographic characteristic, 2008)

	yes, definitely	yes, probably	no, probably not	no, definitely not
TREND				
2008	63.7%	21.2%	9.1%	6.0%
1998	67.8	18.2	7.8	6.2
2008 PROFILE				
Total people	**63.7**	**21.2**	**9.1**	**6.0**
Men	52.5	25.2	14.1	8.2
Women	73.4	17.7	4.8	4.1
Black	75.9	18.7	1.8	3.6
Hispanic	65.5	23.0	5.2	6.3
White	62.1	22.1	9.6	6.2
Aged 18 to 44	61.8	20.1	11.2	6.9
Aged 45 to 64	64.9	22.3	6.9	5.9
Aged 65 or older	65.7	22.8	8.0	3.5
Not a college graduate	67.1	21.3	7.3	4.2
Bachelor's degree or more	54.0	20.9	14.1	11.0

Source: Survey Documentation and Analysis, Computer-assisted Survey Methods Program, University of California, Berkeley, General Social Surveys, 1972–2008 Cumulative Data Files, Internet site http://sda.berkeley.edu/cgi-bin/hsda?harcsda+gss08; calculations by New Strategist

Table 4.10 Belief in Hell, 1998 and 2008

"Do you believe in hell?"

(percent of people aged 18 or older responding, 1998 and 2008; and percent responding by demographic characteristic, 2008)

	yes, definitely	yes, probably	no, probably not	no, definitely not
TREND				
2008	52.2%	20.6%	14.9%	12.3%
1998	56.9	18.2	13.1	11.8
2008 PROFILE				
Total people	**52.2**	**20.6**	**14.9**	**12.3**
Men	46.7	21.6	17.9	13.8
Women	57.1	19.6	12.4	10.9
Black	66.5	17.7	7.6	8.3
Hispanic	53.2	23.3	10.5	13.0
White	49.9	21.2	16.0	12.9
Aged 18 to 44	51.4	20.7	16.0	11.9
Aged 45 to 64	54.6	19.2	14.4	11.8
Aged 65 or older	49.0	23.2	13.3	14.5
Not a college graduate	55.5	20.6	13.4	10.6
Bachelor's degree or more	43.0	20.5	19.4	17.0

Source: Survey Documentation and Analysis, Computer-assisted Survey Methods Program, University of California, Berkeley, General Social Surveys, 1972–2008 Cumulative Data Files, Internet site http://sda.berkeley.edu/cgi-bin/hsda?harcsda+gss08; calculations by New Strategist

Table 4.11 Belief in Religious Miracles, 1998 and 2008

"Do you believe in religious miracles?"

(percent of people aged 18 or older responding, 1998 and 2008; and percent responding by demographic characteristic, 2008)

	yes, definitely	yes, probably	no, probably not	no, definitely not
TREND				
2008	54.9%	23.4%	14.0%	7.7%
1998	52.5	26.4	12.5	8.5
2008 PROFILE				
Total people	**54.9**	**23.4**	**14.0**	**7.7**
Men	45.9	26.2	17.2	10.7
Women	62.8	20.9	11.2	5.1
Black	61.0	27.1	6.8	5.2
Hispanic	60.1	28.2	8.0	3.7
White	54.5	22.3	15.2	7.9
Aged 18 to 44	52.1	24.4	15.1	8.4
Aged 45 to 64	58.9	21.0	13.4	6.7
Aged 65 or older	54.6	25.3	12.6	7.4
Not a college graduate	58.1	23.7	11.7	6.5
Bachelor's degree or more	46.4	22.1	20.4	11.0

Source: Survey Documentation and Analysis, Computer-assisted Survey Methods Program, University of California, Berkeley, General Social Surveys, 1972–2008 Cumulative Data Files, Internet site http://sda.berkeley.edu/cgi-bin/hsda?harcsda+gss08; calculations by New Strategist

Many Believe the Bible Is the Literal Word of God

Four decades after the Supreme Court decision banning Bible readings in public schools, the 58 percent majority of Americans still disapprove of the decision. Nearly half of the public believes the Bible is the inspired word of God and not to be taken literally. A substantial 32 percent believe the Bible is the literal word of God. Two-thirds of the public thinks religious leaders should avoid trying to influence government decisions and an even larger 73 percent thinks religious leaders should avoid trying to influence voters.

(percent distribution of people aged 18 or older by their belief in the Bible, 2008)

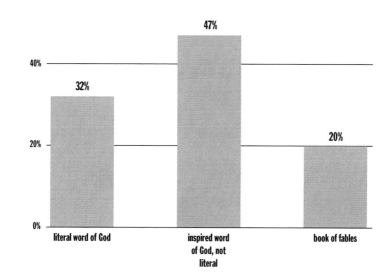

Table 4.12 Belief in the Bible, 1988 to 2008

"Which of these statements comes closest to describing your feelings about the Bible? 1) The Bible is the actual word of God and is to be taken literally, word for word; 2) The Bible is the inspired word of God but not everything in it should be taken literally, word for word; 3) The Bible is an ancient book of fables, legends, history, and moral precepts recorded by men."

(percent of people aged 18 or older responding, 1988 to 2008; and percent responding by demographic characteristic, 2008)

	word of God	inspired word	book of fables	other
TREND				
2008	32.0%	47.0%	19.6%	1.4%
1998	32.0	50.9	16.0	1.1
1988	34.7	48.3	16.3	0.7
2008 PROFILE				
Total people	**32.0**	**47.0**	**19.6**	**1.4**
Men	28.4	44.6	25.3	1.7
Women	35.2	49.2	14.4	1.2
Black	47.4	40.8	9.9	2.0
Hispanic	43.0	39.8	15.6	1.5
White	29.0	49.0	21.0	1.0
Aged 18 to 44	29.5	47.8	20.7	2.0
Aged 45 to 64	33.0	46.2	20.0	0.7
Aged 65 or older	37.0	46.6	15.3	1.1
Not a college graduate	37.2	45.7	16.2	0.8
Bachelor's degree or more	16.8	50.8	29.1	3.2

Source: Survey Documentation and Analysis, Computer-assisted Survey Methods Program, University of California, Berkeley, General Social Surveys, 1972–2008 Cumulative Data Files, Internet site http://sda.berkeley.edu/cgi-bin/hsda?harcsda+gss08; calculations by New Strategist

Table 4.13 Bible in the Public Schools, 1988 to 2008

"The United States Supreme Court has ruled that no state or local government may require the reading of the Lord's Prayer or Bible verses in public schools. What are your views on this? Do you approve or disapprove of the court ruling?"

(percent of people aged 18 or older responding, 1988 to 2008; and percent responding by demographic characteristic, 2008)

	approve	disapprove
TREND		
2008	41.8%	58.2%
1998	44.7	55.3
1988	39.4	60.6
2008 PROFILE		
Total people	**41.8**	**58.2**
Men	43.6	56.4
Women	40.1	59.9
Black	26.6	73.4
Hispanic	42.8	57.2
White	42.9	57.1
Aged 18 to 44	48.9	51.1
Aged 45 to 64	37.8	62.2
Aged 65 or older	29.3	70.7
Not a college graduate	36.5	63.5
Bachelor's degree or more	57.0	43.0

Source: Survey Documentation and Analysis, Computer-assisted Survey Methods Program, University of California, Berkeley, General Social Surveys, 1972–2008 Cumulative Data Files, Internet site http://sda.berkeley.edu/cgi-bin/hsda?harcsda+gss08; calculations by New Strategist

Table 4.14 Clergy Should Not Try to Influence Government Decisions, 1998 and 2008

"How much do you agree or disagree with the following statement:
Religious leaders should not try to influence government decisions?"

(percent of people aged 18 or older responding, 1998 and 2008; and percent responding by demographic characteristic, 2008)

	strongly agree	agree	neither agree nor disagree	disagree	strongly disagree
TREND					
2008	37.6%	29.4%	15.4%	14.1%	3.5%
1998	31.2	28.7	18.4	16.1	5.4
2008 PROFILE					
Total people	**37.6**	**29.4**	**15.4**	**14.1**	**3.5**
Men	36.3	29.3	14.8	15.9	3.8
Women	38.8	29.6	15.9	12.5	3.2
Black	28.1	35.5	16.9	15.9	3.7
Hispanic	29.2	34.8	22.1	7.7	6.1
White	39.5	28.5	14.7	14.4	2.9
Aged 18 to 44	36.1	30.5	17.9	12.4	3.1
Aged 45 to 64	38.0	27.2	14.2	16.4	4.3
Aged 65 or older	42.1	31.0	10.9	14.0	2.1
Not a college graduate	36.1	31.2	16.7	12.8	3.2
Bachelor's degree or more	41.9	24.6	11.4	17.8	4.2

Source: Survey Documentation and Analysis, Computer-assisted Survey Methods Program, University of California, Berkeley, General Social Surveys, 1972–2008 Cumulative Data Files, Internet site http://sda.berkeley.edu/cgi-bin/hsda?harcsda+gss08; calculations by New Strategist

Table 4.15 Clergy Should Not Try to Influence Voters, 1998 and 2008

"How much do you agree or disagree with the following statement:
Religious leaders should not try to influence how people vote in elections?"

(percent of people aged 18 or older responding, 1998 and 2008; and percent responding by demographic characteristic, 2008)

	strongly agree	agree	neither agree nor disagree	disagree	strongly disagree
TREND					
2008	43.5%	29.1%	14.6%	10.5%	2.4%
1998	37.5	28.6	17.1	12.4	4.4
2008 PROFILE					
Total people	**43.5**	**29.1**	**14.6**	**10.5**	**2.4**
Men	41.1	30.1	15.1	11.3	2.4
Women	45.6	28.2	14.1	9.7	2.3
Black	37.4	32.9	12.0	13.9	3.8
Hispanic	34.7	34.0	19.9	8.6	2.8
White	44.5	28.9	14.8	9.5	2.3
Aged 18 to 44	39.0	29.9	18.5	10.8	1.8
Aged 45 to 64	47.5	26.9	13.0	10.0	2.5
Aged 65 or older	49.1	31.9	6.2	9.6	3.2
Not a college graduate	42.2	29.7	16.5	9.6	2.1
Bachelor's degree or more	47.1	27.4	9.4	12.9	3.2

Source: Survey Documentation and Analysis, Computer-assisted Survey Methods Program, University of California, Berkeley, General Social Surveys, 1972–2008 Cumulative Data Files, Internet site http://sda.berkeley.edu/cgi-bin/hsda?harcsda+gss08; calculations by New Strategist

Americans Feel More Spiritual than Religious

Only 18 percent of the public says it is very religious. A larger 26 percent say they are very spiritual. Forty-two percent of Americans say they have had a religious or spiritual experience that changed their life. Thirty-seven percent say they have been born again, including 60 percent of blacks.

(percent distribution of people aged 18 or older by religiosity, 2008)

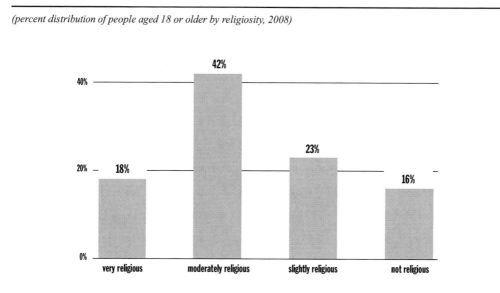

Table 4.16 Degree of Religiosity, 1998 and 2008

"To what extent do you consider yourself a religious person?"

(percent of people aged 18 or older responding, 1998 and 2008; and percent responding by demographic characteristic, 2008)

	very religious	moderately religious	slightly religious	not religious
TREND				
2008	18.2%	42.2%	23.4%	16.2%
1998	18.7	42.9	23.5	14.9
2008 PROFILE				
Total people	**18.2**	**42.2**	**23.4**	**16.2**
Men	13.4	38.9	26.9	20.7
Women	22.5	45.1	20.3	12.1
Black	25.6	47.9	18.5	8.0
Hispanic	16.6	41.0	29.1	13.4
White	17.2	42.0	23.7	17.1
Aged 18 to 44	12.7	37.6	27.0	22.7
Aged 45 to 64	21.0	45.9	21.4	11.7
Aged 65 or older	28.2	47.4	17.4	7.0
Not a college graduate	18.7	42.3	24.5	14.5
Bachelor's degree or more	16.6	42.0	20.3	21.0

Source: Survey Documentation and Analysis, Computer-assisted Survey Methods Program, University of California, Berkeley, General Social Surveys, 1972–2008 Cumulative Data Files, Internet site http://sda.berkeley.edu/cgi-bin/hsda?harcsda+gss08; calculations by New Strategist

Table 4.17 Degree of Spirituality, 1998 and 2008

"To what extent do you consider yourself a spiritual person?"

(percent of people aged 18 or older responding, 1998 and 2008; and percent responding by demographic characteristic, 2008)

	very spiritual	moderately spiritual	slightly spiritual	not spiritual
TREND				
2008	26.2%	41.4%	22.7%	9.8%
1998	21.7	40.1	26.6	11.7
2008 PROFILE				
Total people	**26.2**	**41.4**	**22.7**	**9.8**
Men	19.0	40.2	27.2	13.7
Women	32.5	42.4	18.7	6.4
Black	31.3	40.6	21.3	6.8
Hispanic	24.2	41.3	25.4	9.1
White	26.0	40.8	23.0	10.2
Aged 18 to 44	22.3	39.0	26.9	11.8
Aged 45 to 64	30.0	43.0	19.8	7.2
Aged 65 or older	29.2	44.5	16.6	9.7
Not a college graduate	25.8	40.4	23.9	9.8
Bachelor's degree or more	27.2	44.1	19.1	9.7

Source: Survey Documentation and Analysis, Computer-assisted Survey Methods Program, University of California, Berkeley, General Social Surveys, 1972–2008 Cumulative Data Files, Internet site http://sda.berkeley.edu/cgi-bin/hsda?harcsda+gss08; calculations by New Strategist

Table 4.18 Religious Experience Changed Life, 1998 and 2008

"Did you ever have a religious or spiritual experience that changed your life?"

(percent of people aged 18 or older responding, 1998 and 2008; and percent responding by demographic characteristic, 2008)

	yes	no
TREND		
2008	41.6%	58.4%
1998	39.5	60.5
2008 PROFILE		
Total people	**41.6**	**58.4**
Men	37.8	62.2
Women	44.9	55.1
Black	54.3	45.7
Hispanic	38.8	61.2
White	39.1	60.9
Aged 18 to 44	38.5	61.5
Aged 45 to 64	45.4	54.6
Aged 65 or older	41.6	58.4
Not a college graduate	43.5	56.5
Bachelor's degree or more	36.3	63.7

Source: Survey Documentation and Analysis, Computer-assisted Survey Methods Program, University of California, Berkeley, General Social Surveys, 1972–2008 Cumulative Data Files, Internet site http://sda.berkeley.edu/cgi-bin/hsda?harcsda+gss08; calculations by New Strategist

Table 4.19 Ever Been Born Again, 1988 to 2008

"Would you say you have been born again or have had a born again experience—
that is, a turning point in your life when you committed yourself to Christ?"

(percent of people aged 18 or older responding, 1988 to 2008; and percent responding by demographic charac-
teristic, 2008)

	yes	no
TREND		
2008	37.4%	62.6%
1998	37.5	62.5
1988	36.6	63.4
2008 PROFILE		
Total people	**37.4**	**62.6**
Men	34.3	65.7
Women	40.1	59.9
Black	60.3	39.7
Hispanic	33.4	66.6
White	33.9	66.1
Aged 18 to 44	32.0	68.0
Aged 45 to 64	42.4	57.6
Aged 65 or older	42.4	57.6
Not a college graduate	40.8	59.2
Bachelor's degree or more	27.6	72.4

Source: Survey Documentation and Analysis, Computer-assisted Survey Methods Program, University of California, Berkeley,
General Social Surveys, 1972–2008 Cumulative Data Files, Internet site http://sda.berkeley.edu/cgi-bin/hsda?harcsda+gss08;
calculations by New Strategist

Table 4.20 Ever Tried to Convince Others to Accept Jesus, 1988 to 2008

"Have you ever tried to encourage someone to believe in Jesus Christ
or to accept Jesus Christ as his or her savior?"

(percent of people aged 18 or older responding, 1988 to 2008; and percent responding by demographic characteristic, 2008)

	yes	no
TREND		
2008	44.2%	55.8%
1998	43.6	56.4
1988	46.5	53.5
2008 PROFILE		
Total people	**44.2**	**55.8**
Men	39.0	61.0
Women	48.8	51.2
Black	62.3	37.7
Hispanic	44.6	55.4
White	41.7	58.3
Aged 18 to 44	40.5	59.5
Aged 45 to 64	46.5	53.5
Aged 65 or older	50.4	49.6
Not a college graduate	47.3	52.7
Bachelor's degree or more	35.5	64.5

Source: Survey Documentation and Analysis, Computer-assisted Survey Methods Program, University of California, Berkeley, General Social Surveys, 1972–2008 Cumulative Data Files, Internet site http://sda.berkeley.edu/cgi-bin/hsda?harcsda+gss08; calculations by New Strategist

Table 4.21 Carry Religioius Beliefs into Other Dealings, 1998 and 2008

"Do you agree or disagree with the following statement: I try hard to carry my religious beliefs over into all my other dealings in life?"

(percent of people aged 18 or older responding, 1998 and 2008; and percent responding by demographic characteristic, 2008)

	strongly agree	agree	disagree	strongly disagree
TREND				
2008	27.1%	43.6%	20.2%	9.1%
1998	27.0	45.8	20.2	6.9
2008 PROFILE				
Total people	**27.1**	**43.6**	**20.2**	**9.1**
Men	20.8	42.1	25.3	11.8
Women	32.8	45.0	15.6	6.6
Black	41.7	42.7	13.6	1.9
Hispanic	20.7	48.5	24.5	6.3
White	25.6	42.9	21.4	10.1
Aged 18 to 44	21.8	42.8	24.4	11.0
Aged 45 to 64	31.0	43.1	17.4	8.4
Aged 65 or older	34.2	47.0	13.8	4.9
Not a college graduate	27.5	44.2	21.1	7.2
Bachelor's degree or more	26.2	41.7	17.5	14.5

Source: Survey Documentation and Analysis, Computer-assisted Survey Methods Program, University of California, Berkeley, General Social Surveys, 1972–2008 Cumulative Data Files, Internet site http://sda.berkeley.edu/cgi-bin/hsda?harcsda+gss08; calculations by New Strategist

Table 4.22 We Trust Too Much in Science, Not Enough in Religion, 1998 and 2008

"We trust too much in science and not enough in religious faith."

(percent of people aged 18 or older responding, 1998 and 2008; and percent responding by demographic characteristic, 2008)

	strongly agree	agree	neither agree nor disagree	disagree	strongly disagree
TREND					
2008	6.8%	24.8%	25.0%	31.3%	12.2%
1998	8.7	22.3	27.6	29.0	12.5
2008 PROFILE					
Total people	**6.8**	**24.8**	**25.0**	**31.3**	**12.2**
Men	5.2	21.6	24.3	34.0	14.9
Women	8.2	27.6	25.7	28.8	9.7
Black	12.2	36.3	22.8	25.6	3.1
Hispanic	10.2	37.4	24.0	20.7	7.7
White	5.8	23.1	25.6	32.4	13.0
Aged 18 to 44	6.1	25.3	24.4	30.3	14.0
Aged 45 to 64	7.5	24.8	22.7	32.9	12.0
Aged 65 or older	7.4	22.5	32.2	31.3	6.5
Not a college graduate	8.1	27.6	26.1	30.2	7.9
Bachelor's degree or more	3.1	17.0	21.8	34.3	23.8

Source: Survey Documentation and Analysis, Computer-assisted Survey Methods Program, University of California, Berkeley, General Social Surveys, 1972–2008 Cumulative Data Files, Internet site http://sda.berkeley.edu/cgi-bin/hsda?harcsda+gss08; calculations by New Strategist

Table 4.23 How Much Truth in Religion, 1998 and 2008

"Which of the following statements comes closest to your own views:
1) There is very little truth in any religion; 2) There are basic truths in many religions;
3) There is truth in one religion?"

(percent of people aged 18 or older responding, 1998 and 2008; and percent responding by demographic characteristic, 2008)

	little truth any	basic truth many	truth in one
TREND			
2008	4.9%	83.5%	11.6%
1998	3.7	84.4	11.9
2008 PROFILE			
Total people	**4.9**	**83.5**	**11.6**
Men	6.8	82.2	11.1
Women	3.3	84.6	12.1
Black	2.1	78.2	19.7
Hispanic	6.1	73.1	20.8
White	5.3	85.4	9.3
Aged 18 to 44	6.4	81.1	12.5
Aged 45 to 64	4.1	85.6	10.4
Aged 65 or older	2.0	86.3	11.7
Not a college graduate	5.2	82.0	12.8
Bachelor's degree or more	4.2	87.4	8.5

Source: Survey Documentation and Analysis, Computer-assisted Survey Methods Program, University of California, Berkeley, General Social Surveys, 1972–2008 Cumulative Data Files, Internet site http://sda.berkeley.edu/cgi-bin/hsda?harcsda+gss08; calculations by New Strategist

Attitudes toward Religion Changed after 9/11

In 1998, well before the terrorist attacks of September 11, 2001, only 34 percent of Americans agreed that religion brings more conflict than peace. By 2008, the figure had climbed to 61 percent. In 1998, fully 64 percent of the public agreed that people who violated God's rules should be punished. By 2008, the figure had fallen to 46 percent. The percentage of Americans who think religious people are intolerant climbed from 48 percent in 1998 to 67 percent in 2008.

(percent of people aged 18 or older who agree with the statement, "Religions bring more conflict than peace," 1998 and 2008)

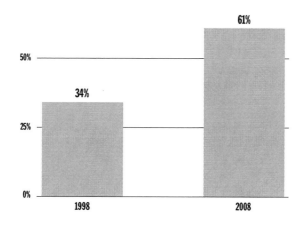

(percent of people aged 18 or older who agree with the statement, "Those who violate God's rules must be punished," 1998 and 2008)

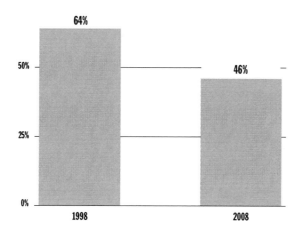

Table 4.24 **Committed to Religion, 2008**

"Has there ever been a turning point in your life when
you became less committed to religion?"

(percent of people aged 18 or older responding by demographic characteristic, 2008)

	yes	no
Total people	**37.1%**	**62.9%**
Men	36.1	63.9
Women	38.0	62.0
Black	33.3	66.7
Hispanic	35.9	64.1
White	38.2	61.8
Aged 18 to 44	37.2	62.8
Aged 45 to 64	39.3	60.7
Aged 65 or older	31.6	68.4
Not a college graduate	36.7	63.3
Bachelor's degree or more	38.3	61.7

*Source: Survey Documentation and Analysis, Computer-assisted Survey Methods Program, University of California, Berkeley,
General Social Surveys, 1972–2008 Cumulative Data Files, Internet site http://sda.berkeley.edu/cgi-bin/hsda?harcsda+gss08;
calculations by New Strategist*

Table 4.25 Religious People Are Too Intolerant, 1998 and 2008

"Do you agree or disagree with the following statement:
People with very strong religious beliefs are often intolerant of others?"

(percent of people aged 18 or older responding, 1998 and 2008; and percent responding by demographic characteristic, 2008)

	strongly agree	agree	neither agree nor disagree	disagree	strongly disagree
TREND					
2008	21.6%	45.6%	15.9%	14.8%	2.2%
1998	12.3	35.7	23.1	22.9	5.9
2008 PROFILE					
Total people	**21.6**	**45.6**	**15.9**	**14.8**	**2.2**
Men	22.2	48.6	14.6	13.4	1.3
Women	21.1	42.9	17.0	16.0	3.0
Black	16.7	41.8	18.6	21.4	1.6
Hispanic	21.7	40.7	20.7	15.8	1.0
White	22.5	46.9	15.2	13.6	1.8
Aged 18 to 44	20.4	44.4	17.5	15.2	2.4
Aged 45 to 64	22.5	45.1	15.2	15.4	1.8
Aged 65 or older	23.6	49.7	12.5	12.2	1.9
Not a college graduate	21.0	44.7	15.9	16.9	1.5
Bachelor's degree or more	23.4	48.1	15.6	9.0	3.9

Source: Survey Documentation and Analysis, Computer-assisted Survey Methods Program, University of California, Berkeley, General Social Surveys, 1972–2008 Cumulative Data Files, Internet site http://sda.berkeley.edu/cgi-bin/hsda?harcsda+gss08; calculations by New Strategist

Table 4.26 Religion Brings More Conflict than Peace, 1998 and 2008

"Do you agree or disagree with the following statement: Looking around the world, religions bring more conflict than peace?"

(percent of people aged 18 or older responding, 1998 and 2008; and percent responding by demographic characteristic, 2008)

	strongly agree	agree	neither agree nor disagree	disagree	strongly disagree
TREND					
2008	19.1%	41.8%	15.8%	20.0%	3.4%
1998	7.7	26.4	22.4	34.1	9.4
2008 PROFILE					
Total people	**19.1**	**41.8**	**15.8**	**20.0**	**3.4**
Men	23.0	44.1	14.4	15.1	3.4
Women	15.6	39.7	17.1	24.2	3.4
Black	14.5	39.4	18.9	22.4	4.8
Hispanic	13.8	35.7	18.7	24.6	7.1
White	20.2	42.4	15.5	19.0	2.9
Aged 18 to 44	17.6	39.6	18.2	20.5	4.1
Aged 45 to 64	21.5	43.5	12.9	19.6	2.5
Aged 65 or older	18.5	44.5	14.5	19.2	3.4
Not a college graduate	18.2	41.3	15.5	20.9	4.1
Bachelor's degree or more	21.4	43.5	16.8	16.8	1.5

Source: Survey Documentation and Analysis, Computer-assisted Survey Methods Program, University of California, Berkeley, General Social Surveys, 1972–2008 Cumulative Data Files, Internet site http://sda.berkeley.edu/cgi-bin/hsda?harcsda+gss08; calculations by New Strategist

Table 4.27 Sinners Must Be Punished, 1988 and 2008

"Do you agree strongly, agree somewhat, disagree somewhat, or disagree strongly with the statement: Those who violate God's rules must be punished?"

(percent of people aged 18 or older responding, 1988 and 2008; and percent responding by demographic characteristic, 2008)

	agree strongly	agree somewhat	disagree somewhat	disagree strongly
TREND				
2008	16.0%	29.6%	30.9%	23.6%
1988	24.0	39.7	26.2	10.1
2008 PROFILE				
Total people	**16.0**	**29.6**	**30.9**	**23.6**
Men	14.1	29.4	31.1	25.3
Women	17.7	29.7	30.6	22.0
Black	24.2	34.7	25.8	15.3
Hispanic	20.5	33.1	26.8	19.6
White	14.5	28.5	32.3	24.7
Aged 18 to 44	13.3	28.1	31.7	26.9
Aged 45 to 64	15.7	32.2	30.4	21.7
Aged 65 or older	25.2	27.2	30.0	17.6
Not a college graduate	18.1	31.5	30.1	20.2
Bachelor's degree or more	10.0	24.2	32.8	33.0

Note: Data for 1998 are not available.
Source: Survey Documentation and Analysis, Computer-assisted Survey Methods Program, University of California, Berkeley, General Social Surveys, 1972–2008 Cumulative Data Files, Internet site http://sda.berkeley.edu/cgi-bin/hsda?harcsda+gss08; calculations by New Strategist

The Public Tolerates Moral Ambiguity

The 71 percent majority of the American public agrees that there is a God who concerns himself with every human being personally. But that still leaves a lot of room for individuals to choose their course of action. Eighty-three percent of people aged 18 or older agree that there are many shades of gray in determining right from wrong. Seventy-six percent agree that morality is a personal matter and society should not force everyone to follow one standard. Most also agree, however, that the immoral actions of one person can corrupt society in general.

(percent of people aged 18 or older who agree with selected statements, 2008)

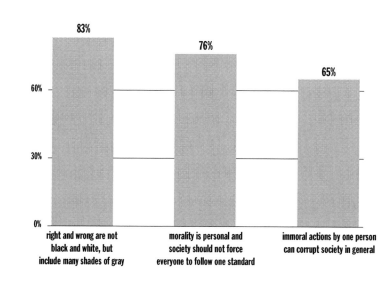

Table 4.28 God Is Concerned with Human Beings Personally, 1998 and 2008

"Do you agree or disagree with the following: There is a God who
concerns Himself with every human being personally?"

(percent of people aged 18 or older responding, 1998 and 2008; and percent responding by demographic characteristic, 2008)

	strongly agree	agree	neither agree nor disagree	disagree	strongly disagree
TREND					
2008	40.1%	30.7%	13.5%	10.3%	5.4%
1998	42.0	31.2	11.8	9.2	5.8
2008 PROFILE					
Total people	**40.1**	**30.7**	**13.5**	**10.3**	**5.4**
Men	31.7	30.7	15.3	14.8	7.6
Women	47.5	30.7	11.9	6.4	3.5
Black	50.6	34.5	8.3	3.6	3.0
Hispanic	37.0	41.3	11.7	6.1	3.8
White	39.2	27.2	14.5	11.2	5.9
Aged 18 to 44	33.9	32.8	15.8	11.9	5.7
Aged 45 to 64	45.8	28.6	10.7	9.3	5.7
Aged 65 or older	45.5	29.3	13.3	8.1	3.8
Not a college graduate	41.3	33.1	12.6	9.2	3.8
Bachelor's degree or more	36.9	23.9	15.9	13.4	9.9

Source: Survey Documentation and Analysis, Computer-assisted Survey Methods Program, University of California, Berkeley, General Social Surveys, 1972–2008 Cumulative Data Files, Internet site http://sda.berkeley.edu/cgi-bin/hsda?harcsda+gss08; calculations by New Strategist

Table 4.29 Right and Wrong, 1988 and 2008

"Do you agree strongly, agree somewhat, disagree somewhat, or
disagree strongly with the statement: Right and wrong are not usually
a simple matter of black and white; there are many shades of gray?"

(percent of people aged 18 or older responding, 1988 and 2008; and percent responding by demographic characteristic, 2008)

	agree strongly	agree somewhat	disagree somewhat	disagree strongly
TREND				
2008	43.9%	38.7%	10.1%	7.3%
1988	40.1	44.1	8.8	7.0
2008 PROFILE				
Total people	**43.9**	**38.7**	**10.1**	**7.3**
Men	39.9	43.2	10.4	6.4
Women	47.4	34.6	9.8	8.1
Black	52.8	33.4	8.2	5.6
Hispanic	35.2	43.9	13.7	7.2
White	42.2	39.2	10.7	7.9
Aged 18 to 44	45.6	37.3	11.6	5.6
Aged 45 to 64	41.7	41.3	8.4	8.6
Aged 65 or older	43.8	36.9	9.4	9.8
Not a college graduate	42.6	39.1	10.3	8.0
Bachelor's degree or more	47.7	37.2	9.6	5.4

Note: Data for 1998 are not available.
*Source: Survey Documentation and Analysis, Computer-assisted Survey Methods Program, University of California, Berkeley,
General Social Surveys, 1972–2008 Cumulative Data Files, Internet site http://sda.berkeley.edu/cgi-bin/hsda?harcsda+gss08;
calculations by New Strategist*

Table 4.30 Morality Is a Personal Matter, 1988 and 2008

"Do you agree strongly, agree somewhat, disagree somewhat, or
disagree strongly with the statement: Morality is a personal matter and
society should not force everyone to follow one standard?"

(percent of people aged 18 or older responding, 1988 and 2008; and percent responding by demographic characteristic, 2008)

	agree strongly	agree somewhat	disagree somewhat	disagree strongly
TREND				
2008	35.8%	40.3%	15.3%	8.6%
1988	32.8	41.3	18.0	7.9
2008 PROFILE				
Total people	**35.8**	**40.3**	**15.3**	**8.6**
Men	39.7	39.2	13.1	8.0
Women	32.4	41.4	17.2	9.1
Black	40.5	40.2	10.7	8.7
Hispanic	32.4	44.8	18.3	4.6
White	35.1	40.4	15.9	8.6
Aged 18 to 44	36.5	40.8	15.7	7.1
Aged 45 to 64	32.8	41.7	16.4	9.1
Aged 65 or older	41.4	35.7	11.5	11.4
Not a college graduate	36.8	40.7	14.1	8.4
Bachelor's degree or more	32.9	39.2	18.7	9.2

Note: Data for 1998 are not available.
Source: Survey Documentation and Analysis, Computer-assisted Survey Methods Program, University of California, Berkeley, General Social Surveys, 1972–2008 Cumulative Data Files, Internet site http://sda.berkeley.edu/cgi-bin/hsda?harcsda+gss08; calculations by New Strategist

Table 4.31 An Immoral Person Corrupts Society, 1988 and 2008

"Do you agree strongly, agree somewhat, disagree somewhat, or disagree strongly with the statement: Immoral actions by one person can corrupt society in general?"

(percent of people aged 18 or older responding, 1988 and 2008; and percent responding by demographic characteristic, 2008)

	agree strongly	agree somewhat	disagree somewhat	disagree strongly
TREND				
2008	25.0%	40.3%	22.8%	11.9%
1988	18.3	34.6	28.7	18.5
2008 PROFILE				
Total people	**25.0**	**40.3**	**22.8**	**11.9**
Men	25.4	39.6	21.5	13.5
Women	24.6	40.9	24.0	10.5
Black	31.9	37.2	17.0	13.9
Hispanic	26.0	42.0	22.6	9.4
White	23.0	40.6	24.8	1.5
Aged 18 to 44	23.5	43.7	21.8	11.1
Aged 45 to 64	25.3	39.6	22.3	12.7
Aged 65 or older	28.3	31.7	27.5	12.5
Not a college graduate	26.6	39.7	22.5	11.2
Bachelor's degree or more	20.2	42.2	23.7	13.8

Note: Data for 1998 are not available.
Source: Survey Documentation and Analysis, Computer-assisted Survey Methods Program, University of California, Berkeley, General Social Surveys, 1972–2008 Cumulative Data Files, Internet site http://sda.berkeley.edu/cgi-bin/hsda?harcsda+gss08; calculations by New Strategist

5

Work and Money

Most Americans are satisfied with their work and at least more or less satisfied with their financial situation. But the Great Recession may be changing some long held attitudes toward the American Dream.

Little or no change

• **Job satisfaction.** If anything, Americans were even more satisfied with their work in 2008 than in any previous year, as the proportion of people who say they are very satisfied topped the 50 percent threshold in 2008.

• **Satisfaction with finances.** The plurality of Americans is more or less satisfied with their present financial situation, a figure that has barely budged over the past decade. Only 29 percent are not at all satisfied with their finances, slightly higher than the 23 to 25 percent of past decades.

• **Class identification.** Americans strongly identify with the working (46 percent) or middle (43 percent) classes. The proportions have barely changed since 1978.

Big changes

• **Family income compared with others**. When asked how their family income ranks relative to others, the share who say it is average fell from 53 to 47 percent between 1978 and 2008. Thirty-one percent say their family income is below average, up from 25 percent who felt that way in 1978.

• **Belief in the American Dream.** Belief in the American Dream is slipping. Only 59 percent agree that the United States provides opportunities for people like them to improve their standard of living, down sharply from 75 percent 10 years earlier. Twenty-seven percent disagree that they have an opportunity to get ahead, up from 14 percent 10 years earlier.

Most Are Satisfied with Their Work

More than half of Americans are very satisfied with the work they do (including both workers and those not in the labor force). Surprisingly, in the midst of the deepest recession since the Great Depression, the 59 percent majority of workers think it is not likely that they will lose their job—although this figure is down from 66 percent who felt confident 10 years earlier. Forty-four percent of workers say it would not be easy to find a comparable job, up from 32 percent who felt that way in 1998. Many have experienced unemployment, with 34 percent of workers saying they have been unemployed for at least a month during the past 10 years.

(percent distribution of people aged 18 or older by satisfaction with the work they do, 2008)

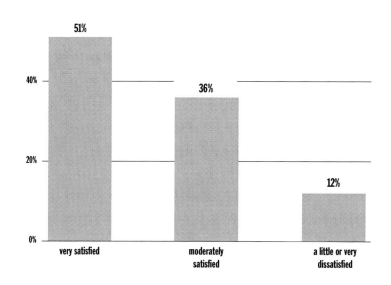

Table 5.1 Satisfaction with Work, 1978 to 2008

"On the whole, how satisfied are you with the work you do?"

(percent of people aged 18 or older responding, 1978 to 2008; and percent responding by demographic characteristic, 2008)

	very satisfied	moderately satisfied	a little dissatisfied	very dissatisfied
TREND				
2008	51.5%	36.3%	9.1%	3.1%
1998	48.4	38.7	9.7	3.2
1988	46.1	39.6	10.3	4.0
1978	49.1	36.0	10.3	4.6
2008 PROFILE				
Total people	**51.5**	**36.3**	**9.1**	**3.1**
Men	50.3	37.0	10.0	2.7
Women	52.5	35.7	8.4	3.4
Black	44.1	35.9	13.9	6.1
Hispanic	47.5	37.0	11.6	3.9
White	52.7	35.9	8.4	2.9
Aged 18 to 44	46.5	38.9	11.1	3.5
Aged 45 to 64	55.2	35.0	7.2	2.6
Aged 65 or older	74.3	18.7	3.5	3.5
Not a college graduate	49.6	37.1	9.9	3.5
Bachelor's degree or more	56.9	34.0	7.0	2.1

Source: Survey Documentation and Analysis, Computer-assisted Survey Methods Program, University of California, Berkeley, General Social Surveys, 1972–2008 Cumulative Data Files, Internet site http://sda.berkeley.edu/cgi-bin/hsda?harcsda+gss08; calculations by New Strategist

Table 5.2 Likely to Lose Job, 1978 to 2008

"Thinking about the next 12 months, how likely is it that
you will lose your job or be laid off?"

(percent of workers aged 18 or older responding, 1978 to 2008; and percent responding by demographic characteristic, 2008)

	very likely	fairly likely	not too likely	not likely
TREND				
2008	5.5%	5.8%	29.3%	59.4%
1998	3.3	4.3	26.7	65.7
1988	4.2	4.4	25.7	65.7
1978	3.7	2.7	19.2	74.4
2008 PROFILE				
Total people	**5.5**	**5.8**	**29.3**	**59.4**
Men	5.9	7.1	224.6	62.4
Women	5.1	4.3	34.6	56.0
Black	11.0	8.3	36.1	44.6
Hispanic	13.9	10.2	22.0	53.9
White	3.9	5.0	28.9	62.1
Aged 18 to 44	6.2	4.4	30.5	58.8
Aged 45 to 64	4.5	7.2	27.9	60.4
Aged 65 or older	9.7	6.4	22.6	61.3
Not a college graduate	7.2	7.1	28.6	57.2
Bachelor's degree or more	1.4	2.6	31.0	65.0

Source: Survey Documentation and Analysis, Computer-assisted Survey Methods Program, University of California, Berkeley, General Social Surveys, 1972–2008 Cumulative Data Files, Internet site http://sda.berkeley.edu/cgi-bin/hsda?harcsda+gss08; calculations by New Strategist

Table 5.3 Ease of Finding Equally Good Job, 1978 to 2008

"About how easy would it be for you to find a job with another employer with
approximately the same income and fringe benefits you now have?"

(percent of workers aged 18 or older responding, 1978 to 2008; and percent responding by demographic characteristic, 2008)

	very easy	somewhat easy	not easy
TREND			
2008	22.0%	34.0%	44.0%
1998	31.9	36.2	31.9
1988	28.2	36.9	34.9
1978	28.8	32.8	38.4
2008 PROFILE			
Total people	**22.0**	**34.0**	**44.0**
Men	22.3	32.8	44.9
Women	21.7	35.5	42.9
Black	20.5	27.6	51.8
Hispanic	19.3	31.1	49.5
White	22.7	34.1	43.1
Aged 18 to 44	25.3	41.4	33.3
Aged 45 to 64	18.0	25.3	56.7
Aged 65 or older	22.4	28.8	48.8
Not a college graduate	22.8	31.7	45.5
Bachelor's degree or more	20.2	39.8	40.0

Source: Survey Documentation and Analysis, Computer-assisted Survey Methods Program, University of California, Berkeley, General Social Surveys, 1972–2008 Cumulative Data Files, Internet site http://sda.berkeley.edu/cgi-bin/hsda?harcsda+gss08; calculations by New Strategist

Table 5.4 Unemployed in Last 10 Years, 1978 to 2008

"At any time during the last 10 years, have you been unemployed
and looking for work for as long as a month?"

(percent of workers aged 18 or older responding, 1978 to 2008; and percent responding by demographic characteristic, 2008)

	yes	no
TREND		
2008	34.0%	66.0%
1998	30.3	69.7
1988	32.0	68.0
1978	28.6	71.4
2008 PROFILE		
Total people	**34.0**	**66.0**
Men	36.5	63.5
Women	31.7	68.3
Black	43.6	56.4
Hispanic	46.4	53.6
White	30.9	69.1
Aged 18 to 44	48.4	51.6
Aged 45 to 64	26.3	73.7
Aged 65 or older	6.1	93.9
Not a college graduate	36.5	63.5
Bachelor's degree or more	26.9	73.1

Source: Survey Documentation and Analysis, Computer-assisted Survey Methods Program, University of California, Berkeley, General Social Surveys, 1972–2008 Cumulative Data Files, Internet site http://sda.berkeley.edu/cgi-bin/hsda?harcsda+gss08; calculations by New Strategist

Table 5.5 Health Insurance through Employer, 2008

"Do you receive your health insurance from your employer?"

(percent of workers aged 18 to 64 responding by demographic characteristic, 2008)

	yes	no
Total people	**33.8%**	**66.2%**
Men	35.7	64.3
Women	33.1	66.9
Black	34.8	65.2
Hispanic	25.4	74.6
White	35.1	64.9
Aged 18 to 44	29.8	70.2
Aged 45 to 64	37.7	62.3
Not a college graduate	27.9	72.1
Bachelor's degree or more	47.9	52.1

Source: Survey Documentation and Analysis, Computer-assisted Survey Methods Program, University of California, Berkeley, General Social Survey, 2008 Cumulative Data Files, Internet site http://sda.berkeley.edu/cgi-bin/hsda?harcsda+gss08; calculations by New Strategist

Pay Is Not Keeping Up with Cost of Living

The 41 percent plurality of workers say their pay has not kept up with the cost of living. A substantial 31 percent say their starting pay at their current employer was lower than their earnings at their last employer. Many workers (32 percent) think free trade has taken jobs away from Americans. Only 15 percent think free trade has created more jobs in the United States.

(percent distribution of workers aged 18 to 64 by how pay has changed since they started their current job, 2008)

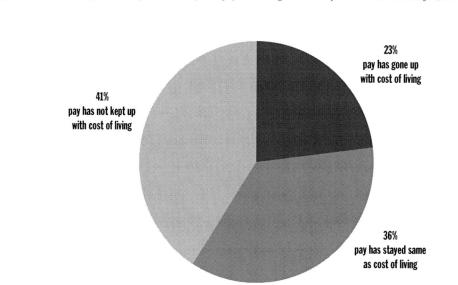

41%
pay has not kept up
with cost of living

23%
pay has gone up
with cost of living

36%
pay has stayed same
as cost of living

Table 5.6 Full-Time Jobs in Past Three Years, 2008

"How many full-time jobs have you had in the past three years,
that is since 2005 (counting the current job)?"

(percent of workers aged 18 to 64 responding by demographic characteristic, 2008)

	one	more than one	none
Total people	**59.6%**	**21.0%**	**19.4%**
Men	68.9	20.6	10.6
Women	51.0	21.4	27.6
Black	58.0	27.0	15.0
Hispanic	52.3	31.2	16.5
White	60.2	19.3	20.5
Aged 18 to 44	54.1	29.9	16.0
Aged 45 to 64	65.1	12.1	22.8
Not a college graduate	57.3	22.8	19.9
Bachelor's degree or more	65.2	16.6	18.2

Source: Survey Documentation and Analysis, Computer-assisted Survey Methods Program, University of California, Berkeley, General Social Survey, 2008 Cumulative Data Files, Internet site http://sda.berkeley.edu/cgi-bin/hsda?harcsda+gss08; calculations by New Strategist

Table 5.7 Pay Change Since Began Job, 2008

"Thinking about your current employer, how much has
your pay changed on your current job since you began?"

(percent of workers aged 18 to 64 responding by demographic characteristic, 2008)

	my pay has gone up with the cost of living	my pay has stayed about the same as the cost of living	my pay has not kept up with the cost of living
Total people	**23.5%**	**35.6%**	**40.9%**
Men	29.4	33.7	36.9
Women	15.2	38.3	46.5
Black	17.9	32.6	49.5
Hispanic	15.3	44.2	40.5
White	25.6	35.3	39.1
Aged 18 to 44	24.6	38.7	36.7
Aged 45 to 64	22.3	32.3	45.4
Not a college graduate	18.8	36.0	45.2
Bachelor's degree or more	34.0	34.9	31.2

Source: Survey Documentation and Analysis, Computer-assisted Survey Methods Program, University of California, Berkeley, General Social Survey, 2008 Cumulative Data Files, Internet site http://sda.berkeley.edu/cgi-bin/hsda?harcsda+gss08; calculations by New Strategist

Table 5.8 Starting Pay at Current and Past Job, 2008

"When you went to work for your current employer, was your starting pay higher, lower, or about the same as what you were earning in your previous (full-time) job?"

(percent of workers aged 18 to 64 responding by demographic characteristic, 2008)

	higher	about the same	lower	current employer is first job
Total people	**44.4%**	**22.1%**	**30.7%**	**2.8%**
Men	44.4	25.9	26.9	2.8
Women	42.6	20.8	34.0	2.6
Black	54.0	18.4	27.6	0.0
Hispanic	35.0	29.4	32.0	3.5
White	41.9	23.3	31.5	3.3
Aged 18 to 44	47.5	23.9	25.8	2.8
Aged 45 to 64	39.7	23.5	34.2	2.6
Not a college graduate	39.8	24.8	33.4	2.0
Bachelor's degree or more	52.2	21.3	22.2	4.4

Source: Survey Documentation and Analysis, Computer-assisted Survey Methods Program, University of California, Berkeley, General Social Survey, 2008 Cumulative Data Files, Internet site http://sda.berkeley.edu/cgi-bin/hsda?harcsda+gss08; calculations by New Strategist

Table 5.9 More Trade, Fewer Jobs, 2008

"Suppose two friends of yours are talking about trade with other countries. One friend thinks that increased trade has created a lot of jobs in the United States for people with jobs like yours. The other friend thinks that increased trade has taken jobs away. Which friend do you agree with?"

(percent of workers aged 18 to 64 responding by demographic characteristic, 2008)

	created more jobs	about the same	taken jobs away	not relevant for my job
Total people	**14.8%**	**20.8%**	**32.0%**	**32.4%**
Men	17.3	21.2	34.3	27.3
Women	11.3	20.4	28.8	39.5
Black	10.0	25.5	39.0	25.4
Hispanic	17.4	28.1	23.9	30.6
White	15.9	18.1	31.9	34.0
Aged 18 to 44	17.4	22.7	27.7	32.2
Aged 45 to 64	12.0	18.9	36.4	32.7
Not a college graduate	12.2	20.0	36.4	31.3
Bachelor's degree or more	20.4	22.6	22.1	34.9

Source: Survey Documentation and Analysis, Computer-assisted Survey Methods Program, University of California, Berkeley, General Social Survey, 2008 Cumulative Data Files, Internet site http://sda.berkeley.edu/cgi-bin/hsda?harcsda+gss08; calculations by New Strategist

Table 5.10 Meeting Face-to-Face with Customers and Clients, 2008

"How often do you meet face-to-face with customers, clients, patients, or others to whom you provide products or services?"

(percent of workers aged 18 to 64 responding by demographic characteristic, 2008)

	never	less than daily	daily
Total people	**17.3%**	**24.6%**	**58.1%**
Men	17.3	28.8	53.9
Women	17.2	19.0	63.8
Black	14.9	12.0	73.1
Hispanic	27.9	21.0	51.2
White	17.3	25.9	56.8
Aged 18 to 44	15.7	27.1	57.3
Aged 45 to 64	18.9	22.1	59.0
Not a college graduate	21.4	20.6	57.9
Bachelor's degree or more	7.7	33.8	58.4

Source: Survey Documentation and Analysis, Computer-assisted Survey Methods Program, University of California, Berkeley, General Social Survey, 2008 Cumulative Data Files, Internet site http://sda.berkeley.edu/cgi-bin/hsda?harcsda+gss08; calculations by New Strategist

Table 5.11 Meeting Face-to-Face with Co-Workers, 2008

"How often do you meet face-to-face with co-workers to work on projects, for example solving special problems or improving products or services?"

(percent of workers aged 18 to 64 responding by demographic characteristic, 2008)

	never	less than daily	daily
Total people	**11.3%**	**20.0%**	**68.7%**
Men	12.1	20.5	67.4
Women	10.1	19.5	70.5
Black	12.2	15.1	72.7
Hispanic	22.1	23.7	54.2
White	10.8	21.4	67.7
Aged 18 to 44	10.3	22.2	67.5
Aged 45 to 64	12.3	17.8	69.9
Not a college graduate	14.0	19.7	66.3
Bachelor's degree or more	5.0	20.8	74.1

Source: Survey Documentation and Analysis, Computer-assisted Survey Methods Program, University of California, Berkeley, General Social Survey, 2008 Cumulative Data Files, Internet site http://sda.berkeley.edu/cgi-bin/hsda?harcsda+gss08; calculations by New Strategist

Table 5.12 Information Exchange with Co-Workers outside the United States, 2008

"How often do you exchange information with co-workers
located outside the United States?"

(percent of workers aged 18 to 64 responding by demographic characteristic, 2008)

	never	less than daily	daily
Total people	**80.1%**	**13.5%**	**6.4%**
Men	78.6	15.8	5.6
Women	82.1	10.4	7.5
Black	87.6	7.9	4.5
Hispanic	81.5	8.8	9.8
White	79.3	14.3	6.4
Aged 18 to 44	78.0	14.6	7.5
Aged 45 to 64	82.3	12.4	5.3
Not a college graduate	87.5	7.9	4.6
Bachelor's degree or more	63.0	26.4	10.6

Source: Survey Documentation and Analysis, Computer-assisted Survey Methods Program, University of California, Berkeley, General Social Survey, 2008 Cumulative Data Files, Internet site http://sda.berkeley.edu/cgi-bin/hsda?harcsda+gss08; calculations by New Strategist

Many Own Their Own Business

More than one in eight people aged 18 or older say they own their own business, including the self-employed. Among the business owners, only 32 percent have paid employees. Nearly half (46 percent) of business owners have a gross income of $15,000 or less, but a substantial 22 percent say their gross income is greater than $100,000. Most say they started their business because they saw an opportunity, while 22 percent said they started it out of necessity.

(percent of people aged 18 or older who own a business, including the self-employed, by age, 2008)

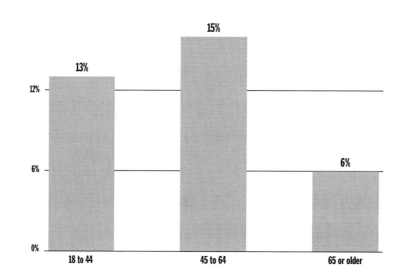

Table 5.13 Business Ownership, 2008

"Are you, alone or with others, currently the owner of a business you help manage, including any self employment or selling any goods or services to others?"

(percent of people aged 18 or older responding by demographic characteristic, 2008)

	yes	no
Total people	**12.6%**	**87.4%**
Men	16.2	83.8
Women	9.5	90.5
Black	6.8	93.2
Hispanic	12.9	87.1
White	13.7	86.3
Aged 18 to 44	12.9	87.1
Aged 45 to 64	15.0	85.0
Aged 65 or older	6.1	93.9
Not a college graduate	10.7	89.3
Bachelor's degree or more	18.1	81.9

Source: Survey Documentation and Analysis, Computer-assisted Survey Methods Program, University of California, Berkeley, General Social Survey, 2008 Cumulative Data Files, Internet site http://sda.berkeley.edu/cgi-bin/hsda?harcsda+gss08; calculations by New Strategist

Table 5.14 Paid Employees, 2008

"Do you have any paid employees?"

(percent of business owners aged 18 or older responding by demographic characteristic, 2008)

	yes	no
Total business owners	**32.1%**	**67.9%**
Men	39.4	60.6
Women	21.2	78.8
Black	40.0	60.0
Hispanic	23.1	76.9
White	32.5	67.5
Aged 18 to 44	24.0	76.0
Aged 45 to 64	38.1	61.9
Aged 65 or older	52.2	47.8
Not a college graduate	31.9	68.1
Bachelor's degree or more	32.5	67.5

Source: Survey Documentation and Analysis, Computer-assisted Survey Methods Program, University of California, Berkeley, General Social Survey, 2008 Cumulative Data Files, Internet site http://sda.berkeley.edu/cgi-bin/hsda?harcsda+gss08; calculations by New Strategist

Table 5.15 Business Revenue Last Year, 2008

"In which of these groups did the revenues from this business fall for last year?"

(percent of business owners aged 18 or older responding by demographic characteristic, 2008)

	$15,000 or less	$15,001 to $25,000	$25,001 to $50,000	$50,001 to $100,000	$100,001 or more
Total business owners	**45.9%**	**5.3%**	**15.2%**	**11.2%**	**22.4%**
Men	38.2	4.5	17.7	10.5	29.1
Women	58.0	6.5	11.4	12.1	11.9
Black	81.3	2.5	16.2	0.0	0.0
Hispanic	57.0	0.0	9.4	21.2	12.4
White	41.6	6.1	15.9	11.8	24.5
Aged 18 to 44	59.2	3.2	13.8	8.4	15.4
Aged 45 to 64	35.6	7.6	16.8	12.2	27.8
Aged 65 or older	20.5	5.1	15.4	22.8	36.1
Not a college graduate	46.5	4.7	19.2	10.8	18.8
Bachelor's degree or more	45.0	6.2	8.7	11.8	28.3

Source: Survey Documentation and Analysis, Computer-assisted Survey Methods Program, University of California, Berkeley, General Social Survey, 2008 Cumulative Data Files, Internet site http://sda.berkeley.edu/cgi-bin/hsda?harcsda+gss08; calculations by New Strategist

Table 5.16 **Business Contribution to Household Income, 2008**

"In which of these groups did your earnings from this business fall in contributing towards your household income for last year?"

(percent of business owners aged 18 or older responding by demographic characteristic, 2008)

	$15,000 or less	$15,001 to $25,000	$25,001 to $50,000	$50,001 to $100,000	$100,001 or more
Total business owners	**51.4%**	**6.8%**	**16.2%**	**14.1%**	**11.5%**
Men	40.2	6.8	20.8	17.4	14.9
Women	68.5	6.9	9.3	15.4	0.0
Black	79.3	14.7	6.0	0.0	0.0
Hispanic	50.7	6.3	17.3	13.3	12.4
White	47.9	6.8	16.9	15.8	12.5
Aged 18 to 44	64.4	5.5	11.9	9.0	9.3
Aged 45 to 64	38.4	7.7	21.3	20.2	12.4
Aged 65 or older	39.5	10.5	15.8	12.9	21.3
Not a college graduate	52.1	7.7	20.8	10.9	8.4
Bachelor's degree or more	50.2	5.3	8.3	19.4	16.7

Source: Survey Documentation and Analysis, Computer-assisted Survey Methods Program, University of California, Berkeley, General Social Survey, 2008 Cumulative Data Files, Internet site http://sda.berkeley.edu/cgi-bin/hsda?harcsda+gss08; calculations by New Strategist

Table 5.17 Why Did You Start Business, 2008

"All in all, would you say your started, or are starting, your business because you saw an opportunity or you started it out of necessity?"

(percent of business owners aged 18 or older responding by demographic characteristic, 2008)

	opportunity	necessity	both
Total business owners	**63.6%**	**21.9%**	**14.5%**
Men	66.9	17.7	15.4
Women	58.6	28.2	13.3
Black	55.8	22.1	22.1
Hispanic	70.2	24.5	5.3
White	64.2	21.0	14.8
Aged 18 to 44	62.5	24.1	13.4
Aged 45 to 64	65.6	16.7	17.6
Aged 65 or older	56.9	38.6	4.6
Not a college graduate	62.9	24.8	12.3
Bachelor's degree or more	64.8	16.7	18.4

Source: Survey Documentation and Analysis, Computer-assisted Survey Methods Program, University of California, Berkeley, General Social Survey, 2008 Cumulative Data Files, Internet site http://sda.berkeley.edu/cgi-bin/hsda?harcsda+gss08; calculations by New Strategist

Most Think Employers Should Make Special Efforts to Hire Women

The 66 percent majority of the public thinks that employers should make special efforts to hire and promote qualified women. Even the majority of men feel this way. Most (58 percent) also think it is at least somewhat likely that a man will not get a job or promotion because of these efforts. An even larger percentage (74 percent), however, think a woman will not get a job or promotion while an equally or less qualified man gets the job instead.

(percent distribution of people aged 18 or older by agreement with the statement, "because of past discrimination, employers should make special efforts to hire and promote qualified women," 2008)

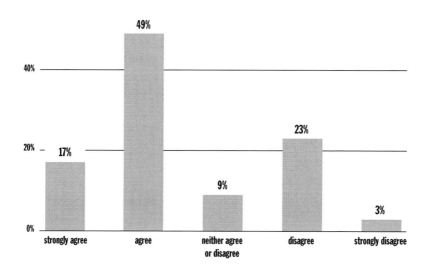

Table 5.18 Affirmative Action for Women, 2008

"Tell me whether you strongly agree, agree, neither agree nor disagree, disagree, or strongly disagree: Because of past discrimination, employers should make special efforts to hire and promote qualified women."

(percent of people aged 18 or older responding by demographic characteristic, 2008)

	strongly agree	agree	neither agree nor disagree	disagree	strongly disagree
Total people	**16.9%**	**48.6%**	**8.7%**	**22.6%**	**3.3%**
Men	12.1	47.7	7.6	28.3	4.3
Women	21.6	49.5	9.7	17.0	2.2
Black	28.3	55.7	4.2	11.7	–
Hispanic	26.3	53.7	5.9	13.7	0.5
White	13.4	47.9	10.0	24.9	3.9
Aged 18 to 44	18.0	45.9	9.9	23.5	2.6
Aged 45 to 64	15.1	49.7	7.2	23.0	5.0
Aged 65 or older	18.4	55.1	7.4	18.3	0.9
Not a college graduate	19.2	50.4	7.0	20.2	3.2
Bachelor's degree or more	9.9	43.1	13.6	30.0	3.3

Note: "–" means sample is too small to make a reliable estimate.
Source: Survey Documentation and Analysis, Computer-assisted Survey Methods Program, University of California, Berkeley, General Social Survey, 2008 Cumulative Data Files, Internet site http://sda.berkeley.edu/cgi-bin/hsda?harcsda+gss08; calculations by New Strategist

Table 5.19 Man Won't Get Job or Promotion, 2008

"What do you think the chances are these days that a man won't get a job or a promotion while an equally or less qualified woman gets one instead?"

(percent of people aged 18 or older responding by demographic characteristic, 2008)

	very likely	somewhat likely	somewhat unlikely	very unlikely
Total people	**13.3%**	**44.7%**	**28.9%**	**13.1%**
Men	12.7	47.6	30.3	9.4
Women	13.8	42.2	27.8	16.3
Black	25.4	37.3	21.6	15.7
Hispanic	14.3	50.3	15.4	20.0
White	11.5	45.4	31.1	12.0
Aged 18 to 44	13.9	44.9	32.6	8.7
Aged 45 to 64	13.6	47.1	23.1	16.2
Aged 65 or older	10.0	38.9	32.3	18.8
Not a college graduate	16.3	43.4	29.5	10.7
Bachelor's degree or more	4.9	48.2	27.3	19.6

Source: Survey Documentation and Analysis, Computer-assisted Survey Methods Program, University of California, Berkeley, General Social Survey, 2008 Cumulative Data Files, Internet site http://sda.berkeley.edu/cgi-bin/hsda?harcsda+gss08; calculations by New Strategist

Table 5.20 Woman Won't Get Job or Promotion, 2008

"What do you think the chances are these days that a woman won't get a job or a promotion while an equally or less qualified man gets one instead?"

(percent of people aged 18 or older responding by demographic characteristic, 2008)

	very likely	somewhat likely	somewhat unlikely	very unlikely
Total people	**22.8%**	**51.2%**	**18.2%**	**7.8%**
Men	18.6	52.7	22.2	6.6
Women	27.0	49.8	14.2	9.0
Black	34.5	41.7	16.9	7.0
Hispanic	19.0	49.3	19.3	12.6
White	21.6	53.9	17.0	7.5
Aged 18 to 44	19.1	51.1	21.4	8.4
Aged 45 to 64	27.4	51.0	16.2	5.4
Aged 65 or older	22.3	53.5	12.3	12.1
Not a college graduate	25.1	46.7	18.9	9.3
Bachelor's degree or more	15.8	65.0	16.1	3.1

Source: Survey Documentation and Analysis, Computer-assisted Survey Methods Program, University of California, Berkeley, General Social Survey, 2008 Cumulative Data Files, Internet site http://sda.berkeley.edu/cgi-bin/hsda?harcsda+gss08; calculations by New Strategist

Most Are Satisfied with Their Finances

In good times and bad, Americans tend to be upbeat about their work and money. Most would continue to work even if they were rich. Most think people get ahead through hard work rather than luck. In 2008, 71 percent of people aged 18 or older were satisfied or more or less satisfied with their financial situation. This figure is only slightly lower than in past decades. A growing share says their financial situation is getting worse, however. The figure climbed from 15 percent in 1998 to 28 percent in 2008.

(percent distribution of people aged 18 or older by satisfaction with their financial situation, 2008)

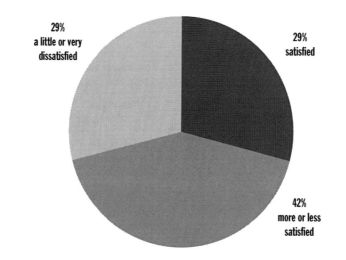

29%
a little or very
dissatisfied

29%
satisfied

42%
more or less
satisfied

Table 5.21 Satisfaction with Financial Situation, 1978 to 2008

"We are interested in how people are getting along financially these days. So far as you and your family are concerned, would you say that you are pretty well satisfied with your present financial situation, more or less satisfied, or not satisfied at all?"

(percent of people aged 18 or older responding, 1978 to 2008; and percent responding by demographic characteristic, 2008)

	satisfied	more or less satisfied	not at all sarisfied
TREND			
2008	28.9%	41.7%	29.4%
1998	30.6	44.3	25.1
1988	30.7	46.3	23.0
1978	34.4	41.8	23.8
2008 PROFILE			
Total people	**28.9**	**41.7**	**29.4**
Men	29.0	42.6	28.4
Women	28.8	40.9	30.3
Black	19.0	35.3	45.8
Hispanic	14.2	51.4	34.4
White	31.7	42.4	25.9
Aged 18 to 44	23.2	43.4	33.5
Aged 45 to 64	28.1	44.0	27.9
Aged 65 or older	48.2	31.7	20.1
Not a college graduate	24.5	41.9	33.6
Bachelor's degree or more	41.6	40.9	17.5

Source: Survey Documentation and Analysis, Computer-assisted Survey Methods Program, University of California, Berkeley, General Social Surveys, 1972–2008 Cumulative Data Files, Internet site http://sda.berkeley.edu/cgi-bin/hsda?harcsda+gss08; calculations by New Strategist

Table 5.22 Change in Financial Situation, 1978 to 2008

"During the last few years, has your financial situation been
getting better, worse, or has it stayed the same?"

(percent of people aged 18 or older responding, 1978 to 2008; and percent responding by demographic characteristic, 2008)

	better	worse	stayed same
TREND			
2008	31.7%	28.3%	40.0%
1998	46.0	15.4	38.5
1988	41.5	18.3	40.2
1978	41.9	19.0	39.1
2008 PROFILE			
Total people	**31.7**	**28.3**	**40.0**
Men	33.9	27.4	38.7
Women	29.8	29.2	41.0
Black	31.6	29.0	39.4
Hispanic	31.5	33.2	35.3
White	32.4	27.9	39.7
Aged 18 to 44	38.5	24.4	37.1
Aged 45 to 64	30.2	32.5	37.3
Aged 65 or older	14.7	30.4	55.0
Not a college graduate	29.1	29.7	41.2
Bachelor's degree or more	39.2	24.4	36.4

Source: Survey Documentation and Analysis, Computer-assisted Survey Methods Program, University of California, Berkeley, General Social Surveys, 1972–2008 Cumulative Data Files, Internet site http://sda.berkeley.edu/cgi-bin/hsda?harcsda+gss08; calculations by New Strategist

Table 5.23 Would Continue to Work If Rich, 1988 to 2008

"If you were to get enough money to live as comfortably as you would like for the rest of your life, would you continue to work or would you stop working?"

(percent of people aged 18 or older responding, 1988 to 2008; and percent responding by demographic characteristic, 2008)

	continue working	stop working
TREND		
2008	72.0%	28.0%
1998	68.8	31.2
1988	70.9	29.1
2008 PROFILE		
Total people	**72.0**	**28.0**
Men	73.7	26.3
Women	70.1	29.9
Black	74.3	25.7
Hispanic	82.9	17.1
White	70.8	29.2
Aged 18 to 44	81.0	19.0
Aged 45 to 64	60.4	39.6
Aged 65 or older	69.9	30.1
Not a college graduate	70.9	29.1
Bachelor's degree or more	74.8	25.2

Source: Survey Documentation and Analysis, Computer-assisted Survey Methods Program, University of California, Berkeley, General Social Surveys, 1972–2008 Cumulative Data Files, Internet site http://sda.berkeley.edu/cgi-bin/hsda?harcsda+gss08; calculations by New Strategist

Table 5.24 How People Get Ahead, 1988 to 2008

"Some people say that people get ahead by their own hard work;
others say that lucky breaks or help from other people are more important.
Which do you think is most important?"

(percent of people aged 18 or older responding, 1988 to 2008; and percent responding by demographic charac-teristic, 2008)

	hard work	both equally	luck or help
TREND			
2008	67.1%	20.8%	12.1%
1998	67.9	21.7	10.4
1988	67.6	20.4	12.0
2008 PROFILE			
Total people	**67.1**	**20.8**	**12.1**
Men	64.6	21.4	14.0
Women	69.2	20.3	10.5
Black	59.4	22.6	18.0
Hispanic	71.2	20.9	7.9
White	67.6	21.1	11.3
Aged 18 to 44	70.5	18.9	10.6
Aged 45 to 64	63.7	24.1	12.2
Aged 65 or older	64.6	19.3	16.1
Not a college graduate	68.2	18.8	13.0
Bachelor's degree or more	64.2	26.2	9.7

Source: Survey Documentation and Analysis, Computer-assisted Survey Methods Program, University of California, Berkeley, General Social Surveys, 1972–2008 Cumulative Data Files, Internet site http://sda.berkeley.edu/cgi-bin/hsda?harcsda+gss08; calculations by New Strategist

More Think Their Family Income Is below Average

When asked to identify their social class, 46 percent of Americans say "working class" and 43 percent say "middle class." Only 4 percent identify themselves as upper class. When asked how their family income ranks relative to others, only 47 percent say it is average. Thirty-one percent say their family income is below average, up from 25 percent in 1978.

(percent of people aged 18 or older who estimate that their family income is below average, 1978 to 2008)

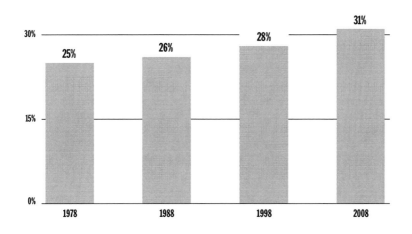

Table 5.25 Class Identification, 1978 to 2008

"If you were asked to use one of four names for your social class, which would you say you belong in: the lower class, the working class, the middle class, or the upper class?"

(percent of people aged 18 or older responding, 1978 to 2008; and percent responding by demographic characteristic, 2008)

	lower class	working class	middle class	upper class
TREND				
2008	7.3%	45.7%	43.4%	3.6%
1998	5.0	45.5	45.7	3.8
1988	4.4	45.5	47.4	2.7
1978	4.7	47.2	45.9	2.2
2008 PROFILE				
Total people	**7.3**	**45.7**	**43.4**	**3.6**
Men	6.1	47.5	42.6	3.8
Women	8.3	44.1	44.1	3.4
Black	12.5	57.1	28.4	2.0
Hispanic	8.8	58.0	32.5	0.7
White	6.1	43.6	46.1	4.2
Aged 18 to 44	7.3	50.4	38.7	3.6
Aged 45 to 64	7.5	44.9	44.5	3.0
Aged 65 or older	6.3	33.4	55.1	5.2
Not a college graduate	9.4	53.1	35.7	1.7
Bachelor's degree or more	1.0	24.2	65.8	9.1

Source: Survey Documentation and Analysis, Computer-assisted Survey Methods Program, University of California, Berkeley, General Social Surveys, 1972–2008 Cumulative Data Files, Internet site http://sda.berkeley.edu/cgi-bin/hsda?harcsda+gss08; calculations by New Strategist

Table 5.26 Family Income Relative to Others, 1978 to 2008

"Compared with American families in general, would you say your family income is far below average, below average, average, above average, or far above average?"

(percent of people aged 18 or older responding, 1978 to 2008; and percent responding by demographic characteristic, 2008)

	far below average	below average	average	above average	far above average
TREND					
2008	6.3%	25.2%	46.7%	19.8%	2.0%
1998	5.5	22.0	48.5	21.6	2.3
1988	4.1	22.3	52.0	19.3	2.4
1978	3.9	20.9	52.8	20.0	2.4
2008 PROFILE					
Total people	**6.3**	**25.2**	**46.7**	**19.8**	**2.0**
Men	5.8	24.1	43.9	23.6	2.7
Women	6.7	26.2	49.2	16.5	1.4
Black	10.1	35.2	44.2	9.8	0.7
Hispanic	10.0	31.5	48.7	9.6	0.2
White	4.9	23.0	47.1	22.6	2.4
Aged 18 to 44	7.1	25.6	46.8	19.0	1.5
Aged 45 to 64	5.7	23.3	46.2	21.8	2.9
Aged 65 or older	4.6	28.4	47.6	17.8	1.6
Not a college graduate	7.9	29.4	48.7	13.4	0.6
Bachelor's degree or more	1.4	13.0	40.9	38.5	6.2

Source: Survey Documentation and Analysis, Computer-assisted Survey Methods Program, University of California, Berkeley, General Social Surveys, 1972–2008 Cumulative Data Files, Internet site http://sda.berkeley.edu/cgi-bin/hsda?harcsda+gss08; calculations by New Strategist

Fewer Believe in the American Dream

The great majority of Americans say their standard of living is better than their parents' standard of living at the same age. Similarly, most parents think their children's standard of living will be even better. But belief in the American Dream is slipping. Only 59 percent agree that the United States provides opportunities for people like them to improve their standard of living, down from 75 percent 10 years earlier. Twenty-seven percent disagree that they have an opportunity to get ahead, up from 14 percent 10 years earlier.

(percent of people aged 18 or older who agree with the statement, "The way things are in America, people like me and my family have a good chance of improving our standard of living," 2008)

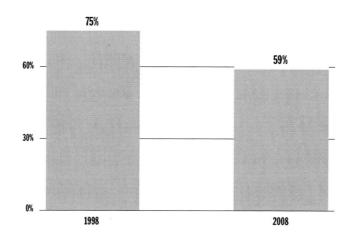

Table 5.27 Parents' Standard of Living, 1998 and 2008

"Compared to your parents when they were the age you are now,
do you think your own standard of living now is much better, somewhat better,
about the same, somewhat worse, or much worse than theirs was?"

(percent of people aged 18 or older responding, 1998 and 2008; and percent responding by demographic characteristic, 2008)

	much better	somewhat better	about the same	somewhat worse	much worse
TREND					
2008	31.6%	31.1%	21.1%	11.5%	4.6%
1998	33.7	32.5	21.5	9.7	2.6
2008 PROFILE					
Total people	**31.6**	**31.1**	**21.1**	**11.5**	**4.6**
Men	30.2	33.7	19.3	12.5	4.2
Women	32.9	28.8	22.7	10.6	4.9
Black	31.3	36.8	13.0	10.3	8.6
Hispanic	39.6	26.1	22.9	6.9	4.6
White	30.5	30.9	22.8	11.9	3.8
Aged 18 to 44	27.7	33.0	21.4	12.9	5.1
Aged 45 to 64	30.0	30.0	22.5	12.5	5.0
Aged 65 or older	47.6	27.7	17.4	5.3	2.0
Not a college graduate	31.9	30.5	20.2	11.7	5.7
Bachelor's degree or more	30.9	32.8	23.8	11.1	1.4

Source: Survey Documentation and Analysis, Computer-assisted Survey Methods Program, University of California, Berkeley, General Social Surveys, 1972–2008 Cumulative Data Files, Internet site http://sda.berkeley.edu/cgi-bin/hsda?harcsda+gss08; calculations by New Strategist

Table 5.28 Children's Standard of Living, 1998 and 2008

"When your children are at the age you are now, do you think
their standard of living will be much better, somewhat better,
about the same, somewhat worse, or much worse than yours is now?"

(percent of parents aged 18 or older responding, 1998 and 2008; and percent responding by demographic characteristic, 2008)

	much better	somewhat better	about the same	somewhat worse	much worse
TREND					
2008	30.7%	29.2%	20.0%	14.3%	5.8%
1998	24.7	38.4	22.6	10.6	3.6
2008 PROFILE					
Total people	**30.7**	**29.2**	**20.0**	**14.3**	**5.8**
Men	26.9	29.9	19.2	17.4	6.7
Women	33.9	28.6	20.6	11.8	5.0
Black	52.2	19.6	6.6	14.6	7.1
Hispanic	47.8	30.4	11.7	4.3	5.8
White	24.7	31.5	22.8	15.1	5.8
Aged 18 to 44	32.5	31.9	20.9	10.2	4.6
Aged 45 to 64	28.4	29.0	17.9	18.0	6.7
Aged 65 or older	29.2	22.4	22.4	18.5	7.5
Not a college graduate	33.2	28.7	16.1	15.3	6.6
Bachelor's degree or more	23.9	30.3	30.9	11.5	3.3

Source: Survey Documentation and Analysis, Computer-assisted Survey Methods Program, University of California, Berkeley, General Social Surveys, 1972–2008 Cumulative Data Files, Internet site http://sda.berkeley.edu/cgi-bin/hsda?harcsda+gss08; calculations by New Strategist

Table 5.29 Standard of Living Will Improve, 1998 and 2008

"The way things are in America, people like me and my family have a good chance of improving our standard of living. Do you agree or disagree?"

(percent of people aged 18 or older responding, 1998 and 2008; and percent responding by demographic characteristic, 2008)

	strongly agree	agree	neither	disagree	strongly disagree
TREND					
2008	14.7%	44.7%	13.9%	22.9%	3.8%
1998	18.5	56.0	11.0	11.9	2.5
2008 PROFILE					
Total people	**14.7**	**44.7**	**13.9**	**22.9**	**3.8**
Men	15.8	46.8	13.2	21.0	3.1
Women	13.8	42.8	14.5	24.5	4.3
Black	17.7	45.3	14.0	15.3	7.7
Hispanic	19.5	50.2	9.5	15.3	5.4
White	14.4	42.7	14.6	25.6	2.8
Aged 18 to 44	16.9	49.0	12.0	18.6	3.5
Aged 45 to 64	12.4	44.9	12.2	26.8	3.7
Aged 65 or older	13.3	30.3	24.3	27.1	4.9
Not a college graduate	13.2	44.4	13.8	24.4	4.2
Bachelor's degree or more	18.9	45.3	14.2	19.0	2.6

Source: Survey Documentation and Analysis, Computer-assisted Survey Methods Program, University of California, Berkeley, General Social Surveys, 1972–2008 Cumulative Data Files, Internet site http://sda.berkeley.edu/cgi-bin/hsda?harcsda+gss08; calculations by New Strategist

6

Family and Friends

Some pundits worry that Americans are becoming increasingly isolated from one another, geographically separated from their families and staring at a computer screen rather than socializing. Those stories may make interesting headlines, but the facts contradict them. Most Americans live close to where they grew up, and they socialize with relatives more frequently than anyone else. Some things have changed, however. Here is a look at trends in relationships over the past decade.

Little or no change

• **Geographic mobility.** Although many believe otherwise, most Americans do not move far from home when they grow up—a pattern that has been fairly stable for decades. Forty percent of the population lives in the same city they lived in at age 16, and most still live in the same state.

• **Marital happiness.** Marital happiness has been relatively stable for the past three decades. More than six out of ten married people say their marriage is very happy.

• **Disciplining children.** The public schools may have banned spanking, but the nation's parents have not. The public still believes that it is sometimes necessary to discipline a child with a good, hard spanking.

• **Socializing with family.** Americans are most likely to socialize with family members, a fact that has not changed over the years.

Big changes

• **Sex roles.** Attitudes toward sex roles have changed profoundly over the decades as younger generations replaced older ones. Most Americans no longer believe traditional sex roles are best, nor do they believe working mothers harm children.

• **Ideal number of children.** Two is still the ideal number of children for the largest share of Americans, but the share has declined over the past decade from 57 to 48 percent. Behind the decline is the rise of the Hispanic population, with many Hispanics favoring larger families.

• **Multigeneration households.** The percentage of people who think it is a good idea for older Americans to share a home with grown children has increased from 36 percent in 1978 to 51 percent in 2008. Interestingly, this living arrangement is favored by 53 to 54 percent of people under age 65, but only 37 percent of those aged 65 or older.

Americans Are Not So Mobile

Most Americans live in the same state they lived in at age 16, and a substantial 40 percent live in the same city. The percentage of people who grew up in big cities or their suburbs has climbed over the past three decades, from 23 percent in 1978 to 30 percent in 2008. The percentage of Americans who grew up on a farm fell from 21 to 11 percent during those years.

(percent distribution of people aged 18 or older by mobility since age 16, 2008)

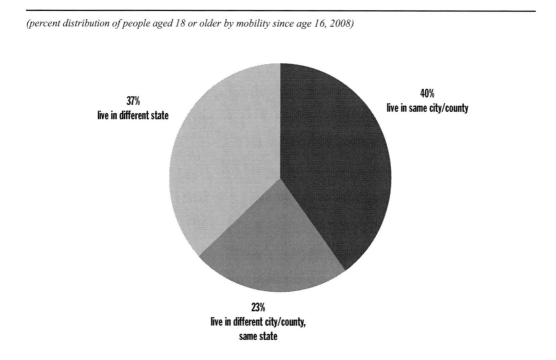

37%
live in different state

40%
live in same city/county

23%
live in different city/county,
same state

Table 6.1 Geographic Mobility since Age 16, 1978 to 2008

"When you were 16 years old, were you living in this same (city/town/county)?"

(percent of people aged 18 or older responding, 1978 to 2008; and percent responding by demographic characteristic, 2008)

	same city	same state, different city	different state
TREND			
2008	40.0%	23.2%	36.8%
1998	40.1	25.4	34.6
1988	41.8	25.4	32.8
1978	41.4	28.6	30.0
2008 PROFILE			
Total people	**40.0**	**23.2**	**36.8**
Men	39.2	24.8	35.9
Women	40.7	21.7	37.6
Black	57.6	15.8	26.6
Hispanic	33.3	13.1	53.7
White	38.3	25.6	36.1
Aged 18 to 44	44.5	20.3	35.2
Aged 45 to 64	37.6	26.7	35.7
Aged 65 or older	31.9	24.2	43.9
Not a college graduate	45.9	22.4	31.7
Bachelor's degree or more	23.3	25.5	51.2

Source: Survey Documentation and Analysis, Computer-assisted Survey Methods Program, University of California, Berkeley, General Social Surveys, 1972–2008 Cumulative Data Files, Internet site http://sda.berkeley.edu/cgi-bin/hsda?harcsda+gss08; calculations by New Strategist

Table 6.2 Type of Place Lived in at Age 16, 1978 to 2008

"Which comes closest to the type of place you were
living in when you were 16 years old?"

(percent of people aged 18 or older responding, 1978 to 2008; and percent responding by demographic characteristic, 2008)

	country, not a farm	farm	town, less than 50,000	town, 50,000–250,000	big-city suburb	city, more than 250,000
TREND						
2008	11.1%	10.5%	32.0%	16.8%	12.6%	16.9%
1998	12.1	12.8	30.3	16.4	12.7	15.7
1988	12.0	16.7	32.1	14.6	10.3	14.3
1978	11.0	20.5	30.8	14.9	9.9	12.9
2008 PROFILE						
Total people	**11.1**	**10.5**	**32.0**	**16.8**	**12.6**	**16.9**
Men	12.5	12.6	30.5	15.2	13.2	16.1
Women	9.9	8.7	33.3	18.3	12.2	17.6
Black	10.8	5.4	31.3	18.9	13.4	20.1
Hispanic	12.1	4.1	29.0	21.6	7.6	25.6
White	11.8	11.9	33.3	16.7	13.8	12.4
Aged 18 to 44	10.8	5.4	31.3	18.9	13.4	20.1
Aged 45 to 64	11.6	14.1	31.0	15.1	13.5	14.6
Aged 65 or older	11.2	18.0	36.0	13.8	8.5	12.6
Not a college graduate	11.8	11.4	33.0	16.4	10.2	17.2
Bachelor's degree or more	9.3	8.0	29.2	18.0	19.6	16.0

Source: Survey Documentation and Analysis, Computer-assisted Survey Methods Program, University of California, Berkeley, General Social Surveys, 1972–2008 Cumulative Data Files, Internet site http://sda.berkeley.edu/cgi-bin/hsda?harcsda+gss08; calculations by New Strategist

Divorce Is Main Reason Children Live with Only One Parent

Among people who lived with only one parent when they were 16, the death of a parent was the primary reason in 1978. By 2008, divorce had become the primary reason, rising from 37 to 55 percent of the total. The percentage of people who say their family income at age 16 was average fell from 57 percent in 1988 to 45 percent in 2008.

(percent distribution of people aged 18 or older by reason they were not living with both parents at age 16, 1978 and 2008)

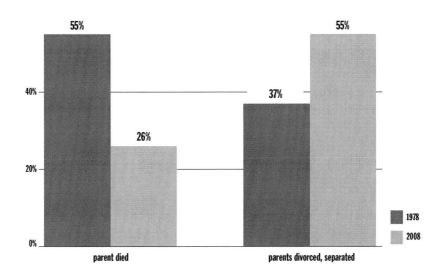

Table 6.3 Family Type at Age 16, 1978 to 2008

"Who were you living with around the time you were 16?"

(percent of people aged 18 or older responding, 1978 to 2008; and percent responding by demographic characteristic, 2008)

	mother and father	father and stepmother	mother and stepfather	father only	mother only	other
TREND						
2008	69.1%	1.2%	5.9%	2.9%	13.9%	7.0%
1998	69.9	3.4	5.5	1.8	13.2	6.2
1988	73.1	1.9	6.1	2.2	11.3	5.4
1978	76.8	1.5	3.6	1.6	10.6	5.9
2008 PROFILE						
Total people	**69.1**	**1.2**	**5.9**	**2.9**	**13.9**	**7.0**
Men	71.4	1.1	4.7	2.8	14.5	5.5
Women	67.0	1.4	7.0	3.1	13.3	8.2
Black	48.4	1.3	9.7	4.0	25.3	11.2
Hispanic	67.8	0.7	2.7	5.6	12.9	10.3
White	72.4	1.2	5.8	2.6	11.7	6.2
Aged 18 to 44	64.0	1.3	8.5	3.9	15.8	6.5
Aged 45 to 64	74.7	1.5	4.5	2.1	11.3	6.0
Aged 65 or older	71.0	0.6	1.4	1.9	14.3	10.9
Not a college graduate	65.4	1.5	6.5	2.8	14.9	8.8
Bachelor's degree or more	79.4	0.5	4.1	3.3	11.0	1.6

Source: Survey Documentation and Analysis, Computer-assisted Survey Methods Program, University of California, Berkeley, General Social Surveys, 1972–2008 Cumulative Data Files, Internet site http://sda.berkeley.edu/cgi-bin/hsda?harcsda+gss08; calculations by New Strategist

Table 6.4 Why Not Living with Both Parents at Age 16, 1978 to 2008

"If you were not living with both your own mother and father at age 16, what happened?"

(percent of people aged 18 or older who were not living with both parents at age 16 responding, 1978 to 2008; and percent responding by demographic characteristic, 2008)

	parent died	parents were divorced or separated	other
TREND			
2008	26.1%	55.2%	18.7%
1998	27.8	53.6	18.6
1988	38.8	48.6	12.6
1978	55.3	36.8	7.9
2008 PROFILE			
Total people	**26.1**	**55.2**	**18.7**
Men	28.8	53.7	17.5
Women	24.0	56.3	19.7
Black	25.7	50.9	23.3
Hispanic	22.5	39.2	38.2
White	25.6	58.6	15.9
Aged 18 to 44	18.3	61.7	20.1
Aged 45 to 64	31.8	48.3	19.9
Aged 65 or older	44.3	44.3	11.5
Not a college graduate	25.6	53.3	21.1
Bachelor's degree or more	28.4	64.3	7.3

Source: Survey Documentation and Analysis, Computer-assisted Survey Methods Program, University of California, Berkeley, General Social Surveys, 1972–2008 Cumulative Data Files, Internet site http://sda.berkeley.edu/cgi-bin/hsda?harcsda+gss08; calculations by New Strategist

Table 6.5 Family Income at Age 16, 1978 to 2008

"Thinking about the time when you were 16 years old, compared with American families in general then, would you say your family income was far below average, below average, average, above average, or far above average?"

(percent of people aged 18 or older responding, 1978 to 2008; and percent responding by demographic characteristic, 2008)

	far below average	below average	average	above average	far above average
TREND					
2008	9.6%	26.0%	45.3%	16.9%	2.2%
1988	7.4	23.3	52.2	15.3	1.8
1978	6.7	23.4	56.6	11.7	1.6
2008 PROFILE					
Total people	**9.6**	**26.0**	**45.3**	**16.9**	**2.2**
Men	9.6	27.7	43.4	16.5	2.7
Women	9.6	24.5	46.8	17.2	1.7
Black	16.4	29.7	40.4	10.1	3.3
Hispanic	23.8	26.2	36.9	11.6	1.5
White	7.6	25.5	46.4	18.6	1.8
Aged 18 to 44	8.3	23.3	45.3	19.9	3.2
Aged 45 to 64	9.3	28.1	46.5	14.9	1.3
Aged 65 or older	14.7	29.9	41.6	12.9	0.9
Not a college graduate	11.4	27.3	45.3	14.2	1.8
Bachelor's degree or more	4.6	22.5	44.9	24.7	3.3

Note: Data for 1998 are not available.
Source: Survey Documentation and Analysis, Computer-assisted Survey Methods Program, University of California, Berkeley, General Social Surveys, 1972–2008 Cumulative Data Files, Internet site http://sda.berkeley.edu/cgi-bin/hsda?harcsda+gss08; calculations by New Strategist

Many Have Grandparents Born outside the United States

Although the 59 percent majority of Americans say all four of their grandparents were born in the United States, a substantial 41 percent say one or more of their grandparents was born in another country. These proportions have not changed in three decades. Twenty-two percent of the population had a parent born outside the United States.

(percent distribution of people aged 18 or older by place of birth of grandparents, 2008)

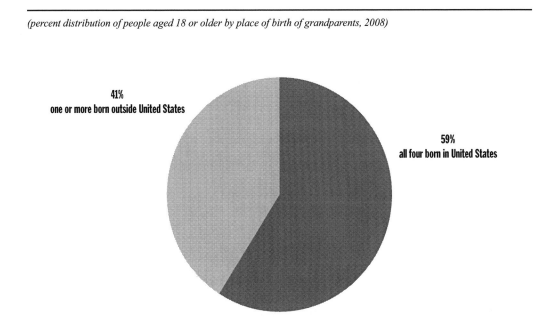

41%
one or more born outside United States

59%
all four born in United States

Table 6.6 Born in the United States, 1978 to 2008

"Were you born in this country?"

(percent of people aged 18 or older responding, 1978 to 2008; and percent responding by demographic characteristic, 2008)

	yes	no
TREND		
2008	86.1%	13.9%
1998	90.8	9.2
1988	93.6	6.4
1978	93.5	6.5
2008 PROFILE		
Total people	**86.1**	**13.9**
Men	86.2	13.8
Women	85.9	14.1
Black	91.5	8.5
Hispanic	43.2	56.8
White	91.1	8.9
Aged 18 to 44	81.1	18.9
Aged 45 to 64	91.1	8.9
Aged 65 or older	89.7	10.3
Not a college graduate	86.4	13.6
Bachelor's degree or more	85.4	14.6

Source: Survey Documentation and Analysis, Computer-assisted Survey Methods Program, University of California, Berkeley, General Social Surveys, 1972–2008 Cumulative Data Files, Internet site http://sda.berkeley.edu/cgi-bin/hsda?harcsda+gss08; calculations by New Strategist

Table 6.7 Were Your Parents Born in the United States, 1978 to 2008

"Were both your parents born in this country?"

(percent of people aged 18 or older responding, 1978 to 2008; and percent responding by demographic characteristic, 2008)

	born in United States			neither born in	don't
	both	mother only	father only	United States	know
TREND					
2008	78.3%	3.1%	1.8%	16.6%	0.2%
1998	82.4	3.1	1.6	12.4	0.5
1988	83.6	3.2	1.9	10.8	0.5
1978	81.8	4.1	2.4	11.2	0.5
2008 PROFILE					
Total people	**78.3**	**3.1**	**1.8**	**16.6**	**0.2**
Men	77.2	3.5	1.7	17.2	0.3
Women	79.2	2.7	1.8	16.1	0.2
Black	88.0	2.7	1.2	7.8	0.3
Hispanic	20.2	6.3	2.8	69.6	1.1
White	83.9	3.2	1.9	10.9	0.1
Aged 18 to 44	72.7	3.0	1.8	22.1	0.5
Aged 45 to 64	85.9	2.9	1.9	9.4	0.0
Aged 65 or older	77.9	3.8	1.4	16.6	0.3
Not a college graduate	78.5	3.0	1.7	16.4	0.3
Bachelor's degree or more	77.8	3.3	1.8	17.0	0.2

Source: Survey Documentation and Analysis, Computer-assisted Survey Methods Program, University of California, Berkeley, General Social Surveys, 1972–2008 Cumulative Data Files, Internet site http://sda.berkeley.edu/cgi-bin/hsda?harcsda+gss08; calculations by New Strategist

Table 6.8 How Many Grandparents Were Born outside the United States, 1978 to 2008

"How many of your grandparents were born outside the United States?"

(percent of people aged 18 or older responding, 1978 to 2008; and percent responding by demographic characteristic, 2008)

	none	one	two	three	four
TREND					
2008	58.6%	6.6%	10.9%	2.1%	21.8%
1998	60.8	6.5	11.6	2.3	18.7
1988	59.5	6.9	11.5	3.4	18.7
1978	58.7	7.0	10.5	3.4	20.4
2008 PROFILE					
Total people	**58.6**	**6.6**	**10.9**	**2.1**	**21.8**
Men	57.1	7.6	11.4	1.7	22.2
Women	59.9	5.8	10.4	2.4	21.4
Black	84.4	2.7	3.5	0.4	9.1
Hispanic	8.7	3.0	9.8	2.1	76.4
White	60.0	7.8	12.7	2.5	16.9
Aged 18 to 44	57.7	6.5	9.1	1.7	25.1
Aged 45 to 64	61.8	6.5	13.3	2.2	16.2
Aged 65 or older	53.6	7.3	11.2	3.2	24.9
Not a college graduate	59.9	6.3	10.0	2.0	21.8
Bachelor's degree or more	55.0	7.5	13.3	2.4	21.7

Source: Survey Documentation and Analysis, Computer-assisted Survey Methods Program, University of California, Berkeley, General Social Surveys, 1972–2008 Cumulative Data Files, Internet site http://sda.berkeley.edu/cgi-bin/hsda?harcsda+gss08; calculations by New Strategist

One in Four Has Divorced

Among the married, the great majority says their marriage is "very happy"–perhaps because those who are not happily married get divorced. Twenty-five percent of ever-married adults say they have been divorced or legally separated. The proportion peaks among 45-to-64-year-olds at 33 percent. Interestingly, the percentage of the public that thinks it is a good idea for older people to share a home with grown children has increased from 36 percent in 1978 to the 51 percent majority in 2008.

(percent of ever-married people aged 18 or older who have ever been divorced or legally separated, 1978 and 2008)

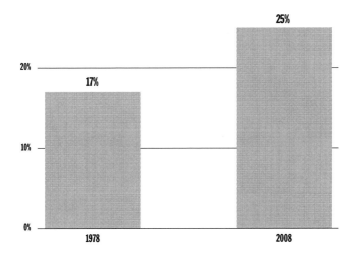

Table 6.9 Happiness of Marriage, 1978 to 2008

"Taking all things together, how would you describe your marriage?"

(percent of married people aged 18 or older responding, 1978 to 2008; and percent responding by demographic characteristic, 2008)

	very happy	pretty happy	not too happy
TREND			
2008	62.1%	35.3%	2.6%
1998	63.6	33.7	2.7
1988	62.0	34.5	3.5
1978	64.8	32.0	3.2
2008 PROFILE			
Total ever-married	**62.1**	**35.3**	**2.6**
Men	64.1	34.0	1.9
Women	60.2	36.5	3.3
Black	50.1	42.6	7.3
Hispanic	42.1	54.3	3.6
White	63.4	34.6	2.0
Aged 18 to 44	62.9	34.8	2.3
Aged 45 to 64	60.4	36.4	3.2
Aged 65 or older	64.6	33.3	2.0
Not a college graduate	57.5	39.7	2.8
Bachelor's degree or more	72.1	25.6	2.3

Source: Survey Documentation and Analysis, Computer-assisted Survey Methods Program, University of California, Berkeley, General Social Surveys, 1972–2008 Cumulative Data Files, Internet site http://sda.berkeley.edu/cgi-bin/hsda?harcsda+gss08; calculations by New Strategist

Table 6.10 Ever Been Divorced, 1978 to 2008

"Have you ever been divorced or legally separated?"

(percent of ever-married people aged 18 or older responding, 1978 to 2008; and percent responding by demographic characteristic, 2008)

	yes	no
TREND		
2008	25.0%	75.0%
1998	22.5	77.5
1988	19.2	80.8
1978	16.5	83.5
2008 PROFILE		
Total people	**25.0**	**75.0**
Men	26.4	73.6
Women	23.9	76.1
Black	20.9	79.1
Hispanic	23.6	76.4
White	27.0	73.0
Aged 18 to 44	16.1	83.9
Aged 45 to 64	33.1	66.9
Aged 65 or older	23.5	76.5
Not a college graduate	28.6	71.4
Bachelor's degree or more	16.6	83.4

Source: Survey Documentation and Analysis, Computer-assisted Survey Methods Program, University of California, Berkeley, General Social Surveys, 1972–2008 Cumulative Data Files, Internet site http://sda.berkeley.edu/cgi-bin/hsda?harcsda+gss08; calculations by New Strategist

Table 6.11 Divorce Laws, 1978 to 2008

"Should divorce in this country be easier or more difficult to obtain than it is now?"

(percent of people aged 18 or older responding, 1978 to 2008; and percent responding by demographic characteristic, 2008)

	easier	more difficult	stay same
TREND			
2008	27.4%	48.7%	23.9%
1998	24.6	56.3	19.1
1988	25.2	52.2	22.6
1978	28.0	44.6	27.4
2008 PROFILE			
Total people	**27.4**	**48.7**	**23.9**
Men	27.7	47.4	25.0
Women	27.1	50.0	22.9
Black	54.3	34.4	11.3
Hispanic	41.5	39.0	19.5
White	21.7	51.3	27.0
Aged 18 to 44	31.1	46.6	22.3
Aged 45 to 64	27.0	49.6	23.5
Aged 65 or older	16.7	53.5	29.8
Not a college graduate	31.2	48.8	20.0
Bachelor's degree or more	16.0	48.6	35.5

Source: Survey Documentation and Analysis, Computer-assisted Survey Methods Program, University of California, Berkeley, General Social Surveys, 1972–2008 Cumulative Data Files, Internet site http://sda.berkeley.edu/cgi-bin/hsda?harcsda+gss08; calculations by New Strategist

Table 6.12 Should Aged Share Home with Grown Children, 1978 to 2008

"As you know, many older people share a home with their grown children.
Do you think this is generally a good idea or a bad idea?"

(percent of people aged 18 or older responding, 1978 to 2008; and percent responding by demographic characteristic, 2008)

	good idea	bad idea	depends
TREND			
2008	50.9%	31.7%	17.3%
1998	46.7	34.1	19.3
1988	46.0	40.1	13.9
1978	36.3	46.7	16.9
2008 PROFILE			
Total people	**50.9**	**31.7**	**17.3**
Men	51.2	31.0	17.8
Women	50.7	32.4	17.0
Black	42.8	33.4	23.8
Hispanic	60.6	22.8	16.6
White	50.8	32.5	16.7
Aged 18 to 44	54.0	29.6	16.4
Aged 45 to 64	52.6	29.4	18.0
Aged 65 or older	37.4	43.7	18.9
Not a college graduate	51.4	32.1	16.5
Bachelor's degree or more	49.8	30.8	19.4

Source: Survey Documentation and Analysis, Computer-assisted Survey Methods Program, University of California, Berkeley, General Social Surveys, 1972–2008 Cumulative Data Files, Internet site http://sda.berkeley.edu/cgi-bin/hsda?harcsda+gss08; calculations by New Strategist

Young and Middle-Aged Adults Reject Traditional Sex Roles

Only 26 percent of the American public agrees that it is the husband's job to earn money and the wife's job to look after the family. Fifty-three percent disagree with the notion of traditional sex roles. Most Americans also say working mothers do not hurt children (72 percent) and that preschoolers do not suffer if their mother works (65 percent). More than two-thirds of today's adults had working mothers.

(percent who disagree with the statement, "A husband's job is to earn money; a wife's job is to look after the home and family," 2008)

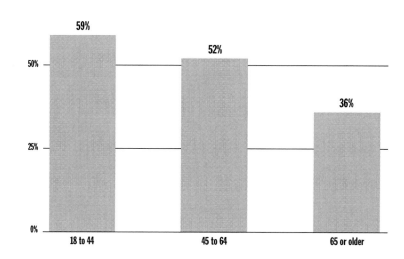

Table 6.13 Husband Should Work, Wife Should Look After Home, 1988 to 2008

"Do you agree or disagree: A husband's job is to earn money; a wife's job is to look after the home and family."

(percent of people aged 18 or older responding, 1988 to 2008; and percent responding by demographic characteristic, 2008)

	strongly agree	agree	neither agree nor disagree	disagree	strongly disagree
TREND					
2008	11.3%	14.9%	20.6%	31.9%	21.2%
1998	9.5	12.1	19.7	25.0	33.7
1988	8.2	19.0	20.5	32.7	19.5
2008 PROFILE					
Total people	**11.3**	**14.9**	**20.6**	**31.9**	**21.2**
Men	12.5	16.3	23.0	29.7	18.5
Women	10.3	13.7	18.5	33.9	23.6
Black	16.6	17.4	18.1	31.6	16.2
Hispanic	15.5	15.0	15.8	34.3	19.4
White	10.5	15.0	21.9	31.1	21.5
Aged 18 to 44	7.7	12.8	20.5	34.4	24.5
Aged 45 to 64	11.5	15.0	21.3	31.2	20.9
Aged 65 or older	21.9	21.6	20.1	25.8	10.6
Not a college graduate	13.9	17.1	19.6	31.3	18.1
Bachelor's degree or more	4.1	8.8	23.4	33.7	30.1

Source: Survey Documentation and Analysis, Computer-assisted Survey Methods Program, University of California, Berkeley, General Social Surveys, 1972–2008 Cumulative Data Files, Internet site http://sda.berkeley.edu/cgi-bin/hsda?harcsda+gss08; calculations by New Strategist

Table 6.14 Better for Man to Work, Woman to Tend Home, 1988 to 2008

"It is much better for everyone involved if the man is the achiever
outside the home and the woman takes care of the home and family."

(percent of people aged 18 or older responding, 1988 to 2008; and percent responding by demographic characteristic, 2008)

	strongly agree	agree	disagree	strongly disagree
TREND				
2008	8.2%	27.0%	47.2%	17.5%
1998	6.8	27.2	47.2	18.7
1988	9.0	32.0	43.3	15.8
2008 PROFILE				
Total people	**8.2**	**27.0**	**47.2**	**17.5**
Men	6.8	27.2	47.2	18.7
Women	8.4	24.2	45.2	22.2
Black	9.5	17.4	54.8	18.4
Hispanic	15.1	38.3	36.6	10.0
White	7.1	27.4	47.9	17.7
Aged 18 to 44	8.3	24.0	46.8	20.9
Aged 45 to 64	6.7	25.1	50.4	17.8
Aged 65 or older	12.3	41.6	40.4	5.6
Not a college graduate	9.5	30.2	45.2	15.2
Bachelor's degree or more	4.6	18.0	53.2	24.2

Source: Survey Documentation and Analysis, Computer-assisted Survey Methods Program, University of California, Berkeley, General Social Surveys, 1972–2008 Cumulative Data Files, Internet site http://sda.berkeley.edu/cgi-bin/hsda?harcsda+gss08; calculations by New Strategist

Table 6.15 Working Mother Doesn't Hurt Children, 1988 to 2008

"A working mother can establish just as warm and secure a relationship
with her children as a mother who does not work."

(percent of people aged 18 or older responding, 1988 to 2008; and percent responding by demographic charac-teristic, 2008)

	strongly agree	agree	disagree	strongly disagree
TREND				
2008	26.3%	46.0%	22.2%	5.4%
1998	22.1	45.8	25.2	7.0
1988	22.4	40.1	28.4	9.1
2008 PROFILE				
Total people	**26.3**	**46.0**	**22.2**	**5.4**
Men	16.1	46.3	30.3	7.3
Women	35.8	45.8	14.7	3.7
Black	32.4	45.7	17.9	3.9
Hispanic	15.1	43.7	37.5	3.6
White	26.3	46.6	21.5	5.6
Aged 18 to 44	28.8	45.9	21.1	4.2
Aged 45 to 64	26.0	47.7	20.2	6.1
Aged 65 or older	19.9	42.4	30.0	7.7
Not a college graduate	24.7	45.0	24.7	5.5
Bachelor's degree or more	30.9	49.0	14.9	5.2

Source: Survey Documentation and Analysis, Computer-assisted Survey Methods Program, University of California, Berkeley, General Social Surveys, 1972–2008 Cumulative Data Files, Internet site http://sda.berkeley.edu/cgi-bin/hsda?harcsda+gss08; calculations by New Strategist

Table 6.16 Preschool Children Suffer If Mother Works, 1988 to 2008

"A preschool child is likely to suffer if his or her mother works."

(percent of people aged 18 or older responding, 1988 to 2008; and percent responding by demographic characteristic, 2008)

	strongly agree	agree	disagree	strongly disagree
TREND				
2008	7.2%	27.7%	52.8%	12.2%
1998	8.7	33.6	47.6	10.1
1988	10.5	37.9	41.1	10.5
2008 PROFILE				
Total people	**7.2**	**27.7**	**52.8**	**12.2**
Men	8.7	33.8	52.4	5.2
Women	5.8	22.2	53.2	18.7
Black	6.1	17.3	60.8	15.7
Hispanic	9.6	45.7	39.9	4.7
White	6.8	27.8	53.4	12.1
Aged 18 to 44	5.6	25.7	53.2	15.5
Aged 45 to 64	8.5	26.1	55.0	10.5
Aged 65 or older	9.2	38.3	46.4	6.1
Not a college graduate	8.5	28.9	50.7	11.9
Bachelor's degree or more	3.3	24.3	59.0	13.3

Source: Survey Documentation and Analysis, Computer-assisted Survey Methods Program, University of California, Berkeley, General Social Surveys, 1972–2008 Cumulative Data Files, Internet site http://sda.berkeley.edu/cgi-bin/hsda?harcsda+gss08; calculations by New Strategist

Table 6.17 Mother Worked while You Were Growing Up, 1998 and 2008

"Did your mother ever work for pay for as long as a year while you were growing up?"

(percent of people aged 18 or older responding, 1998 and 2008; and percent responding by demographic characteristic, 2008)

	yes	no
TREND		
2008	68.8%	31.2%
1998	62.9	37.1
2008 PROFILE		
Total people	**68.8**	**31.2**
Men	68.4	31.6
Women	69.2	30.8
Black	85.4	14.6
Hispanic	51.4	48.6
White	67.6	32.4
Aged 18 to 44	77.8	22.2
Aged 45 to 64	66.1	33.9
Aged 65 or older	48.7	51.3
Not a college graduate	69.3	30.7
Bachelor's degree or more	67.6	32.4

Source: Survey Documentation and Analysis, Computer-assisted Survey Methods Program, University of California, Berkeley, General Social Surveys, 1972–2008 Cumulative Data Files, Internet site http://sda.berkeley.edu/cgi-bin/hsda?harcsda+gss08; calculations by New Strategist

Children Should Learn to Think for Themselves

A 48 percent plurality of Americans says two is the ideal number of children, a figure that has dropped from the 57 percent majority in 1998. What should those children learn? Most important is learning to think for themselves, according to the largest share of the public (45 percent). Working hard is in second place (23 percent), and learning to obey is in fourth place (15.5 percent)—slightly behind helping others.

(percent who say selected characteristic is the most important for a child to learn, 2008)

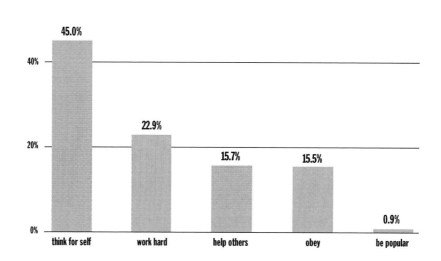

Table 6.18 Ideal Number of Children, 1978 to 2008

"What do you think is the ideal number of children for a family to have?"

(percent of people aged 18 or older responding, 1978 to 2008; and percent responding by demographic characteristic, 2008)

	none	one	two	three	four	five	six	seven+	as many as want
TREND									
2008	1.0%	2.5%	47.7%	26.6%	7.9%	1.5%	0.5%	0.2%	12.1%
1998	1.5	2.4	56.8	20.2	8.5	0.9	0.7	0.5	8.6
1988	4.6	1.7	51.3	26.6	10.9	1.8	1.0	0.3	4.9
1978	1.4	2.0	51.0	24.1	13.3	2.2	0.8	0.4	4.8
2008 PROFILE									
Total people	**1.0**	**2.5**	**47.7**	**26.6**	**7.9**	**1.5**	**0.5**	**0.2**	**12.1**
Men	1.4	2.4	50.8	25.1	7.2	1.9	0.6	0.2	10.5
Women	0.6	2.6	44.9	27.9	8.5	1.2	0.4	0.2	13.6
Black	0.3	2.7	39.8	30.0	11.4	4.6	–	–	11.2
Hispanic	–	3.9	40.1	35.7	9.9	1.0	2.3	0.5	6.6
White	1.2	2.2	49.0	25.8	7.3	1.2	0.5	0.1	12.6
Aged 18 to 44	0.4	3.1	41.9	32.2	8.8	1.7	0.8	0.1	11.2
Aged 45 to 64	1.9	2.0	55.9	18.5	7.6	0.8	0.2	0.2	12.8
Aged 65 or older	0.4	1.9	46.1	28.7	5.9	2.7	0.4	0.4	13.4
Not a college graduate	1.1	2.7	46.0	26.6	9.8	1.8	0.7	0.2	11.0
Bachelor's degree or more	0.5	1.9	52.9	26.4	2.0	0.7	–	0.1	15.4

Source: Survey Documentation and Analysis, Computer-assisted Survey Methods Program, University of California, Berkeley, General Social Surveys, 1972–2008 Cumulative Data Files, Internet site http://sda.berkeley.edu/cgi-bin/hsda?harcsda+gss08; calculations by New Strategist

Table 6.19 Child Should Learn to Obey, 1988 to 2008

"How important is it for a child to learn to obey to prepare him or her for life?"

(percent of people aged 18 or older responding, 1988 to 2008; and percent responding by demographic characteristic, 2008)

	importance of learning to obey				
	most important	second most important	third most important	fourth most important	least important
TREND					
2008	15.5%	11.4%	16.6%	41.7%	14.8%
1998	18.5	12.8	17.0	37.0	14.7
1988	22.6	11.8	19.6	30.3	15.7
2008 PROFILE					
Total people	**15.5**	**11.4**	**16.6**	**41.7**	**14.8**
Men	16.6	12.5	16.0	38.6	16.3
Women	14.6	10.4	17.0	44.4	13.5
Black	20.6	20.0	18.2	31.6	9.6
Hispanic	24.6	13.8	16.2	34.1	11.3
White	14.4	9.4	16.3	44.5	15.3
Aged 18 to 44	14.4	14.3	15.8	38.5	16.9
Aged 45 to 64	14.6	8.6	17.7	46.6	12.6
Aged 65 or older	21.6	8.1	16.6	39.8	14.0
Not a college graduate	19.2	13.0	17.3	38.5	12.0
Bachelor's degree or more	5.3	6.9	14.4	50.7	22.7

Source: Survey Documentation and Analysis, Computer-assisted Survey Methods Program, University of California, Berkeley, General Social Surveys, 1972–2008 Cumulative Data Files, Internet site http://sda.berkeley.edu/cgi-bin/hsda?harcsda+gss08; calculations by New Strategist

Table 6.20 Child Should Learn to Think for Self, 1988 to 2008

"How important is it for a child to learn to think for
himself or herself to prepare him or her for life?"

(percent of people aged 18 or older responding, 1988 to 2008; and percent responding by demographic charac-teristic, 2008)

| | importance of thinking for self | | | | |
	most important	second most important	third most important	fourth most important	least important
TREND					
2008	45.0%	21.6%	14.2%	14.8%	4.4%
1998	49.4	18.1	13.9	14.1	4.6
1988	50.1	17.1	12.8	13.1	6.8
2008 PROFILE					
Total people	**45.0**	**21.6**	**14.2**	**14.8**	**4.4**
Men	41.3	22.7	13.9	16.1	6.0
Women	48.2	20.7	14.4	13.6	3.1
Black	36.3	26.8	18.8	15.8	2.3
Hispanic	34.7	19.7	15.7	22.6	7.3
White	48.0	21.3	12.9	13.8	4.0
Aged 18 to 44	40.7	21.9	17.1	15.6	4.6
Aged 45 to 64	49.8	23.5	9.2	13.6	3.9
Aged 65 or older	47.4	16.5	15.8	15.2	5.1
Not a college graduate	40.6	22.2	15.3	16.8	5.1
Bachelor's degree or more	57.2	19.9	11.0	9.2	2.6

Source: Survey Documentation and Analysis, Computer-assisted Survey Methods Program, University of California, Berkeley, General Social Surveys, 1972–2008 Cumulative Data Files, Internet site http://sda.berkeley.edu/cgi-bin/hsda?harcsda+gss08; calculations by New Strategist

Table 6.21 Child Should Learn to Be Popular, 1988 to 2008

"How important is it for a child to learn to be well-liked
or popular to prepare him or her for life?"

(percent of people aged 18 or older responding, 1988 to 2008; and percent responding by demographic characteristic, 2008)

	importance of being well-liked or popular				
	most important	second most important	third most important	fourth most important	least important
TREND					
2008	0.9%	0.9%	3.0%	18.1%	77.1%
1998	1.0	2.0	3.3	16.7	77.0
1988	0.7	4.7	5.0	19.8	69.8
2008 PROFILE					
Total people	**0.9**	**0.9**	**3.0**	**18.1**	**77.1**
Men	0.9	1.5	3.4	20.5	73.8
Women	0.9	0.4	2.7	16.1	79.9
Black	2.0	1.3	4.2	10.4	82.1
Hispanic	0.3	3.1	9.7	20.0	67.0
White	0.9	0.7	2.5	18.5	77.4
Aged 18 to 44	1.3	1.0	3.6	19.9	74.1
Aged 45 to 64	0.6	0.6	1.8	15.8	81.1
Aged 65 or older	0.4	1.1	3.5	17.9	77.1
Not a college graduate	1.0	1.0	3.1	16.5	78.3
Bachelor's degree or more	0.7	0.5	2.7	22.6	73.4

Source: Survey Documentation and Analysis, Computer-assisted Survey Methods Program, University of California, Berkeley, General Social Surveys, 1972–2008 Cumulative Data Files, Internet site http://sda.berkeley.edu/cgi-bin/hsda?harcsda+gss08; calculations by New Strategist

Table 6.22 Child Should Learn to Work Hard, 1988 to 2008

"How important is it for a child to learn to work hard to prepare him or her for life?"

(percent of people aged 18 or older responding, 1988 to 2008; and percent responding by demographic characteristic, 2008)

	importance of learning to work hard				
	most important	second most important	third most important	fourth most important	least important
TREND					
2008	22.9%	34.7%	28.7%	11.8%	1.8%
1998	17.8	36.6	31.8	12.4	1.4
1988	14.5	32.6	32.7	16.8	3.4
2008 PROFILE					
Total people	**22.9**	**34.7**	**28.7**	**11.8**	**1.8**
Men	25.9	31.0	30.6	10.5	2.1
Women	20.3	37.9	27.1	13.1	1.7
Black	26.8	25.7	26.0	18.7	2.7
Hispanic	24.2	28.7	25.4	13.8	7.9
White	21.4	36.1	29.6	11.1	1.8
Aged 18 to 44	27.0	32.4	27.3	11.3	1.9
Aged 45 to 64	20.0	32.7	33.3	12.5	1.6
Aged 65 or older	16.5	47.0	22.3	11.8	2.4
Not a college graduate	22.6	33.6	27.1	14.3	2.4
Bachelor's degree or more	23.6	37.9	33.2	4.9	0.4

Source: Survey Documentation and Analysis, Computer-assisted Survey Methods Program, University of California, Berkeley, General Social Surveys, 1972–2008 Cumulative Data Files, Internet site http://sda.berkeley.edu/cgi-bin/hsda?harcsda+gss08; calculations by New Strategist

Table 6.23 Child Should Learn to Help Others, 1988 to 2008

"How important is it for a child to learn to help others to prepare him or her for life?"

(percent of people aged 18 or older responding, 1988 to 2008; and percent responding by demographic characteristic, 2008)

	importance of learning to help others				
	most important	second most important	third most important	fourth most important	least important
TREND					
2008	15.7%	31.4%	37.6%	13.6%	1.8%
1998	13.3	30.5	34.0	19.9	2.3
1988	12.4	33.3	29.6	20.1	4.5
2008 PROFILE					
Total people	**15.7**	**31.4**	**37.6**	**13.6**	**1.8**
Men	15.3	32.3	36.1	14.4	1.9
Women	16.0	30.6	38.8	12.9	1.8
Black	14.2	26.1	32.8	23.4	3.3
Hispanic	16.2	34.8	32.9	9.5	6.6
White	15.3	32.5	38.7	12.1	1.4
Aged 18 to 44	16.5	30.3	36.2	14.6	2.4
Aged 45 to 64	15.0	34.6	38.0	11.6	0.8
Aged 65 or older	14.1	27.3	41.9	15.4	1.4
Not a college graduate	16.5	30.1	37.2	13.9	2.2
Bachelor's degree or more	13.2	34.8	38.6	12.5	0.9

Source: Survey Documentation and Analysis, Computer-assisted Survey Methods Program, University of California, Berkeley, General Social Surveys, 1972–2008 Cumulative Data Files, Internet site http://sda.berkeley.edu/cgi-bin/hsda?harcsda+gss08; calculations by New Strategist

Spanking Is OK

Americans are not easy on criminals or children. Most agree that spanking is OK. They do not flinch in their approval even if the punishment is described as a "good, hard spanking." More than 70 percent of Americans approve.

(percent distribution of people aged 18 or older by attitude toward the statement, "It is sometimes necessary to discipline a child with a good, hard spanking," 2008)

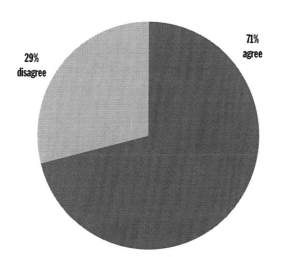

Table 6.24 Favor Spanking to Discipline Child, 1988 to 2008

"Do you strongly agree, agree, disagree, or strongly disagree that it is
sometimes necessary to discipline a child with a good, hard spanking?"

(percent of people aged 18 or older responding, 1988 to 2008; and percent responding by demographic characteristic, 2008)

	strongly agree	agree	disagree	strongly disagree
TREND				
2008	24.7%	46.2%	23.1%	6.0%
1998	26.7	48.6	17.9	6.8
1988	30.7	49.1	15.2	5.0
2008 PROFILE				
Total people	**24.7**	**46.2**	**23.1**	**6.0**
Men	25.8	51.7	18.2	4.3
Women	23.7	41.1	27.6	7.6
Black	41.4	45.3	12.2	1.1
Hispanic	21.0	43.4	28.5	7.1
White	22.3	46.6	24.7	6.4
Aged 18 to 44	25.1	46.0	23.2	5.7
Aged 45 to 64	24.8	46.6	22.1	6.5
Aged 65 or older	22.4	46.0	25.7	5.8
Not a college graduate	28.0	46.7	20.2	5.1
Bachelor's degree or more	15.2	44.6	31.4	8.7

Source: Survey Documentation and Analysis, Computer-assisted Survey Methods Program, University of California, Berkeley, General Social Surveys, 1972–2008 Cumulative Data Files, Internet site http://sda.berkeley.edu/cgi-bin/hsda?harcsda+gss08; calculations by New Strategist

Americans Socialize Most Frequently with Relatives

One of the myths rampant in our society is the notion that Americans are growing increasingly distant from their families. Results from the General Social Survey show this to be decidedly untrue. The average American socializes more frequently with family members than with friends or neighbors. Few frequent bars on a weekly basis, although more than one-third of adults under age 45 socialize in bars at least once a month.

(percent of people aged 18 or older who socialize at least several times a week, 2008)

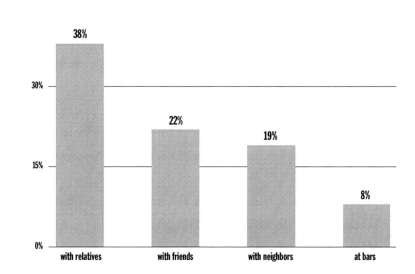

Table 6.25 Spend Evening with Relatives, 1978 to 2008

"How often do you spend a social evening with relatives?"

(percent of people aged 18 or older responding, 1978 to 2008; and percent responding by demographic characteristic, 2008)

	almost daily	several times a week	several times a month	once a month	several times a year	once a year	never
TREND							
2008	13.8%	24.3%	19.7%	15.1%	16.6%	6.5%	4.0%
1998	8.9	28.0	16.6	17.6	18.3	7.0	3.6
1988	10.8	25.9	18.6	15.1	18.2	7.7	3.6
1978	7.0	27.3	19.2	14.4	19.7	7.7	4.6
2008 PROFILE							
Total people	**13.8**	**24.3**	**19.7**	**15.1**	**16.6**	**6.5**	**4.0**
Men	14.6	22.1	18.2	16.3	17.3	6.8	4.7
Women	13.2	26.3	21.0	14.0	15.9	6.2	3.4
Black	20.7	25.9	19.2	13.8	11.1	5.5	3.8
Hispanic	22.3	25.3	15.6	11.4	6.7	12.3	6.4
White	12.2	23.8	20.3	15.2	18.7	6.1	3.6
Aged 18 to 44	19.2	25.0	19.4	14.8	12.5	5.4	3.8
Aged 45 to 64	9.6	25.0	21.1	16.3	17.3	8.2	2.6
Aged 65 or older	7.8	20.2	17.5	13.6	28.1	4.9	8.0
Not a college graduate	16.0	24.7	19.3	14.6	14.5	6.5	4.4
Bachelor's degree or more	7.6	23.0	20.7	16.5	22.7	6.5	3.0

Source: Survey Documentation and Analysis, Computer-assisted Survey Methods Program, University of California, Berkeley, General Social Surveys, 1972–2008 Cumulative Data Files, Internet site http://sda.berkeley.edu/cgi-bin/hsda?harcsda+gss08; calculations by New Strategist

Table 6.26 Spend Evening with Neighbors, 1978 to 2008

"How often do you spend a social evening with someone
who lives in your neighborhood?"

(percent of people aged 18 or older responding, 1978 to 2008; and percent responding by demographic characteristic, 2008)

	almost daily	several times a week	several times a month	once a month	several times a year	once a year	never
TREND							
2008	5.1%	14.3%	10.8%	14.9%	13.2%	11.6%	30.1%
1998	5.0	15.4	10.5	16.3	14.6	10.6	27.6
1988	4.4	20.5	11.1	15.1	13.5	7.4	27.9
1978	4.9	23.5	10.7	12.0	113.9	8.9	26.2
2008 PROFILE							
Total people	**5.1**	**14.3**	**10.8**	**14.9**	**13.2**	**11.6**	**30.1**
Men	5.9	12.5	11.2	13.4	15.8	12.1	29.1
Women	4.4	15.9	10.4	16.2	10.8	11.2	31.0
Black	9.3	18.1	10.2	14.1	7.6	9.0	31.8
Hispanic	6.7	11.4	4.8	16.0	10.2	6.1	45.0
White	4.4	13.6	11.5	15.1	14.2	11.8	29.3
Aged 18 to 44	7.2	14.3	9.3	17.1	13.3	9.6	29.2
Aged 45 to 64	3.3	13.0	11.9	14.4	14.3	14.5	28.7
Aged 65 or older	3.4	17.2	12.7	9.1	10.2	11.3	36.1
Not a college graduate	6.0	14.5	10.1	15.2	10.6	10.2	33.5
Bachelor's degree or more	2.5	13.8	12.8	14.0	20.7	16.0	20.2

Source: Survey Documentation and Analysis, Computer-assisted Survey Methods Program, University of California, Berkeley, General Social Surveys, 1972–2008 Cumulative Data Files, Internet site http://sda.berkeley.edu/cgi-bin/hsda?harcsda+gss08; calculations by New Strategist

Table 6.27 Spend Evening with Friends, 1978 to 2008

"How often do you spend a social evening with friends
who live outside the neighborhood?"

(percent of people aged 18 or older responding, 1978 to 2008; and percent responding by demographic characteristic, 2008)

	almost daily	several times a week	several times a month	once a month	several times a year	once a year	never
TREND							
2008	4.5%	17.6%	20.4%	21.2%	18.7%	7.8%	9.8%
1998	3.6	18.0	21.1	21.4	21.1	6.7	8.0
1988	3.2	17.2	20.9	24.3	18.0	6.4	10.0
1978	1.7	20.3	20.4	16.6	21.3	8.6	11.2
2008 PROFILE							
Total people	**4.5**	**17.6**	**20.4**	**21.2**	**18.7**	**7.8**	**9.8**
Men	5.8	18.5	20.2	18.5	17.1	9.2	10.7
Women	3.3	16.7	20.6	23.7	20.1	6.5	9.0
Black	8.7	24.6	15.3	18.5	14.1	9.6	9.2
Hispanic	5.3	16.5	12.4	28.4	11.4	6.0	20.1
White	3.6	16.5	21.7	21.3	20.2	7.6	9.2
Aged 18 to 44	7.9	22.2	22.2	22.2	13.7	6.2	5.5
Aged 45 to 64	1.3	12.7	20.4	22.7	22.6	8.6	11.6
Aged 65 or older	1.5	14.6	15.3	14.3	24.6	11.0	18.7
Not a college graduate	5.3	17.9	17.7	22.5	16.9	7.9	11.8
Bachelor's degree or more	2.2	16.6	28.3	17.5	23.8	7.6	4.0

Source: Survey Documentation and Analysis, Computer-assisted Survey Methods Program, University of California, Berkeley, General Social Surveys, 1972–2008 Cumulative Data Files, Internet site http://sda.berkeley.edu/cgi-bin/hsda?harcsda+gss08; calculations by New Strategist

Table 6.28 Spend Evening at Bar, 1978 to 2008

"How often do you go to a bar or tavern?"

(percent of people aged 18 or older responding, 1978 to 2008; and percent responding by demographic characteristic, 2008)

	almost daily	several times a week	several times a month	once a month	several times a year	once a year	never
TREND							
2008	0.6%	7.2%	5.6%	11.7%	14.0%	11.9%	49.0%
1998	1.5	6.3	6.4	10.4	12.6	13.1	49.7
1988	0.9	8.8	6.6	9.8	10.4	12.1	51.4
1978	1.6	8.8	8.9	7.7	13.3	9.7	50.0
2008 PROFILE							
Total people	**0.6**	**7.2**	**5.6**	**11.7**	**14.0**	**11.9**	**49.0**
Men	1.0	9.9	6.4	14.3	12.0	9.4	47.0
Women	0.3	4.7	4.9	9.3	15.8	14.2	50.9
Black	0.0	8.6	5.3	12.9	11.6	12.3	49.3
Hispanic	1.3	9.7	3.5	8.0	10.9	6.3	60.3
White	0.8	7.0	6.0	11.7	14.7	12.3	47.4
Aged 18 to 44	0.7	11.3	8.2	17.1	15.9	10.8	36.0
Aged 45 to 64	0.3	4.4	3.8	8.0	16.3	14.3	52.9
Aged 65 or older	1.3	1.3	2.0	3.5	2.5	9.0	80.4
Not a college graduate	0.5	6.1	5.5	11.8	12.2	11.2	52.8
Bachelor's degree or more	1.1	10.2	6.1	11.4	19.2	14.1	38.0

Source: Survey Documentation and Analysis, Computer-assisted Survey Methods Program, University of California, Berkeley, General Social Surveys, 1972–2008 Cumulative Data Files, Internet site http://sda.berkeley.edu/cgi-bin/hsda?harcsda+gss08; calculations by New Strategist

7

Race

The election of the first black president holds out the promise that America may be becoming a postracial society. Results from the General Social Survey both support and dispute that notion. Integration is now the norm in neighborhoods and the workplace, but questions about hard work and intelligence reveal deep-seated prejudices against blacks.

No change

• **Most continue to oppose affirmative action.** More than 80 percent of the public is against affirmative action for blacks—a figure that has not changed in the past decade. Even the majority of blacks are against it.

• **Most think affirmative action could hurt whites.** Only about one-third of Americans think it is unlikely that a black would get a job over an equally qualified white. Most think it is at least somewhat likely—including the majority of blacks.

Big changes

• **Fewer think discrimination explains the lower socioeconomic status of blacks.** The percentage of Americans who think blacks lag behind whites because of discrimination has fallen from 45 percent in 1988 to 35 percent in 2008.

• **More live in integrated neighborhoods.** The percentage of people who say blacks live in their neighborhood has grown from 50 to 69 percent during the past 30 years.

• **Most now support open housing laws.** The percentage of Americans who believe it should be against the law for a homeowner to refuse to sell his house based on the race of the buyer grew from 43 to 71 percent between 1978 and 2008.

Most Blame Problems of Blacks on Lack of Will

The 51 percent majority of the public believes that the socioeconomic status of blacks is below that of whites mainly because of a lack of motivation. Hispanics are most likely to feel that way. Forty-six percent of the public think the differences are mainly due to a lack of education. Only 35 percent think the differences are rooted in discrimination, and just 11 percent believe they are a consequence of lower ability.

(percent of people aged 18 or older who agree that the reason blacks have worse jobs, income, and housing than whites is because they lack the willpower to pull themselves up out of poverty, by race and Hispanic origin, 2008)

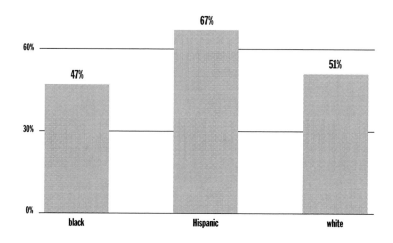

Table 7.1 Reason for Racial Differences: Discrimination, 1988 to 2008

"On the average (blacks/African Americans) have worse jobs, income, and housing than white people. Do you think these differences are mainly due to discrimination?"

(percent of people aged 18 or older responding, 1988 to 2008; and percent responding by demographic characteristic, 2008)

	yes	no
TREND		
2008	34.5%	65.5%
1998	36.8	63.2
1988	44.6	55.4
2008 PROFILE		
Total people	**34.5**	**65.5**
Men	31.6	68.4
Women	37.3	62.7
Black	54.8	45.2
Hispanic	51.4	48.6
White	29.8	70.2
Aged 18 to 44	35.0	65.0
Aged 45 to 64	31.6	68.4
Aged 65 or older	40.2	59.8
Not a college graduate	35.0	65.0
Bachelor's degree or more	33.1	66.9

Source: Survey Documentation and Analysis, Computer-assisted Survey Methods Program, University of California, Berkeley, General Social Surveys, 1972–2008 Cumulative Data Files, Internet site http://sda.berkeley.edu/cgi-bin/hsda?harcsda+gss08; calculations by New Strategist

Table 7.2 Reason for Racial Differences: Inborn Ability, 1988 to 2008

"On the average (blacks/African Americans) have worse jobs, income,
and housing than white people. Do you think these differences
are because most have less in-born ability to learn?"

(percent of people aged 18 or older responding, 1988 to 2008; and percent responding by demographic characteristic, 2008)

	yes	no
TREND		
2008	10.8%	89.2%
1998	9.8	90.2
1988	18.9	81.1
2008 PROFILE		
Total people	**10.8**	**89.2**
Men	11.4	88.6
Women	10.3	89.7
Black	11.8	88.2
Hispanic	20.5	79.5
White	9.2	90.8
Aged 18 to 44	10.5	89.5
Aged 45 to 64	9.1	90.9
Aged 65 or older	16.5	83.5
Not a college graduate	13.3	86.7
Bachelor's degree or more	3.8	96.2

Source: Survey Documentation and Analysis, Computer-assisted Survey Methods Program, University of California, Berkeley, General Social Surveys, 1972–2008 Cumulative Data Files, Internet site http://sda.berkeley.edu/cgi-bin/hsda?harcsda+gss08; calculations by New Strategist

Table 7.3 Reason for Racial Differences: Education, 1978 to 2008

"On the average (blacks/African Americans) have worse jobs, income, and housing than white people. Do you think these differences are because most don't have the chance for education that it takes to rise out of poverty?"

(percent of people aged 18 or older responding, 1978 to 2008; and percent responding by demographic characteristic, 2008)

	yes	no
TREND		
2008	46.3%	53.7%
1998	44.4	55.6
1988	55.0	45.0
2008 PROFILE		
Total people	**46.3**	**53.7**
Men	41.8	58.2
Women	50.4	49.6
Black	52.9	47.1
Hispanic	41.6	58.4
White	46.0	54.0
Aged 18 to 44	43.1	56.9
Aged 45 to 64	48.9	51.1
Aged 65 or older	50.4	49.6
Not a college graduate	41.6	58.4
Bachelor's degree or more	59.8	40.2

Source: Survey Documentation and Analysis, Computer-assisted Survey Methods Program, University of California, Berkeley, General Social Surveys, 1972–2008 Cumulative Data Files, Internet site http://sda.berkeley.edu/cgi-bin/hsda?harcsda+gss08; calculations by New Strategist

Table 7.4 Reason for Racial Differences: Lack of Will, 1988 to 2008

"On the average (blacks/African Americans) have worse jobs, income, and
housing than white people. Do you think these differences are because most just don't
have the motivation or willpower to pull themselves up out of poverty?"

(percent of people aged 18 or older responding, 1988 to 2008; and percent responding by demographic characteristic, 2008)

	yes	no
TREND		
2008	51.6%	48.4%
1998	46.5	53.5
1988	58.9	41.1
2008 PROFILE		
Total people	**51.6**	**48.4**
Men	54.3	45.7
Women	49.1	50.9
Black	46.9	53.1
Hispanic	67.0	33.0
White	51.5	48.5
Aged 18 to 44	48.7	51.3
Aged 45 to 64	50.2	49.8
Aged 65 or older	63.4	36.6
Not a college graduate	57.6	42.4
Bachelor's degree or more	34.8	65.2

*Source: Survey Documentation and Analysis, Computer-assisted Survey Methods Program, University of California, Berkeley,
General Social Surveys, 1972–2008 Cumulative Data Files, Internet site http://sda.berkeley.edu/cgi-bin/hsda?harcsda+gss08;
calculations by New Strategist*

Bias against Blacks Revealed by Hard-Work Questions

When asked to rate whether blacks are hardworking or lazy on a scale of 1 to 7, only 18 percent of the public places them on the hardworking end of the scale, while a larger 34 percent puts them on the lazy end. But when asked how whites rate, a much larger 39 percent say whites are hardworking and only 13 percent think whites are lazy. Blacks rate whites about the same as whites rate themselves. But whites are far less likely than blacks to rate blacks as hardworking (14 percent of whites versus 34 percent of blacks).

(percent of people aged 18 or older who think blacks are hardworking (a rating of 1 to 3) on a scale of 1 (hardworking) to 7 (lazy), by race, 2008)

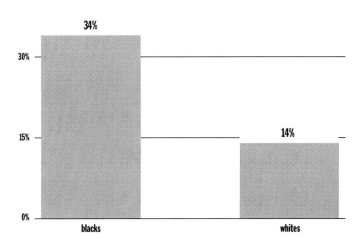

Table 7.5 Are Blacks Hardworking or Lazy? 1998 and 2008

"On a seven-point scale on which the characteristics of people in a group can be rated, a score of 1 means that you think almost all of the people in that group are hardworking. A score of 7 means that you think almost everyone in the group is lazy. A score of 4 means that you think that the group is not towards one end or another, and you may choose any number in between that comes closest to where you think people in that group stand. Are blacks hardworking or do they tend to be lazy?"

(percent of people aged 18 or older responding, 1998 and 2008; and percent responding by demographic characteristic, 2008)

	1 hardworking	2	3	4 neither	5	6	7 lazy
TREND							
2008	2.1%	4.2%	11.2%	49.0%	21.3%	9.0%	3.2%
1998	1.7	5.0	13.9	46.1	20.8	9.3	3.2
2008 PROFILE							
Total people	**2.1**	**4.2**	**11.2**	**49.0**	**21.3**	**9.0**	**3.2**
Men	2.2	5.3	11.6	45.7	22.2	9.4	3.5
Women	2.0	3.2	10.8	52.0	20.5	8.6	2.9
Black	5.1	12.9	15.7	36.0	21.3	6.6	2.4
Hispanic	4.8	3.9	9.3	33.7	25.3	15.0	7.9
White	1.2	2.6	10.6	53.2	20.9	8.6	2.8
Aged 18 to 44	2.9	4.3	12.5	47.6	20.5	8.8	3.3
Aged 45 to 64	1.0	4.6	11.1	52.9	19.1	9.1	2.1
Aged 65 or older	2.5	2.9	7.1	43.8	28.5	9.7	5.4
Not a college graduate	2.1	4.5	11.1	45.8	22.8	9.8	4.0
Bachelor's degree or more	2.3	3.5	11.6	58.3	16.9	6.6	0.8

Source: Survey Documentation and Analysis, Computer-assisted Survey Methods Program, University of California, Berkeley, General Social Surveys, 1972–2008 Cumulative Data Files, Internet site http://sda.berkeley.edu/cgi-bin/hsda?harcsda+gss08; calculations by New Strategist

Table 7.6 Are Whites Hardworking or Lazy? 1998 and 2008

"On a seven-point scale on which the characteristics of people in a group can be rated, a score of 1 means that you think almost all of the people in that group are hardworking. A score of 7 means that you think almost everyone in the group is lazy. A score of 4 means that you think that the group is not towards one end or another, and you may choose any number in between that comes closest to where you think people in that group stand. Are whites hardworking or do they tend to be lazy?"

(percent of people aged 18 or older responding, 1998 and 2008; and percent responding by demographic characteristic, 2008)

	1 hardworking	2	3	4 neither	5	6	7 lazy
TREND							
2008	7.1%	9.9%	22.3%	48.2%	9.6%	2.0%	0.9%
1998	4.4	10.9	24.8	47.3	8.7	3.0	0.9
2008 PROFILE							
Total people	**7.1**	**9.9**	**22.3**	**48.2**	**9.6**	**2.0**	**0.9**
Men	6.5	10.7	22.7	46.4	10.1	2.3	1.2
Women	7.6	9.2	21.9	49.8	9.1	1.8	0.7
Black	8.1	13.6	21.5	43.9	8.5	2.2	2.1
Hispanic	20.7	9.4	15.9	39.4	10.0	4.3	0.3
White	5.7	9.7	22.6	49.9	9.5	1.8	0.8
Aged 18 to 44	8.4	9.4	20.6	47.2	11.0	2.9	0.6
Aged 45 to 64	5.3	11.0	22.0	50.6	9.2	1.1	0.9
Aged 65 or older	7.2	9.0	28.3	45.6	6.0	1.8	2.1
Not a college graduate	8.4	10.8	22.2	45.3	9.6	2.5	1.2
Bachelor's degree or more	3.1	7.1	22.5	56.9	9.7	0.7	0.0

Source: Survey Documentation and Analysis, Computer-assisted Survey Methods Program, University of California, Berkeley, General Social Surveys, 1972–2008 Cumulative Data Files, Internet site http://sda.berkeley.edu/cgi-bin/hsda?harcsda+gss08; calculations by New Strategist

Most Oppose Affirmative Action for Blacks

Sixty-four percent of workers say their workplace is all or mostly white, down from 76 percent who reported a mostly white workplace in 1998. Seventy-five percent of the public thinks blacks should work their way up without special favors. Among blacks, the 55 percent majority agrees. An even larger 83 percent of Americans are against the preferential hiring and promotion of blacks, including the 54 percent majority of blacks. Sixty-three percent of all adults—and 59 percent of blacks—think it is at least somewhat likely that a white person won't get a job while an equally qualified black gets hired.

(percent of people aged 18 or older who think blacks should work their way up without special favors, by race and Hispanic origin, 2008)

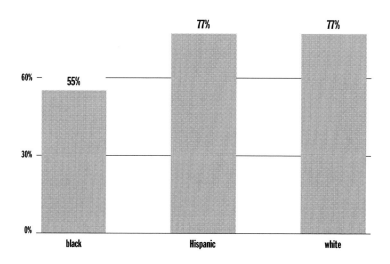

Table 7.7 Racial Makeup of Workplace, 1998 and 2008

"Are the people who work where you work all white, mostly white,
about half and half, mostly black, or all black?"

(percent of workers aged 18 or older responding, 1998 and 2008; and percent responding by demographic characteristic, 2008)

	all white	mostly white	half and half	mostly black	all black
TREND					
2008	21.4%	43.1%	29.1%	5.4%	1.0%
1998	29.9	46.5	18.9	3.5	1.2
2008 PROFILE					
Total people	**21.4**	**43.1**	**29.1**	**5.4**	**1.0**
Men	22.2	47.2	24.7	4.8	1.1
Women	20.5	38.9	33.6	6.1	1.0
Black	4.3	30.1	41.3	18.9	5.4
Hispanic	27.6	34.0	36.3	2.1	0.0
White	25.3	46.7	24.4	3.3	0.2
Aged 18 to 44	21.2	44.2	28.1	5.0	1.5
Aged 45 to 64	20.5	42.6	30.4	6.0	0.5
Aged 65 or older	30.7	36.9	26.0	6.4	0.0
Not a college graduate	22.4	38.0	32.1	6.2	1.3
Bachelor's degree or more	18.7	56.5	21.1	3.4	0.4

Source: Survey Documentation and Analysis, Computer-assisted Survey Methods Program, University of California, Berkeley, General Social Surveys, 1972–2008 Cumulative Data Files, Internet site http://sda.berkeley.edu/cgi-bin/hsda?harcsda+gss08; calculations by New Strategist

Table 7.8 Blacks Should Overcome Prejudice without Favors, 1998 and 2008

"Do you agree strongly, agree somewhat, neither agree nor disagree, disagree somewhat, or disagree strongly with the following statement? Irish, Italian, Jewish and many other minorities overcame prejudice and worked their way up. Blacks should do the same without any special favors."

(percent of people aged 18 or older responding, 1998 and 2008; and percent responding by demographic characteristic, 2008)

	agree strongly	agree somewhat	neither agree nor disagree	disagree somewhat	disagree strongly
TREND					
2008	44.4%	30.2%	12.6%	7.9%	4.8%
1998	42.4	30.7	12.8	8.4	5.8
2008 PROFILE					
Total people	**44.4**	**30.2**	**12.6**	**7.9**	**4.8**
Men	43.4	31.9	13.1	7.3	4.3
Women	45.4	28.7	12.2	8.5	5.3
Black	26.8	28.6	18.7	11.8	14.1
Hispanic	39.1	37.8	13.2	6.3	3.6
White	46.6	30.6	12.1	7.1	3.5
Aged 18 to 44	42.8	30.2	15.2	6.9	4.8
Aged 45 to 64	44.7	30.2	10.8	8.2	6.1
Aged 65 or older	49.0	29.8	9.3	10.7	1.3
Not a college graduate	49.5	30.4	10.7	5.8	3.7
Bachelor's degree or more	29.6	29.8	18.2	14.3	8.1

Source: Survey Documentation and Analysis, Computer-assisted Survey Methods Program, University of California, Berkeley, General Social Surveys, 1972–2008 Cumulative Data Files, Internet site http://sda.berkeley.edu/cgi-bin/hsda?harcsda+gss08; calculations by New Strategist

Table 7.9 Favor Preference in Hiring Blacks, 1998 and 2008

"Some people say that because of past discrimination, blacks should be given preference in hiring and promotion. Others say that such preference in hiring and promotion of blacks is wrong because it discriminates against whites. What about your opinion—are you for or against preferential hiring and promotion of blacks?"

(percent of people aged 18 or older responding, 1998 and 2008; and percent responding by demographic characteristic, 2008)

	strongly support	support	oppose	strongly oppose
TREND				
2008	10.3%	6.7%	27.1%	55.8%
1998	8.3	6.8	24.7	60.3
2008 PROFILE				
Total people	**10.3**	**6.7**	**27.1**	**55.8**
Men	12.1	6.2	25.8	56.0
Women	8.7	7.3	28.4	55.6
Black	33.7	12.7	23.7	29.9
Hispanic	11.3	7.3	42.7	38.7
White	6.1	5.6	27.1	61.2
Aged 18 to 44	11.9	7.0	30.0	51.2
Aged 45 to 64	10.1	6.5	24.0	59.4
Aged 65 or older	5.7	6.8	25.9	61.6
Not a college graduate	11.3	5.8	26.4	56.6
Bachelor's degree or more	7.5	9.6	29.3	53.5

Source: Survey Documentation and Analysis, Computer-assisted Survey Methods Program, University of California, Berkeley, General Social Surveys, 1972–2008 Cumulative Data Files, Internet site http://sda.berkeley.edu/cgi-bin/hsda?harcsda+gss08; calculations by New Strategist

Table 7.10 Whites Hurt by Affirmative Action, 1998 and 2008

"What do you think the chances are these days that a white person won't get a job or promotion while an equally qualified black person gets one instead?"

(percent of people aged 18 or older responding, 1998 and 2008; and percent responding by demographic characteristic, 2008)

	very likely	somewhat likely	not very likely
TREND			
2008	16.7%	46.4%	36.9%
1998	20.3	47.6	32.1
2008 PROFILE			
Total people	**16.7**	**46.4**	**36.9**
Men	15.0	47.3	37.7
Women	18.2	45.6	36.1
Black	19.5	39.7	40.8
Hispanic	18.3	43.2	38.5
White	15.7	49.6	34.7
Aged 18 to 44	15.4	45.2	39.4
Aged 45 to 64	17.7	47.2	35.1
Aged 65 or older	18.1	47.9	34.0
Not a college graduate	20.1	47.7	32.2
Bachelor's degree or more	7.0	42.6	50.3

Source: Survey Documentation and Analysis, Computer-assisted Survey Methods Program, University of California, Berkeley, General Social Surveys, 1972–2008 Cumulative Data Files, Internet site http://sda.berkeley.edu/cgi-bin/hsda?harcsda+gss08; calculations by New Strategist

Most Now Favor Open Housing Laws

The percentage of people who live in an integrated neighborhood has grown during the past three decades. In 2008, 69 percent of the total public and 66 percent of whites said blacks lived in their neighborhood. Most now favor open housing laws that ban discrimination based on race, with the percentage rising from 43 to 71 percent between 1978 and 2008. Most whites and blacks would not oppose living in a neighborhood that was half black or white, respectively. Only 6 percent of blacks and a 25 percent minority of whites would be opposed to a relative marrying a white or black, respectively.

(percentage of people aged 18 or older who support open housing laws that make it illegal for a homeowner to refuse to sell his house to someone because of his or her race, 1978 to 2008)

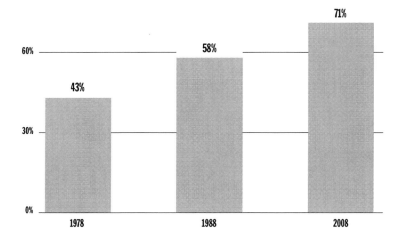

Table 7.11 Blacks Living in Neighborhood, 1978 to 2008

"Are there any blacks/African Americans living in this neighborhood now?"

(percent of people aged 18 or older responding, 1978 to 2008; and percent responding by demographic characteristic, 2008)

	yes	no
TREND		
2008	69.4%	30.6%
1998	65.8	34.2
1988	54.2	45.8
1978	50.1	49.9
2008 PROFILE		
Total people	**69.4**	**30.6**
Men	72.0	28.0
Women	67.0	33.0
Black	86.4	13.6
Hispanic	67.4	32.6
White	66.4	33.6
Aged 18 to 44	72.4	27.6
Aged 45 to 64	69.0	31.0
Aged 65 or older	61.1	38.9
Not a college graduate	67.8	32.2
Bachelor's degree or more	74.1	25.9

Source: Survey Documentation and Analysis, Computer-assisted Survey Methods Program, University of California, Berkeley, General Social Surveys, 1972–2008 Cumulative Data Files, Internet site http://sda.berkeley.edu/cgi-bin/hsda?harcsda+gss08; calculations by New Strategist

Table 7.12 Open Housing Laws, 1978 to 2008

"Suppose there is a community-wide vote on the general housing issue. There are two possible laws to vote on: One law says that a homeowner can decide for himself whom to sell his house to, even if he prefers not to sell to blacks/African Americans, [while the other law specified that] a homeowner cannot refuse to sell to someone because of their race or color. Which law would you vote for?"

(percent of people aged 18 or older responding, 1978 tod 2008; and percent responding by demographic characteristic, 2008)

	owner decides	can't discriminate	neither
TREND			
2008	25.2%	70.9%	3.9%
1988	39.6	58.0	2.4
1978	56.3	42.7	1.0
2008 PROFILE			
Total people	**25.2**	**70.9**	**3.9**
Men	28.8	67.7	3.5
Women	22.1	73.6	4.3
Black	12.2	79.4	8.3
Hispanic	24.0	72.2	3.9
White	28.2	68.6	3.2
Aged 18 to 44	22.0	74.1	3.9
Aged 45 to 64	24.7	72.4	2.9
Aged 65 or older	35.2	58.7	6.1
Not a college graduate	27.3	68.3	4.3
Bachelor's degree or more	18.7	78.4	2.9

Note: Data for 1998 are not available.
Source: Survey Documentation and Analysis, Computer-assisted Survey Methods Program, University of California, Berkeley, General Social Surveys, 1972–2008 Cumulative Data Files, Internet site http://sda.berkeley.edu/cgi-bin/hsda?harcsda+gss08; calculations by New Strategist

Table 7.13 Favor Living in Neighborhood Half Black, 1998 and 2008

"Please tell me whether you would be very much in favor of it happening, somewhat in favor, neither in favor nor opposed to it happening, somewhat opposed, or very much opposed to living in a neighborhood where half of your neighbors were black?"

(percent of people aged 18 or older responding, 1998 and 2008; and percent responding by demographic characteristic, 2008)

	strongly favor	favor	neither favor nor oppose	oppose	strongly oppose
TREND					
2008	9.5%	18.0%	53.4%	13.6%	5.5%
1998	11.3	13.8	46.8	18.6	9.6
2008 PROFILE					
Total people	**9.5**	**18.0**	**53.4**	**13.6**	**5.5**
Men	9.5	17.2	53.8	14.3	5.2
Women	9.5	18.7	53.0	13.0	5.8
Black	23.2	21.5	49.5	4.5	1.3
Hispanic	9.1	15.3	50.6	14.6	10.5
White	7.2	17.7	54.8	14.7	5.6
Aged 18 to 44	10.2	16.2	56.6	12.4	4.6
Aged 45 to 64	9.4	19.4	52.4	12.9	5.9
Aged 65 or older	7.4	20.0	45.3	19.4	7.9
Not a college graduate	9.3	19.5	51.7	13.2	6.3
Bachelor's degree or more	9.9	13.5	58.4	15.0	3.3

Source: Survey Documentation and Analysis, Computer-assisted Survey Methods Program, University of California, Berkeley, General Social Surveys, 1972–2008 Cumulative Data Files, Internet site http://sda.berkeley.edu/cgi-bin/hsda?harcsda+gss08; calculations by New Strategist

Table 7.14 Favor Living in Neighborhood Half White, 2008

"Please tell me whether you would be very much in favor of it happening, somewhat in favor, neither in favor nor opposed to it happening, somewhat opposed, or very much opposed to living in a neighborhood where half of your neighbors were white?"

(percent of people aged 18 or older responding by demographic characteristic, 2008)

	strongly favor	favor	neither favor nor oppose	oppose	strongly oppose
Total people	**19.6%**	**24.5%**	**50.0%**	**4.5%**	**1.3%**
Men	15.7	27.9	51.1	4.1	1.2
Women	23.2	21.4	49.0	4.9	1.5
Black	20.1	24.7	48.1	4.2	2.9
Hispanic	23.8	27.5	43.3	4.7	0.8
White	19.4	24.2	51.1	4.2	1.1
Aged 18 to 44	18.3	24.9	51.8	4.2	0.8
Aged 45 to 64	20.0	23.6	51.0	3.9	1.5
Aged 65 or older	22.8	26.2	41.7	6.5	2.8
Not a college graduate	20.8	26.2	47.1	4.3	1.7
Bachelor's degree or more	16.4	19.6	58.6	5.1	0.4

Source: Survey Documentation and Analysis, Computer-assisted Survey Methods Program, University of California, Berkeley, General Social Surveys, 1972–2008 Cumulative Data Files, Internet site http://sda.berkeley.edu/cgi-bin/hsda?harcsda+gss08; calculations by New Strategist

Table 7.15 Favor Close Relative Marrying an Asian American, 2008

"What about having a close relative marry an Asian American? Would you be very much in favor of it happening, somewhat in favor, neither in favor nor opposed to it happening, somewhat opposed, or very opposed to it happening?"

(percent of people aged 18 or older responding by demographic characteristic, 2008)

	strongly favor	favor	neither favor nor oppose	oppose	strongly oppose
Total people	**16.7%**	**16.1%**	**52.1%**	**10.1%**	**5.1%**
Men	12.8	19.0	50.6	11.8	5.7
Women	20.2	13.4	53.4	8.4	4.6
Black	29.4	20.4	41.4	3.4	5.5
Hispanic	18.1	19.2	60.0	1.3	1.4
White	14.1	14.3	54.2	12.0	5.4
Aged 18 to 44	19.7	16.2	54.6	6.8	2.7
Aged 45 to 64	13.8	16.3	52.5	11.5	6.0
Aged 65 or older	14.5	15.5	42.2	17.0	10.9
Not a college graduate	15.9	16.6	49.6	11.3	6.6
Bachelor's degree or more	18.7	14.6	59.2	6.6	0.9

Source: Survey Documentation and Analysis, Computer-assisted Survey Methods Program, University of California, Berkeley, General Social Surveys, 1972–2008 Cumulative Data Files, Internet site http://sda.berkeley.edu/cgi-bin/hsda?harcsda+gss08; calculations by New Strategist

Table 7.16 Favor Close Relative Marrying a Black Person, 1998 and 2008

"What about having a close relative marry a black person? Would you be
very much in favor of it happening, somewhat in favor, neither in favor nor opposed
to it happening, somewhat opposed, or very opposed to it happening?"

(percent of people aged 18 or older responding, 1998 and 2008; and percent responding by demographic characteristic, 2008)

	strongly favor	favor	neither favor nor oppose	oppose	strongly oppose
TREND					
2008	16.6%	14.6%	47.3%	11.1%	10.4%
1998	13.7	10.7	40.8	16.6	18.2
2008 PROFILE					
Total people	**16.6**	**14.6**	**47.3**	**11.1**	**10.4**
Men	13.8	15.5	46.2	11.5	13.0
Women	19.2	13.9	48.3	10.7	8.0
Black	45.7	13.9	36.2	0.8	3.4
Hispanic	16.5	21.0	52.0	5.4	5.1
White	11.6	13.9	49.4	13.3	11.9
Aged 18 to 44	19.7	15.3	51.8	6.3	7.0
Aged 45 to 64	14.7	14.9	45.2	14.0	11.1
Aged 65 or older	11.8	12.2	37.2	19.3	19.4
Not a college graduate	16.6	16.0	43.6	11.1	12.7
Bachelor's degree or more	16.5	10.8	58.0	11.1	3.6

*Source: Survey Documentation and Analysis, Computer-assisted Survey Methods Program, University of California, Berkeley,
General Social Surveys, 1972–2008 Cumulative Data Files, Internet site http://sda.berkeley.edu/cgi-bin/hsda?harcsda+gss08;
calculations by New Strategist*

Table 7.17 Favor Close Relative Marrying a Hispanic American, 2008

"What about having a close relative marry a Hispanic American? Would you be very much in favor of it happening, somewhat in favor, neither in favor nor opposed to it happening, somewhat opposed, or very opposed to it happening?"

(percent of people aged 18 or older responding by demographic characteristic, 2008)

	strongly favor	favor	neither favor nor oppose	oppose	strongly oppose
Total people	**18.0%**	**16.4%**	**50.3%**	**9.6%**	**5.7%**
Men	15.0	18.7	48.8	10.4	7.1
Women	20.8	14.2	51.7	8.9	4.4
Black	28.6	20.3	42.7	2.9	5.5
Hispanic	37.8	17.4	43.8	0.0	1.0
White	15.3	15.2	52.4	11.3	5.8
Aged 18 to 44	21.9	16.1	52.8	5.3	4.0
Aged 45 to 64	14.4	17.2	50.0	12.7	5.7
Aged 65 or older	15.1	15.7	41.9	16.0	11.2
Not a college graduate	17.5	18.1	46.6	10.4	7.4
Bachelor's degree or more	19.6	11.4	61.0	7.3	0.6

Source: Survey Documentation and Analysis, Computer-assisted Survey Methods Program, University of California, Berkeley, General Social Survey, 2008 Cumulative Data Files, Internet site http://sda.berkeley.edu/cgi-bin/hsda?harcsda+gss08; calculations by New Strategist

Table 7.18 Favor Close Relative Marrying a White Person, 2008

"What about having a close relative marry a white person? Would you be very much in favor of it happening, somewhat in favor, neither in favor nor opposed to it happening, somewhat opposed, or very opposed to it happening?"

(percent of people aged 18 or older responding by demographic characteristic, 2008)

	strongly favor	favor	neither favor nor oppose	oppose	strongly oppose
Total people	**39.6%**	**15.4%**	**42.1%**	**1.9%**	**0.9%**
Men	32.5	20.0	44.5	2.0	0.9
Women	46.2	11.2	39.9	1.8	0.9
Black	32.5	20.6	41.1	2.1	3.6
Hispanic	24.9	24.3	50.0	0.3	0.5
White	42.2	13.9	41.4	1.9	0.5
Aged 18 to 44	35.0	15.3	47.7	1.3	0.7
Aged 45 to 64	40.0	16.8	39.8	2.5	0.9
Aged 65 or older	54.3	12.2	29.6	2.3	1.5
Not a college graduate	39.9	17.3	39.7	1.9	1.2
Bachelor's degree or more	38.8	10.2	49.2	1.8	0.0

Source: Survey Documentation and Analysis, Computer-assisted Survey Methods Program, University of California, Berkeley, General Social Survey, 2008 Cumulative Data Files, Internet site http://sda.berkeley.edu/cgi-bin/hsda?harcsda+gss08; calculations by New Strategist

Deep Seated Prejudice Revealed by Intelligence Question

When asked on a scale of 1 (rich) to 7 (poor) whether blacks are rich or poor, the 64 percent majority of the public places them on the poor side (5 to 7) of the scale. Whites are far less likely to be seen as poor (9 percent). The same type of question asked about intelligence reveals deep-seated prejudices against blacks. A larger share of the public thinks whites are intelligent (43 percent) than thinks blacks are intelligent (29 percent).

(percent of people aged 18 or older who think blacks and whites are intelligent (a rating of 5 to 7) on a scale of 1 (unintelligent) to 7 (intelligent), by race, 2008)

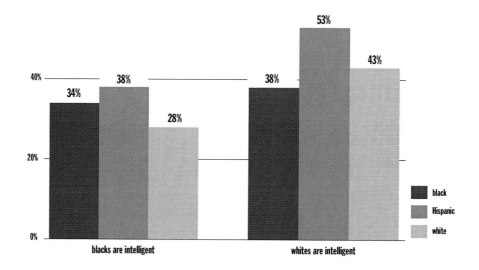

Table 7.19 Are Blacks Rich or Poor? 1998 and 2008

"On a seven-point scale on which the characteristics of people in a group can
be rated, a score of 1 means that you think almost all of the people in that group
are rich. A score of 7 means that you think almost everyone in the group is poor.
A score of 4 means that you think that the group is not towards one end or
another, and you may choose any number in between that comes closest
to where you think people in that group stand. Are blacks rich or poor?"

(percent of people aged 18 or older responding, 1998 and 2008; and percent responding by demographic characteristic, 2008)

	1 rich	2	3	4 neither	5	6	7 poor
TREND							
2008	0.1%	1.9%	6.0%	27.7%	43.5%	17.2%	3.7%
1998	0.5	1.8	7.1	24.1	41.5	22.1	3.0
2008 PROFILE							
Total people	**0.1**	**1.9**	**6.0**	**27.7**	**43.5**	**17.2**	**3.7**
Men	0.2	2.8	7.9	27.4	42.5	15.6	3.5
Women	1.0	4.2	27.9	44.4	18.6	3.9	0.0
Black	0.0	0.5	5.8	35.2	33.8	18.1	6.5
Hispanic	0.0	1.8	12.8	24.8	34.9	18.6	7.1
White	0.1	2.3	5.1	26.4	46.4	16.8	2.8
Aged 18 to 44	0.1	1.7	6.0	33.6	41.8	13.8	2.9
Aged 45 to 64	0.1	2.5	4.6	21.6	49.3	18.9	3.0
Aged 65 or older	0.0	0.8	9.8	24.0	32.9	24.4	8.1
Not a college graduate	0.0	2.0	6.7	30.1	39.5	17.6	4.0
Bachelor's degree or more	0.3	1.6	3.9	20.4	55.2	15.8	2.8

*Source: Survey Documentation and Analysis, Computer-assisted Survey Methods Program, University of California, Berkeley,
General Social Surveys, 1972–2008 Cumulative Data Files, Internet site http://sda.berkeley.edu/cgi-bin/hsda?harcsda+gss08;
calculations by New Strategist*

Table 7.20 Are Whites Rich or Poor? 1998 and 2008

"On a seven-point scale on which the characteristics of people in a group can
be rated, a score of 1 means that you think almost all of the people in that
group are rich. A score of 7 means that you think almost everyone in the
group is poor. A score of 4 means that you think that the group is not towards
one end or another, and you may choose any number in between that comes closest
to where you think people in that group stand. Are whites rich or poor?"

(percent of people aged 18 or older responding, 1998 and 2008; and percent responding by demographic characteristic, 2008)

	1 rich	2	3	4 neither	5	6	7 poor
TREND							
2008	5.5%	6.1%	28.5%	50.9%	7.8%	0.8%	0.5%
1998	4.0	8.7	29.6	49.3	6.6	1.2	0.4
2008 PROFILE							
Total people	**5.5**	**6.1**	**28.5**	**50.9**	**7.8**	**0.8**	**0.5**
Men	5.9	5.4	32.9	45.3	8.8	1.0	0.6
Women	5.1	6.7	24.4	55.9	6.9	0.7	0.3
Black	11.3	9.3	31.7	38.5	8.6	0.5	0.0
Hispanic	12.9	8.2	33.5	33.9	8.2	2.6	0.6
White	4.1	4.7	27.0	55.1	7.7	0.8	0.5
Aged 18 to 44	6.4	8.1	32.2	44.8	7.1	1.1	0.3
Aged 45 to 64	4.5	4.0	28.7	54.6	7.2	0.4	0.6
Aged 65 or older	4.8	4.5	15.4	61.3	12.1	1.1	0.8
Not a college graduate	6.5	6.0	26.5	50.3	9.1	1.1	0.5
Bachelor's degree or more	2.3	6.5	34.4	52.6	4.0	0.0	0.3

Source: Survey Documentation and Analysis, Computer-assisted Survey Methods Program, University of California, Berkeley, General Social Surveys, 1972–2008 Cumulative Data Files, Internet site http://sda.berkeley.edu/cgi-bin/hsda?harcsda+gss08; calculations by New Strategist

Table 7.21 Are Blacks Unintelligent or Intelligent? 1998 and 2008

"On a seven-point scale on which the characteristics of people in a group can
be rated, a score of 1 means that you think almost all of the people in that group
are unintelligent. A score of 7 means that you think almost everyone in the group is
intelligent. A score of 4 means that you think that the group is not towards one end or
another, and you may choose any number in between that comes closest to where you
think people in that group stand. Do blacks tend to be unintelligent or intelligent?"

(percent of people aged 18 or older responding, 1998 and 2008; and percent responding by demographic characteristic, 2008)

	1 unintelligent	2	3	4 neither	5	6	7 intelligent
TREND							
2008	1.1%	2.2%	12.0%	55.8%	18.5%	6.8%	3.7%
1998	0.7	4.1	11.6	52.8	19.4	8.6	2.9
2008 PROFILE							
Total people	**1.1**	**2.2**	**12.0**	**55.8**	**18.5**	**6.8**	**3.7**
Men	1.2	2.3	12.6	58.0	16.6	6.3	3.0
Women	1.0	2.1	11.4	53.7	20.2	7.2	4.4
Black	1.2	0.0	14.1	50.5	16.6	9.6	8.0
Hispanic	2.8	2.9	6.9	49.8	21.2	10.3	6.1
White	0.8	2.2	11.9	57.5	18.7	6.2	2.7
Aged 18 to 44	1.6	2.0	9.6	58.3	17.1	7.2	4.3
Aged 45 to 64	0.5	2.6	12.0	55.5	18.6	7.6	3.2
Aged 65 or older	1.4	1.7	19.7	48.2	23.0	3.6	2.5
Not a college graduate	1.5	2.4	13.0	53.9	17.9	7.4	3.9
Bachelor's degree or more	0.1	1.6	8.9	61.3	20.1	4.8	3.1

*Source: Survey Documentation and Analysis, Computer-assisted Survey Methods Program, University of California, Berkeley,
General Social Surveys, 1972–2008 Cumulative Data Files, Internet site http://sda.berkeley.edu/cgi-bin/hsda?harcsda+gss08;
calculations by New Strategist*

Table 7.22 Are Whites Unintelligent or Intelligent? 1998 and 2008

"On a seven-point scale on which the characteristics of people in a group can be rated, a score of 1 means that you think almost all of the people in that group are unintelligent. A score of 7 means that you think almost everyone in the group is intelligent. A score of 4 means that you think that the group is not towards one end or another, and you may choose any number in between that comes closest to where you think people in that group stand. Do whites tend to be unintelligent or intelligent?"

(percent of people aged 18 or older responding, 1998 and 2008; and percent responding by demographic characteristic, 2008)

	1 unintelligent	2	3	4 neither	5	6	7 intelligent
TREND							
2008	0.7%	1.5%	7.7%	47.0%	22.2%	13.3%	7.6%
1998	0.5	2.3	7.6	44.7	22.9	16.3	5.7
2008 PROFILE							
Total people	**0.7**	**1.5**	**7.7**	**47.0**	**22.2**	**13.3**	**7.6**
Men	1.0	4.6	8.1	49.2	19.2	13.4	7.4
Women	0.4	1.5	7.2	45.0	24.9	13.3	7.8
Black	1.7	2.1	11.5	46.8	17.0	11.2	9.6
Hispanic	2.1	2.9	3.1	38.7	14.0	20.9	18.3
White	0.3	1.4	7.4	47.8	24.0	13.2	6.0
Aged 18 to 44	1.2	1.1	6.8	49.0	20.4	12.6	8.9
Aged 45 to 64	0.2	2.1	9.2	45.7	23.5	13.0	6.3
Aged 65 or older	0.2	1.4	6.6	43.9	24.7	16.6	6.5
Not a college graduate	0.9	1.9	8.0	43.6	21.8	14.9	8.9
Bachelor's degree or more	0.0	0.4	6.6	57.4	23.2	8.7	3.7

Source: Survey Documentation and Analysis, Computer-assisted Survey Methods Program, University of California, Berkeley, General Social Surveys, 1972–2008 Cumulative Data Files, Internet site http://sda.berkeley.edu/cgi-bin/hsda?harcsda+gss08; calculations by New Strategist

Many Whites Feel Close to Blacks

On a scale of 1 (not at all close) to 9 (very close), a substantial 39 percent of whites place themselves on the close side (a rating of 6 to 9). When blacks are asked how close they feel to whites, an even larger 48 percent place themselves on the close end of the scale. Among the public in general, 61 percent say they feel close to whites and 44 percent say they feel close to blacks.

(percent of people aged 18 or older who feel close (a rating of 6 to 9) to whites and blacks on a scale of 1 (not at all close) to 9 (very close), by race, 2008)

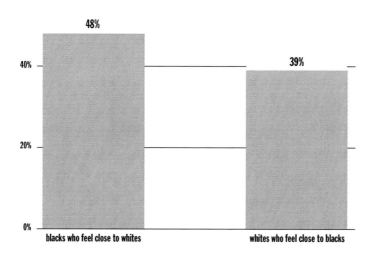

Table 7.23 How Close to Blacks? 1998 and 2008

"In general, how close do you feel to blacks?"

(percent of people aged 18 or older responding, 1998 and 2008; and percent responding by demographic characteristic, 2008)

	1 not at all close	2	3	4	5 neither	6	7	8	9 very close
TREND									
2008	5.8%	2.2%	3.4%	3.2%	41.4%	8.3%	14.5%	7.0%	14.1%
1998	6.5	4.6	5.2	4.2	43.4	7.7	10.8	5.1	12.6
2008 PROFILE									
Total people	**5.8**	**2.2**	**3.4**	**3.2**	**41.4**	**8.3**	**14.5**	**7.0**	**14.1**
Men	6.4	2.3	3.7	4.0	39.6	8.0	16.9	6.0	13.2
Women	5.3	2.1	3.1	2.5	42.9	8.6	12.5	7.9	15.0
Black	1.4	1.2	0.7	1.7	19.8	3.1	13.5	9.4	49.1
Hispanic	16.8	2.6	3.3	1.6	37.3	5.0	11.8	5.5	16.2
White	5.4	2.2	3.5	3.5	46.0	9.7	14.7	6.7	8.3
Aged 18 to 44	6.1	2.5	2.3	4.0	37.0	9.6	15.0	8.5	14.8
Aged 45 to 64	6.2	1.6	4.5	2.4	44.7	6.8	14.8	4.9	14.1
Aged 65 or older	4.3	2.6	4.0	2.4	46.9	7.5	12.3	7.5	12.4
Not a college graduate	6.9	2.3	3.3	2.5	42.0	7.4	13.5	7.1	15.1
Bachelor's degree or more	2.7	1.8	3.7	5.2	39.6	11.0	17.6	7.0	11.4

Source: Survey Documentation and Analysis, Computer-assisted Survey Methods Program, University of California, Berkeley, General Social Surveys, 1972–2008 Cumulative Data Files, Internet site http://sda.berkeley.edu/cgi-bin/hsda?harcsda+gss08; calculations by New Strategist

Table 7.24 How Close to Whites? 1998 and 2008

"In general, how close do you feel to whites?"

(percent of people aged 18 or older responding, 1998 and 2008; and percent responding by demographic characteristic, 2008)

	1 not at all close	2	3	4	5 neither	6	7	8	9 very close
TREND									
2008	1.8%	1.2%	2.3%	1.9%	31.5%	7.0%	14.7%	12.0%	27.5%
1998	1.1	0.9	1.5	2.0	31.5	7.8	14.4	12.6	28.2
2008 PROFILE									
Total people	**1.8**	**1.2**	**2.3**	**1.9**	**31.5**	**7.0**	**14.7**	**12.0**	**27.5**
Men	1.9	1.3	3.1	2.6	33.0	7.8	17.2	9.3	23.8
Women	1.7	1.1	1.6	1.4	30.2	6.3	12.6	14.4	30.6
Black	6.3	1.9	5.8	2.3	35.4	12.4	14.7	5.2	16.1
Hispanic	3.5	3.3	8.0	3.5	40.4	6.4	7.1	8.5	19.3
White	0.5	0.5	1.1	1.7	30.9	6.0	14.8	13.6	30.8
Aged 18 to 44	3.2	1.6	3.1	3.0	30.3	6.8	13.9	12.7	25.3
Aged 45 to 64	0.6	1.2	1.6	1.3	33.0	7.8	16.3	10.3	27.8
Aged 65 or older	0.4	0.0	1.4	0.4	32.2	5.7	12.7	14.2	33.0
Not a college graduate	2.2	1.5	2.4	1.9	33.8	6.9	12.8	10.8	27.8
Bachelor's degree or more	0.8	0.3	2.1	2.0	25.1	7.2	20.2	15.5	26.8

Source: Survey Documentation and Analysis, Computer-assisted Survey Methods Program, University of California, Berkeley, General Social Surveys, 1972–2008 Cumulative Data Files, Internet site http://sda.berkeley.edu/cgi-bin/hsda?harcsda+gss08; calculations by New Strategist

8

Personal Outlook

Most Americans are at least pretty happy, but a growing proportion say they are not happy. The average person does not trust others as much as he once did. The American outlook is shifting, and not necessarily for the better.

Little or no change

• **Life is about as exciting as it ever was.** Americans are split on whether life is exciting (47 percent) or pretty routine (48 percent). These figures have barely budged over the past two decades despite the technological revolution, economic turmoil, and political change.

Big changes

• **Happiness is waning.** Americans are less happy today than they were several decades ago. In 2008, 86 percent of people aged 18 or older said they were "very" or "pretty happy," down from 92 percent in 1978. Fourteen percent of the public reported feeling "not too happy" in 2008, up from 8 percent in 1978.

• **Trust in others has declined.** The percentage of Americans who think other people try to be helpful rather than looking out for themselves has fallen steeply from 60 percent in 1978 to 46 percent in 2008. The percentage who believe you can't be too careful with other people climbed from 56 to 64 percent during those years. Forty-one percent of the public believes others will try to take advantage if they get a chance, up from 31 percent who felt that way in 1978.

Many Find Life Exciting

College graduates get more of a thrill out of life. The 61 percent majority of people with a bachelor's degree say life is exciting compared with only 43 percent of their less-educated counterparts. Older Americans are more likely than younger adults to say they are very happy. Forty percent of people aged 65 or older are very happy compared with 29 to 31 percent of those aged 18 to 64. When the question is asked in a slightly different way, the 55 percent majority of people aged 65 or older say they are very happy.

(percent of people aged 18 or older who find life exciting, by education, 2008)

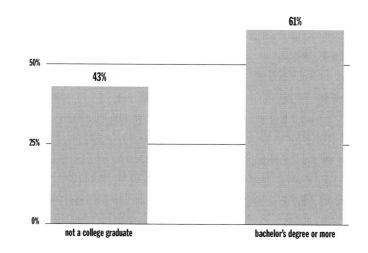

Table 8.1 Life Exciting or Dull, 1988 to 2008

"In general, do you find life exciting, pretty routine, or dull?"

(percent of people aged 18 or older responding, 1988 to 2008; and percent responding by demographic characteristic, 2008)

	exciting	pretty routine	dull
TREND			
2008	47.2%	48.1%	3.8%
1998	45.2	50.0	4.9
1988	46.4	49.2	4.4
2008 PROFILE			
Total people	**47.2**	**48.1**	**3.8**
Men	48.6	48.2	2.5
Women	46.0	48.1	4.9
Black	39.3	55.0	5.2
Hispanic	45.2	48.7	3.8
White	49.3	46.6	3.6
Aged 18 to 44	47.2	48.5	3.3
Aged 45 to 64	47.1	48.0	4.5
Aged 65 or older	47.4	47.3	3.7
Not a college graduate	42.6	51.6	4.8
Bachelor's degree or more	60.6	38.2	1.1

Note: Numbers do not sum to 100 because "other response" is not shown.
Source: Survey Documentation and Analysis, Computer-assisted Survey Methods Program, University of California, Berkeley, General Social Surveys, 1972–2008 Cumulative Data Files, Internet site http://sda.berkeley.edu/cgi-bin/hsda?harcsda+gss08; calculations by New Strategist

Table 8.2 General Happiness, 1978 to 2008

"Taken all together, how would you say things are these days—would you
say that you are very happy, pretty happy, or not too happy?"

(percent of people aged 18 or older responding, 1978 to 2008; and percent responding by demographic characteristic, 2008)

	very happy	pretty happy	not too happy
TREND			
2008	31.6%	54.4%	13.9%
1998	33.3	55.9	10.9
1988	36.1	55.7	8.2
1978	34.4	57.9	7.7
2008 PROFILE			
Total people	**31.6**	**54.4**	**13.9**
Men	30.7	55.6	13.7
Women	32.5	53.3	14.2
Black	22.4	49.1	28.5
Hispanic	26.3	53.0	20.7
White	33.3	55.3	11.4
Aged 18 to 44	29.4	56.6	14.0
Aged 45 to 64	30.6	55.3	14.0
Aged 65 or older	40.4	46.0	13.7
Not a college graduate	29.7	53.8	16.5
Bachelor's degree or more	37.3	56.0	6.7

Source: Survey Documentation and Analysis, Computer-assisted Survey Methods Program, University of California, Berkeley, General Social Surveys, 1972–2008 Cumulative Data Files, Internet site http://sda.berkeley.edu/cgi-bin/hsda?harcsda+gss08; calculations by New Strategist

Table 8.3 Happiness Today, 1998 and 2008

"If you were to consider your life in general these days,
how happy or unhappy would you say you are?"

(percent of people aged 18 or older responding, 1998 and 2008; and percent responding by demographic characteristic, 2008)

	very happy	fairly happy	not very happy	not at all happy
TREND				
2008	45.2%	48.2%	5.3%	1.2%
1998	38.1	51.8	8.5	1.6
2008 PROFILE				
Total people	**45.2**	**48.2**	**5.3**	**1.2**
Men	42.7	50.1	5.8	1.4
Women	47.4	46.6	5.9	1.1
Black	37.1	50.1	11.3	1.5
Hispanic	40.9	53.8	3.1	2.1
White	46.3	48.3	4.5	1.0
Aged 18 to 44	42.6	51.2	4.5	1.7
Aged 45 to 64	44.0	48.6	6.6	0.8
Aged 65 or older	55.3	39.3	4.6	0.8
Not a college graduate	42.9	50.0	5.7	1.3
Bachelor's degree or more	51.7	43.0	4.3	1.0

Source: Survey Documentation and Analysis, Computer-assisted Survey Methods Program, University of California, Berkeley, General Social Surveys, 1972–2008 Cumulative Data Files, Internet site http://sda.berkeley.edu/cgi-bin/hsda?harcsda+gss08; calculations by New Strategist

Fewer Americans Report Excellent Health

Americans' self-reported health status has fallen over the past two decades. The percentage of adults who say their health is excellent fell from 31 to 26 percent between 1988 and 2008. College graduates are much more likely to report excellent health (34 percent) than people without a bachelor's degree (23 percent).

(percent who report excellent health, 1988 and 2008)

Table 8.4 Health Status, 1988 to 2008

"Would you say your own health, in general, is excellent, good, fair, or poor?"

(percent of people aged 18 or older responding, 1988 to 2008; and percent responding by demographic characteristic, 2008)

	excellent	good	fair	poor
TREND				
2008	25.5%	49.0%	20.9%	4.6%
1998	31.8	47.8	15.8	4.5
1988	30.7	46.2	17.8	5.2
2008 PROFILE				
Total people	**25.5**	**49.0**	**20.9**	**4.6**
Men	25.7	49.4	21.0	3.9
Women	25.4	48.7	20.8	5.2
Black	24.7	42.5	26.6	6.1
Hispanic	20.1	45.8	30.3	3.7
White	26.2	48.9	20.4	4.5
Aged 18 to 44	31.2	48.5	18.5	1.8
Aged 45 to 64	22.5	50.4	20.9	6.2
Aged 65 or older	15.8	47.0	28.0	9.1
Not a college graduate	22.6	48.4	23.4	5.6
Bachelor's degree or more	34.2	50.8	13.4	1.7

Source: Survey Documentation and Analysis, Computer-assisted Survey Methods Program, University of California, Berkeley, General Social Surveys, 1972–2008 Cumulative Data Files, Internet site http://sda.berkeley.edu/cgi-bin/hsda?harcsda+gss08; calculations by New Strategist

Americans Do Not Trust Others

Americans are on guard. While the majority still thinks that most people try to be fair versus taking advantage (50 versus 41 percent), they are split pretty evenly on whether other people try to be helpful or are just looking out for themselves (46 to 45 percent). An even smaller proportion says they trust others. The percentage of Americans who believe others can be trusted has fallen from 40 to 32 percent over the past three decades. College graduates are most trusting, 49 percent saying they trust others.

(percent of people aged 18 or older who think most people can be trusted, 1978 to 2008)

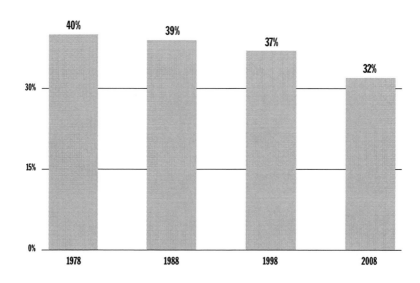

Table 8.5 Helpfulness of Others, 1978 to 2008

"Would you say that most of the time people try to be helpful,
or that they are mostly just looking out for themselves?"

(percent of people aged 18 or older responding, 1978 to 2008; and percent responding by demographic characteristic, 2008)

	helpful	look out for self	depends
TREND			
2008	45.7%	45.1%	9.2%
1998	47.7	43.2	9.1
1988	49.6	46.1	4.3
1978	59.8	35.4	4.8
2008 PROFILE			
Total people	**45.7**	**45.1**	**9.2**
Men	41.4	47.1	11.5
Women	49.5	43.4	7.1
Black	33.2	53.8	13.0
Hispanic	28.4	63.6	8.0
White	47.8	44.2	8.0
Aged 18 to 44	36.0	53.5	10.5
Aged 45 to 64	52.9	38.4	8.7
Aged 65 or older	59.8	34.1	6.1
Not a college graduate	41.7	49.8	8.5
Bachelor's degree or more	56.8	32.2	11.1

Source: Survey Documentation and Analysis, Computer-assisted Survey Methods Program, University of California, Berkeley, General Social Surveys, 1972–2008 Cumulative Data Files, Internet site http://sda.berkeley.edu/cgi-bin/hsda?harcsda+gss08; calculations by New Strategist

Table 8.6 Fairness of Others, 1978 to 2008

"Do you think most people would try to take advantage of you
if they got a chance, or would they try to be fair?"

*(percent of people aged 18 or older responding, 1978 to 2008; and percent responding by demographic charac-
teristic, 2008)*

	take advantage	be fair	depends
TREND			
2008	41.3%	50.1%	8.6%
1998	38.8	52.7	8.6
1988	33.7	60.6	5.7
1978	30.6	64.1	5.3
2008 PROFILE			
Total people	**41.3**	**50.1**	**8.6**
Men	41.2	47.9	10.9
Women	41.5	51.9	6.6
Black	65.3	25.6	9.0
Hispanic	60.9	33.7	5.5
White	36.9	54.4	8.7
Aged 18 to 44	47.7	41.9	10.4
Aged 45 to 64	36.9	56.2	6.9
Aged 65 or older	31.2	61.6	7.2
Not a college graduate	46.8	44.9	8.3
Bachelor's degree or more	26.3	64.2	9.5

*Source: Survey Documentation and Analysis, Computer-assisted Survey Methods Program, University of California, Berkeley,
General Social Surveys, 1972–2008 Cumulative Data Files, Internet site http://sda.berkeley.edu/cgi-bin/hsda?harcsda+gss08;
calculations by New Strategist*

Table 8.7 Trust in Others, 1978 to 2008

"Generally speaking, would you say that most people can
be trusted or that you can't be too careful in life?"

(percent of people aged 18 or older responding, 1978 to 2008; and percent responding by demographic characteristic, 2008)

	can trust	cannot trust	depends
TREND			
2008	31.9%	63.9%	4.3%
1998	37.2	57.4	5.4
1988	39.5	56.1	4.4
1978	40.2	55.6	4.3
2008 PROFILE			
Total people	**31.9**	**63.9**	**4.3**
Men	33.2	61.2	5.6
Women	30.7	66.2	3.1
Black	14.4	81.3	4.3
Hispanic	11.9	83.2	4.9
White	35.3	60.5	4.2
Aged 18 to 44	27.2	68.6	4.2
Aged 45 to 64	34.5	61.4	4.1
Aged 65 or older	40.8	54.6	4.6
Not a college graduate	25.9	70.5	3.6
Bachelor's degree or more	48.6	45.2	6.2

Source: Survey Documentation and Analysis, Computer-assisted Survey Methods Program, University of California, Berkeley, General Social Surveys, 1972–2008 Cumulative Data Files, Internet site http://sda.berkeley.edu/cgi-bin/hsda?harcsda+gss08; calculations by New Strategist

Americans Are Optimists

Philosophically, most Americans are upbeat. A nearly unanimous 93 percent disagrees that life does not serve any purpose. Fully 83 percent disagree that people cannot change the course of their lives. The public is more divided when asked whether they agree or disagree with the statement, "Life is only meaningful if you provide the meaning yourself." Fifty percent agree and 37 percent disagree with the statement.

(percent of people aged 18 or older by response to the statement, "In my opinion, life does not serve any purpose," 2008)

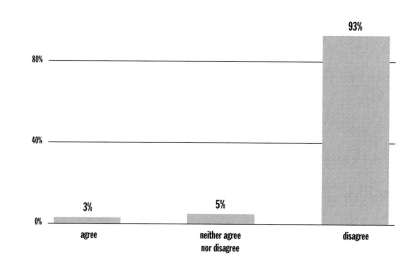

Table 8.8 Life Serves No Purpose, 1998 and 2008

"Do you agree or disagree with the following statement:
In my opinion, life does not serve any purpose."

(percent of people aged 18 or older responding, 1998 and 2008; and percent responding by demographic characteristic, 2008)

	strongly agree	agree	neither agree nor disagree	disagree	strongly disagree
TREND					
2008	0.8%	1.9%	4.5%	38.4%	54.3%
1998	0.7	2.3	6.6	35.1	55.3
2008 PROFILE					
Total people	**0.8**	**1.9**	**4.5**	**38.4**	**54.3**
Men	1.0	1.8	6.0	39.4	51.8
Women	0.7	2.0	3.3	37.6	56.5
Black	0.0	2.0	6.3	36.5	55.2
Hispanic	3.1	7.5	6.7	44.0	38.8
White	0.5	1.8	3.5	38.2	55.9
Aged 18 to 44	0.7	1.7	6.1	40.0	51.5
Aged 45 to 64	0.5	2.2	3.5	35.1	58.7
Aged 65 or older	1.7	1.9	2.3	41.3	52.7
Not a college graduate	1.0	2.3	4.7	41.5	50.5
Bachelor's degree or more	0.4	0.8	4.2	29.6	65.1

Source: Survey Documentation and Analysis, Computer-assisted Survey Methods Program, University of California, Berkeley, General Social Surveys, 1972–2008 Cumulative Data Files, Internet site http://sda.berkeley.edu/cgi-bin/hsda?harcsda+gss08; calculations by New Strategist

Table 8.9 Life Is Meaningful Only If You Provide the Meaning, 1998 and 2008

"Do you agree or disagree with the following statement:
Life is only meaningful if you provide the meaning yourself."

(percent of people aged 18 or older responding, 1998 and 2008; and percent responding by demographic characteristic, 2008)

	strongly agree	agree	neither agree nor disagree	disagree	strongly disagree
TREND					
2008	14.8%	35.1%	13.4%	25.2%	11.5%
1998	11.1	34.8	19.0	21.0	14.0
2008 PROFILE					
Total people	**14.8**	**35.1**	**13.4**	**25.2**	**11.5**
Men	16.1	37.4	13.4	22.2	11.0
Women	13.8	33.1	13.5	27.8	11.9
Black	8.1	36.6	14.3	30.5	10.5
Hispanic	19.4	40.8	12.7	23.0	4.1
White	8.1	36.6	14.3	30.5	10.5
Aged 18 to 44	15.2	38.4	14.8	23.2	8.4
Aged 45 to 64	16.8	28.5	11.7	29.4	13.6
Aged 65 or older	9.1	40.9	13.2	21.4	15.5
Not a college graduate	14.7	35.4	13.2	24.7	12.0
Bachelor's degree or more	15.2	34.4	14.2	26.1	10.0

Source: Survey Documentation and Analysis, Computer-assisted Survey Methods Program, University of California, Berkeley, General Social Surveys, 1972–2008 Cumulative Data Files, Internet site http://sda.berkeley.edu/cgi-bin/hsda?harcsda+gss08; calculations by New Strategist

Table 8.10 People Cannot Change the Course of Their Lives, 1998 and 2008

"Do you agree or disagree with the following: There is little
that people can do to change the course of their lives."

(percent of people aged 18 or older responding, 1998 and 2008; and percent responding by demographic characteristic, 2008)

	strongly agree	agree	neither agree nor disagree	disagree	strongly disagree
TREND					
2008	3.1%	8.0%	5.8%	47.2%	36.0%
1998	3.7	7.7	7.3	44.4	36.9
2008 PROFILE					
Total people	**3.1**	**8.0**	**5.8**	**47.2**	**36.0**
Men	3.5	7.3	5.3	47.2	36.8
Women	2.7	8.5	6.2	47.3	35.3
Black	5.6	14.2	7.5	45.4	27.3
Hispanic	4.8	19.1	8.6	43.6	24.0
White	2.5	6.1	5.8	46.6	39.1
Aged 18 to 44	2.2	8.2	5.7	46.4	37.4
Aged 45 to 64	4.2	8.1	4.7	45.9	37.1
Aged 65 or older	3.2	7.2	8.7	52.9	28.1
Not a college graduate	3.7	9.9	6.5	48.3	31.7
Bachelor's degree or more	1.5	2.7	3.8	44.2	47.9

Source: Survey Documentation and Analysis, Computer-assisted Survey Methods Program, University of California, Berkeley, General Social Surveys, 1972–2008 Cumulative Data Files, Internet site http://sda.berkeley.edu/cgi-bin/hsda?harcsda+gss08; calculations by New Strategist

The Public Wants Fewer Immigrants

More than one in four Americans can speak a language other English. Hispanics are most likely to speak another language, with 67 percent saying they can. Among adults aged 18 to 44, 37 percent are bilingual. The 54 percent majority of the public wants to reduce the number of immigrants coming to the United States. Among Hispanics, however, only 24 percent want to reduce immigration.

(percent distribution of people aged 18 or older by the change they would like to see in the number of immigrants coming to the United States, 2008)

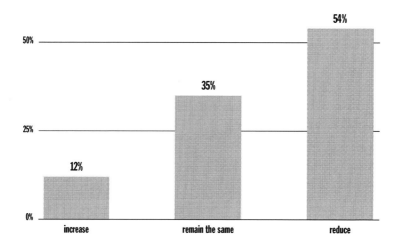

Table 8.11 Can Speak Language Other than English, 2008

"Can you speak a language other than English?"

(percent of people aged 18 or older responding by demographic characteristic, 2008)

	yes	no
Total people	**27.8%**	**72.2%**
Men	28.7	71.3
Women	27.1	72.9
Black	16.3	83.7
Hispanic	66.8	33.2
White	24.0	76.0
Aged 18 to 44	36.7	63.3
Aged 45 to 64	18.9	81.1
Aged 65 or older	20.9	79.1
Not a college graduate	23.9	76.1
Bachelor's degree or more	38.9	61.1

Source: Survey Documentation and Analysis, Computer-assisted Survey Methods Program, University of California, Berkeley, General Social Survey, 2008 Cumulative Data Files, Internet site http://sda.berkeley.edu/cgi-bin/hsda?harcsda+gss08; calculations by New Strategist

Table 8.12 Change in Number of Immigrants, 2008

"Do you think the number of immigrants to America nowadays should be . . . ?"

(percent of people aged 18 or older responding by demographic characteristic, 2008)

	increased a lot	increased a little	remain the same	reduced a little	reduced a lot
Total people	**3.1%**	**8.6%**	**34.8%**	**24.2%**	**29.3%**
Men	3.4	8.6	34.5	23.8	29.8
Women	2.8	8.5	35.2	24.6	28.9
Black	4.7	13.0	30.6	23.4	28.3
Hispanic	6.9	11.8	57.1	14.1	10.1
White	2.3	7.7	32.8	25.3	31.9
Aged 18 to 44	2.7	9.2	39.4	26.1	22.6
Aged 45 to 64	3.9	7.3	31.4	22.2	35.3
Aged 65 or older	2.2	10.0	28.7	23.7	35.4
Not a college graduate	3.0	6.4	31.8	24.5	34.2
Bachelor's degree or more	3.1	14.9	43.8	23.3	14.9

Source: Survey Documentation and Analysis, Computer-assisted Survey Methods Program, University of California, Berkeley, General Social Survey, 2008 Cumulative Data Files, Internet site http://sda.berkeley.edu/cgi-bin/hsda?harcsda+gss08; calculations by New Strategist

Most Visit a Library at Least Once a Year

The 63 percent majority of people aged 18 or older have visited a public library at least once in the past year. More than half have visited a library two or more times. Those most likely to go to the library are college graduates (76 percent), adults aged 18 to 44 (70 percent), and blacks (68 percent). A visit to a zoo is also popular, with half the public doing so in the past year. Only 32 percent visited an art museum in the past year, but the proportion rises to 59 percent among college graduates.

(percent of people aged 18 or older who visited selected institutions at least once in the past year, 2008)

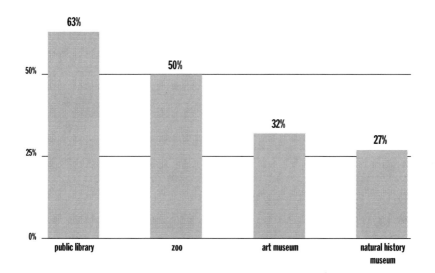

Table 8.13 Visited an Art Museum, 2008

"How often did you visit an art museum last year?"

(percent of people aged 18 or older responding by demographic characteristic, 2008)

	not once	once	two or more times
Total people	**68.1%**	**14.9%**	**17.0%**
Men	69.7	13.9	16.3
Women	66.5	15.8	17.7
Black	73.0	13.6	13.4
Hispanic	73.5	13.3	13.2
White	67.6	15.3	17.0
Aged 18 to 44	65.6	16.1	18.3
Aged 45 to 64	67.9	15.7	16.4
Aged 65 or older	76.4	9.1	14.5
Not a college graduate	77.7	11.3	11.0
Bachelor's degree or more	40.8	25.1	34.1

Source: Survey Documentation and Analysis, Computer-assisted Survey Methods Program, University of California, Berkeley, General Social Survey, 2008 Cumulative Data Files, Internet site http://sda.berkeley.edu/cgi-bin/hsda?harcsda+gss08; calculations by New Strategist

Table 8.14 Visited a Natural History Museum, 2008

"How often did you visit a natural history museum last year?"

(percent of people aged 18 or older responding by demographic characteristic, 2008)

	not once	once	two or more times
Total people	**73.5 %**	**18.3%**	**8.2%**
Men	72.7	18.8	8.6
Women	74.2	17.9	7.9
Black	82.2	11.6	6.2
Hispanic	75.5	20.3	4.1
White	71.8	19.5	8.7
Aged 18 to 44	71.7	21.0	7.2
Aged 45 to 64	71.6	18.1	10.3
Aged 65 or older	83.1	10.6	6.3
Not a college graduate	78.9	15.3	5.8
Bachelor's degree or more	58.0	27.0	15.0

Source: Survey Documentation and Analysis, Computer-assisted Survey Methods Program, University of California, Berkeley, General Social Survey, 2008 Cumulative Data Files, Internet site http://sda.berkeley.edu/cgi-bin/hsda?harcsda+gss08; calculations by New Strategist

Table 8.15 Visited a Zoo, 2008

"How often did you visit a zoo last year?"

(percent of people aged 18 or older responding by demographic characteristic, 2008)

	not once	once	two or more times
Total people	**50.0%**	**27.9%**	**22.1%**
Men	52.6	27.2	20.1
Women	47.6	28.5	23.9
Black	57.3	20.1	22.6
Hispanic	54.2	26.1	19.7
White	49.1	29.5	21.4
Aged 18 to 44	38.5	31.7	29.9
Aged 45 to 64	56.6	27.1	16.4
Aged 65 or older	70.2	17.9	12.0
Not a college graduate	54.7	26.8	18.4
Bachelor's degree or more	36.7	30.8	32.5

Source: Survey Documentation and Analysis, Computer-assisted Survey Methods Program, University of California, Berkeley, General Social Survey, 2008 Cumulative Data Files, Internet site http://sda.berkeley.edu/cgi-bin/hsda?harcsda+gss08; calculations by New Strategist

Table 8.16 Visited a Science Museum, 2008

"How often did you visit a science museum last year?"

(percent of people aged 18 or older responding by demographic characteristic, 2008)

	not once	once	two or more times
Total people	**74.6%**	**17.3%**	**8.1%**
Men	72.9	17.5	9.6
Women	76.2	17.0	6.7
Black	83.6	10.4	5.9
Hispanic	81.0	9.7	9.2
White	73.4	18.3	8.2
Aged 18 to 44	70.8	19.9	9.3
Aged 45 to 64	75.1	16.7	8.2
Aged 65 or older	85.4	10.3	4.3
Not a college graduate	80.5	13.9	5.6
Bachelor's degree or more	57.9	26.8	15.3

Source: Survey Documentation and Analysis, Computer-assisted Survey Methods Program, University of California, Berkeley, General Social Survey, 2008 Cumulative Data Files, Internet site http://sda.berkeley.edu/cgi-bin/hsda?harcsda+gss08; calculations by New Strategist

Table 8.17 Visited a Public Library, 2008

"How often did you visit a public library last year?"

(percent of people aged 18 or older responding by demographic characteristic, 2008)

	not once	once	two or more times
Total people	**36.6%**	**9.1%**	**54.3%**
Men	42.6	12.4	45.0
Women	30.9	5.9	63.2
Black	31.6	10.8	57.6
Hispanic	37.1	8.5	54.5
White	37.5	8.4	54.1
Aged 18 to 44	29.9	9.3	60.8
Aged 45 to 64	40.0	9.9	50.1
Aged 65 or older	49.3	5.9	44.8
Not a college graduate	40.9	10.3	48.8
Bachelor's degree or more	24.0	5.5	70.5

Source: Survey Documentation and Analysis, Computer-assisted Survey Methods Program, University of California, Berkeley, General Social Survey, 2008 Cumulative Data Files, Internet site http://sda.berkeley.edu/cgi-bin/hsda?harcsda+gss08; calculations by New Strategist

Heightened Awareness Is Biggest Impact of Terrorism

The most common response among Americans to the September 11, 2001, terrorist attacks is a heightened awareness of what is going on around them. Sixty-three percent say they or people they know are more aware. Twenty-three percent developed an emergency plan, and 21 percent stockpiled supplies. Only 9 percent avoided travel to certain cities and just 6 percent avoided tall buildings.

(percent of people aged 18 or older who have personally done or know someone who has done selected things because of terrorism since September 11, 2001, 2008)

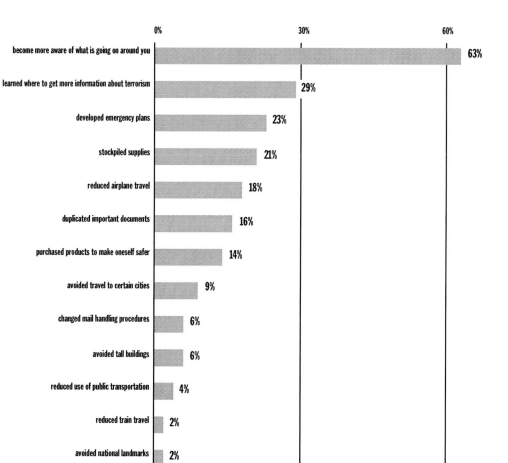

Table 8.18 Developed Emergency Plans, 2008

"Community-wide disasters happen, and these happen for a variety of reasons, such as acts of nature, terrorism, industrial accidents, and other causes. Do you know anyone who has done any of the following things because of terrorism since September 11th, 2001? Developed emergency plans (evacuation, meeting places)?"

(percent of people aged 18 or older responding by demographic characteristic, 2008)

	no	yes, personally	someone you know	personally and someone you know
Total people	**77.0%**	**4.7%**	**9.7%**	**8.6%**
Men	79.4	4.1	9.2	7.3
Women	75.0	5.2	10.1	9.7
Black	75.9	3.9	9.4	10.8
Hispanic	89.5	1.4	6.8	2.3
White	76.0	5.0	10.3	8.7
Aged 18 to 44	77.2	3.9	11.3	7.6
Aged 45 to 64	72.5	6.8	8.5	12.3
Aged 65 or older	87.1	2.4	8.1	2.4
Not a college graduate	80.4	4.4	8.6	6.6
Bachelor's degree or more	67.2	5.6	12.8	14.4

Source: Survey Documentation and Analysis, Computer-assisted Survey Methods Program, University of California, Berkeley, General Social Survey, 2008 Cumulative Data Files, Internet site http://sda.berkeley.edu/cgi-bin/hsda?harcsda+gss08; calculations by New Strategist

Table 8.19 Stockpiled Supplies, 2008

"Do you know anyone who has done any of the following things because of terrorism since September 11th, 2001? Have you or anyone you know stockpiled supplies (food, water, antibiotics, etc.)?"

(percent of people aged 18 or older responding by demographic characteristic, 2008)

	no	yes, personally	someone you know	personally and someone you know
Total people	**78.5%**	**4.7%**	**11.3%**	**5.4%**
Men	81.5	4.3	10.0	4.3
Women	76.0	5.2	12.4	6.4
Black	78.6	1.9	11.4	8.1
Hispanic	81.0	9.4	8.7	0.9
White	78.1	5.5	11.3	5.1
Aged 18 to 44	77.7	3.7	13.7	4.9
Aged 45 to 64	77.1	5.2	11.0	6.8
Aged 65 or older	84.5	7.0	5.0	3.6
Not a college graduate	79.7	5.1	10.4	4.8
Bachelor's degree or more	75.2	3.8	13.7	7.3

Source: Survey Documentation and Analysis, Computer-assisted Survey Methods Program, University of California, Berkeley, General Social Survey, 2008 Cumulative Data Files, Internet site http://sda.berkeley.edu/cgi-bin/hsda?harcsda+gss08; calculations by New Strategist

Table 8.20 Purchased Things to Make You Safer, 2008

"Do you know anyone who has done any of the following things because of terrorism since September 11th, 2001? Have you or anyone you know purchased things to make them safer (gas masks, duct tape, things to make their house safer, etc.)?"

(percent of people aged 18 or older responding by demographic characteristic, 2008)

	no	yes, personally	someone you know	personally and someone you know
Total people	**85.7%**	**2.9%**	**7.9%**	**3.5%**
Men	86.5	3.7	6.5	3.4
Women	85.0	2.3	9.2	3.5
Black	85.7	0.7	9.1	4.4
Hispanic	88.2	6.1	4.6	1.2
White	88.0	3.6	8.1	3.3
Aged 18 to 44	85.1	2.2	9.0	3.7
Aged 45 to 64	84.3	3.2	8.9	3.6
Aged 65 or older	90.7	4.3	3.1	2.0
Not a college graduate	86.3	3.1	7.7	3.0
Bachelor's degree or more	84.1	2.3	8.8	4.9

Source: Survey Documentation and Analysis, Computer-assisted Survey Methods Program, University of California, Berkeley, General Social Survey, 2008 Cumulative Data Files, Internet site http://sda.berkeley.edu/cgi-bin/hsda?harcsda+gss08; calculations by New Strategist

Table 8.21 Learned Where to Get More Information about Terrorism, 2008

"Do you know anyone who has done any of the following things because of terrorism since September 11th, 2001? Have you or anyone you know learned where to get more information about terrorism?"

(percent of people aged 18 or older responding by demographic characteristic, 2008)

	no	yes, personally	someone you know	personally and someone you know
Total people	**71.4%**	**11.1%**	**5.3%**	**12.2%**
Men	68.7	12.2	4.9	14.3
Women	73.8	10.1	5.7	10.4
Black	72.1	8.0	8.8	11.2
Hispanic	84.2	7.4	4.1	4.2
White	70.2	12.5	5.1	12.2
Aged 18 to 44	70.2	10.3	5.9	13.6
Aged 45 to 64	68.4	13.4	4.9	13.3
Aged 65 or older	82.3	8.0	4.3	5.3
Not a college graduate	75.7	9.4	5.1	9.8
Bachelor's degree or more	59.3	15.9	5.9	19.0

Source: Survey Documentation and Analysis, Computer-assisted Survey Methods Program, University of California, Berkeley, General Social Survey, 2008 Cumulative Data Files, Internet site http://sda.berkeley.edu/cgi-bin/hsda?harcsda+gss08; calculations by New Strategist

Table 8.22 Duplicated Important Documents, 2008

"Do you know anyone who has done any of the following things because of terrorism since September 11th, 2001? Have you or anyone you know duplicated important documents?"

(percent of people aged 18 or older responding by demographic characteristic, 2008)

	no	yes, personally	someone you know	personally and someone you know
Total people	**83.9%**	**6.2%**	**2.9%**	**7.0%**
Men	85.2	5.6	2.7	6.4
Women	82.7	6.7	3.0	7.5
Black	82.0	4.9	5.4	7.7
Hispanic	83.5	9.7	3.8	3.0
White	84.2	6.1	2.8	6.9
Aged 18 to 44	82.2	5.9	3.9	8.0
Aged 45 to 64	85.2	6.8	2.2	5.8
Aged 65 or older	86.0	6.0	1.5	6.5
Not a college graduate	85.9	5.6	2.3	6.2
Bachelor's degree or more	78.1	8.0	4.5	9.4

Source: Survey Documentation and Analysis, Computer-assisted Survey Methods Program, University of California, Berkeley, General Social Survey, 2008 Cumulative Data Files, Internet site http://sda.berkeley.edu/cgi-bin/hsda?harcsda+gss08; calculations by New Strategist

Table 8.23 Reduced Airplane Travel, 2008

"Do you know anyone who has done any of the following things because of terrorism since September 11th, 2001? Have you or anyone you know reduced airplane travel?"

(percent of people aged 18 or older responding by demographic characteristic, 2008)

	no	yes, personally	someone you know	personally and someone you know
Total people	**82.4%**	**6.3%**	**7.3%**	**4.0%**
Men	86.8	6.0	5.2	1.9
Women	78.7	6.5	9.0	5.8
Black	82.1	3.7	7.9	6.2
Hispanic	80.5	9.7	7.4	2.4
White	82.5	6.7	7.4	3.5
Aged 18 to 44	82.0	5.4	8.8	3.7
Aged 45 to 64	81.6	7.6	6.2	4.7
Aged 65 or older	85.8	6.0	5.2	3.0
Not a college graduate	84.5	6.1	6.2	3.3
Bachelor's degree or more	76.5	6.9	10.4	6.1

Source: Survey Documentation and Analysis, Computer-assisted Survey Methods Program, University of California, Berkeley, General Social Survey, 2008 Cumulative Data Files, Internet site http://sda.berkeley.edu/cgi-bin/hsda?harcsda+gss08; calculations by New Strategist

Table 8.24 Reduced Train Travel, 2008

"Do you know anyone who has done any of the following things because of terrorism since September 11th, 2001? Have you or anyone you know reduced travel by train?"

(percent of people aged 18 or older responding by demographic characteristic, 2008)

	no	yes, personally	someone you know	personally and someone you know
Total people	**97.6%**	**1.3%**	**0.8%**	**0.4%**
Men	97.6	1.6	0.8	0.0
Women	97.5	1.0	0.8	0.8
Black	93.0	3.0	2.8	1.2
Hispanic	98.1	1.5	0.5	0.0
White	98.4	0.9	0.4	0.2
Aged 18 to 44	97.0	1.5	1.1	0.5
Aged 45 to 64	98.4	1.3	0.4	0.0
Aged 65 or older	97.8	0.7	0.8	0.7
Not a college graduate	97.0	1.6	0.9	0.5
Bachelor's degree or more	99.1	0.3	0.4	0.3

Source: Survey Documentation and Analysis, Computer-assisted Survey Methods Program, University of California, Berkeley, General Social Survey, 2008 Cumulative Data Files, Internet site http://sda.berkeley.edu/cgi-bin/hsda?harcsda+gss08; calculations by New Strategist

Table 8.25 Reduced Use of Public Transportation, 2008

"Do you know anyone who has done any of the following things because of terrorism since September 11th, 2001? Have you or anyone you know reduced use of public transportation?"

(percent of people aged 18 or older responding by demographic characteristic, 2008)

	no	yes, personally	someone you know	personally and someone you know
Total people	**96.2%**	**1.0%**	**2.1%**	**0.7%**
Men	95.9	1.4	2.4	0.3
Women	96.5	0.5	1.9	1.0
Black	91.9	1.4	5.5	1.2
Hispanic	94.1	2.4	2.3	1.2
White	97.5	0.9	1.2	0.4
Aged 18 to 44	94.4	0.9	3.6	1.0
Aged 45 to 64	97.8	1.1	1.0	0.2
Aged 65 or older	98.4	0.8	0.4	0.4
Not a college graduate	96.0	1.3	2.3	0.4
Bachelor's degree or more	96.8	0.0	1.8	1.4

Source: Survey Documentation and Analysis, Computer-assisted Survey Methods Program, University of California, Berkeley, General Social Survey, 2008 Cumulative Data Files, Internet site http://sda.berkeley.edu/cgi-bin/hsda?harcsda+gss08; calculations by New Strategist

Table 8.26 Changed Mail Handling Procedures, 2008

"Do you know anyone who has done any of the following things
because of terrorism since September 11th, 2001? Have you
or anyone you know changed mail handling procedures?"

(percent of people aged 18 or older responding by demographic characteristic, 2008)

	no	yes, personally	someone you know	personally and someone you know
Total people	**93.5%**	**2.7%**	**2.6%**	**1.1%**
Men	95.3	2.6	1.4	0.7
Women	92.1	2.7	3.7	1.5
Black	94.9	1.9	1.7	1.5
Hispanic	94.8	3.3	1.8	0.0
White	93.0	3.0	2.8	1.1
Aged 18 to 44	94.1	1.7	3.0	1.3
Aged 45 to 64	93.3	3.5	2.8	0.4
Aged 65 or older	93.7	3.6	0.8	1.9
Not a college graduate	94.5	2.7	1.9	0.9
Bachelor's degree or more	90.8	2.5	4.7	1.9

Source: Survey Documentation and Analysis, Computer-assisted Survey Methods Program, University of California, Berkeley, General Social Survey, 2008 Cumulative Data Files, Internet site http://sda.berkeley.edu/cgi-bin/hsda?harcsda+gss08; calculations by New Strategist

Table 8.27 Become More Aware of What Is Going On around You, 2008

"Do you know anyone who has done any of the following things because of terrorism since September 11th, 2001? Have you or anyone you know become more vigilant or aware of what is going on around them?"

(percent of people aged 18 or older responding by demographic characteristic, 2008)

	no	yes, personally	someone you know	personally and someone you know
Total people	**37.4%**	**27.2%**	**5.2%**	**30.2%**
Men	40.2	28.3	4.3	27.3
Women	35.0	26.3	5.9	32.7
Black	33.6	26.1	9.0	31.3
Hispanic	48.7	21.7	8.7	20.9
White	36.8	28.2	4.4	30.5
Aged 18 to 44	35.5	25.2	6.8	32.5
Aged 45 to 64	35.0	28.1	3.8	33.0
Aged 65 or older	48.4	31.5	3.4	16.8
Not a college graduate	40.7	26.8	5.0	27.6
Bachelor's degree or more	28.0	28.6	5.6	37.8

Source: Survey Documentation and Analysis, Computer-assisted Survey Methods Program, University of California, Berkeley, General Social Survey, 2008 Cumulative Data Files, Internet site http://sda.berkeley.edu/cgi-bin/hsda?harcsda+gss08; calculations by New Strategist

Table 8.28 Avoided Travel to Certain Cities, 2008

"Do you know anyone who has done any of the following things because of terrorism since September 11th, 2001? Have you or anyone you know avoided travel to certain cities?"

(percent of people aged 18 or older responding by demographic characteristic, 2008)

	no	yes, personally	someone you know	personally and someone you know
Total people	**90.8%**	**3.5%**	**3.4%**	**2.3%**
Men	91.6	4.2	2.8	1.4
Women	90.1	2.9	3.9	3.0
Black	92.5	0.7	3.9	2.9
Hispanic	90.9	5.0	3.0	1.2
White	90.7	3.9	3.3	2.1
Aged 18 to 44	90.3	3.1	4.3	2.3
Aged 45 to 64	90.6	4.2	3.0	2.2
Aged 65 or older	93.1	3.3	1.8	1.8
Not a college graduate	92.4	3.0	3.2	1.4
Bachelor's degree or more	86.2	5.2	3.9	4.8

Source: Survey Documentation and Analysis, Computer-assisted Survey Methods Program, University of California, Berkeley, General Social Survey, 2008 Cumulative Data Files, Internet site http://sda.berkeley.edu/cgi-bin/hsda?harcsda+gss08; calculations by New Strategist

Table 8.29 Avoided Tall Buildings, 2008

"Do you know anyone who has done any of the following things because of terrorism since September 11th, 2001? Have you or anyone you know avoided tall buildings?"

(percent of people aged 18 or older responding by demographic characteristic, 2008)

	no	yes, personally	someone you know	personally and someone you know
Total people	**93.8%**	**3.0%**	**1.6%**	**1.6%**
Men	95.0	2.0	1.4	1.6
Women	92.7	3.8	1.8	1.6
Black	87.6	4.1	3.6	4.7
Hispanic	91.2	5.8	1.6	1.4
White	95.3	2.4	1.3	1.0
Aged 18 to 44	92.5	3.2	2.3	2.1
Aged 45 to 64	94.9	2.9	1.1	1.2
Aged 65 or older	95.6	2.8	1.0	0.6
Not a college graduate	93.7	3.3	1.5	1.5
Bachelor's degree or more	94.0	2.1	2.0	1.9

Source: Survey Documentation and Analysis, Computer-assisted Survey Methods Program, University of California, Berkeley, General Social Survey, 2008 Cumulative Data Files, Internet site http://sda.berkeley.edu/cgi-bin/hsda?harcsda+gss08; calculations by New Strategist

Table 8.30 Avoided National Landmarks, 2008

"Do you know anyone who has done any of the following things because of terrorism since September 11th, 2001? Have you or anyone you know avoided national landmarks?"

(percent of people aged 18 or older responding by demographic characteristic, 2008)

	no	yes, personally	someone you know	personally and someone you know
Total people	**97.7%**	**0.7%**	**0.8%**	**0.8%**
Men	98.6	0.4	0.3	0.7
Women	96.9	0.9	1.3	0.8
Black	96.0	1.7	1.2	1.1
Hispanic	96.4	2.1	0.9	0.6
White	98.6	0.3	0.7	0.5
Aged 18 to 44	96.5	0.8	1.4	1.3
Aged 45 to 64	98.7	0.9	0.4	0.0
Aged 65 or older	99.4	0.0	0.0	0.6
Not a college graduate	97.9	0.9	0.7	0.6
Bachelor's degree or more	97.2	0.1	1.2	1.4

Source: Survey Documentation and Analysis, Computer-assisted Survey Methods Program, University of California, Berkeley, General Social Survey, 2008 Cumulative Data Files, Internet site http://sda.berkeley.edu/cgi-bin/hsda?harcsda+gss08; calculations by New Strategist

9

Sexual Attitudes and Behavior

Some sexual attitudes and behaviors have changed greatly over the past half-century, while others have barely budged. General Social Survey questions that probe sexual activity support the notion that human beings are essentially monogamous, with some backsliding. The results also show that some seemingly controversial issues—such as whether sex education should be taught in the public schools—are not controversial at all.

Little or no change

• **Support for abortion.** No one likes the idea of abortion, but most Americans support abortion in certain circumstances—attitudes that have not changed in decades. Only 41 percent of the public supports abortion for any reason, but 89 percent support abortion if a woman's health is endangered.

• **Sex education in the public schools.** The great majority of the public has supported sex education in the public schools for decades, with more than nine out of ten in favor of it in 2008.

• **Extramarital sex.** At various times throughout history, free thinkers espouse the notion that extramarital relationships are OK. Most people heartily disagree. More than 80 percent of the public says extramarital sex is always wrong.

Big changes

• **Premarital sex.** Big changes have occurred in attitudes toward premarital sex over the past several decades. In 1978, only 40 percent of the public said premarital sex is not wrong at all. In 2008, the figure was 55 percent.

• **Attitudes toward gays and lesbians.** The percentage of Americans who think sexual relations between adults of the same sex are always wrong has dropped from 77 percent in 1988 to 52 percent in 2008. Among adults aged 18 to 44, the 49 percent plurality thinks homosexual couples should have the right to marry. As younger people age and replace older, less tolerant generations, acceptance of gays and lesbians will continue to grow.

Sex Education in the Public Schools Is Widely Supported

There is no controversy over sex education in the public schools. The American public widely supports it, with more than nine out of 10 in favor of sex education. The public also supports making birth control available to teenagers aged 14 to 16, even if their parents do not approve. Despite this tolerance, 72 percent of adults think sex between people in their early teens is always wrong.

(percent distribution of people aged 18 or older by attitude toward sex education in public schools, 2008)

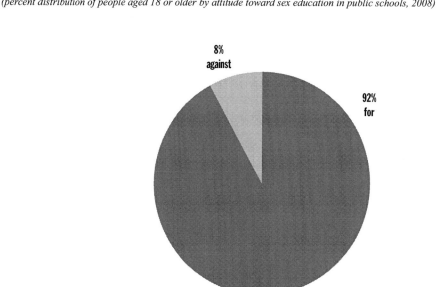

Table 9.1 Sex Education in Public Schools, 1988 to 2008

"Would you be for or against sex education in the public schools?"

(percent of people aged 18 or older responding, 1988 to 2008; and percent responding by demographic characteristic, 2008)

	favor	oppose
TREND		
2008	91.9%	8.1%
1998	87.1	12.9
1988	87.6	12.4
2008 PROFILE		
Total people	**91.9**	**8.1**
Men	91.8	7.2
Women	92.0	8.0
Black	94.0	6.0
Hispanic	90.0	10.0
White	91.7	8.3
Aged 18 to 44	94.1	5.9
Aged 45 to 64	91.8	8.2
Aged 65 or older	85.1	14.9
Not a college graduate	91.0	9.0
Bachelor's degree or more	94.7	5.3

Source: Survey Documentation and Analysis, Computer-assisted Survey Methods Program, University of California, Berkeley, General Social Surveys, 1972–2008 Cumulative Data Files, Internet site http://sda.berkeley.edu/cgi-bin/hsda?harcsda+gss08; calculations by New Strategist

Table 9.2 Birth Control for Teenagers, 1988 to 2008

"Do you strongly agree, agree, or strongly disagree that methods
of birth control should be available to teenagers between the ages
of 14 and 16 even if their parents did not approve?"

(percent of people aged 18 or older responding, 1988 to 2008; and percent responding by demographic characteristic, 2008)

	strongly agree	agree	disagree	strongly disagree
TREND				
2008	23.1%	33.9%	21.4%	21.6%
1998	26.8	30.9	21.0	21.3
1988	28.3	31.0	23.3	17.4
2008 PROFILE				
Total people	**23.1**	**33.9**	**21.4**	**21.6**
Men	20.9	33.2	23.9	22.0
Women	25.0	34.4	19.4	21.2
Black	32.2	32.6	14.0	21.2
Hispanic	19.4	34.3	24.4	21.9
White	21.4	35.3	22.9	20.4
Aged 18 to 44	25.1	38.9	18.0	18.0
Aged 45 to 64	25.3	30.7	23.2	20.8
Aged 65 or older	11.7	26.5	28.3	33.4
Not a college graduate	23.9	32.9	20.8	22.4
Bachelor's degree or more	21.1	36.4	23.1	19.3

Source: Survey Documentation and Analysis, Computer-assisted Survey Methods Program, University of California, Berkeley, General Social Surveys, 1972–2008 Cumulative Data Files, Internet site http://sda.berkeley.edu/cgi-bin/hsda?harcsda+gss08; calculations by New Strategist

Table 9.3 Sexual Relations between Teenagers, 1988 to 2008

"Do you think sex relations before marriage between people in their early teens, say 14 to 16, are always wrong, almost always wrong, wrong only sometimes, or not wrong at all?"

(percent of people aged 18 or older responding, 1988 to 2008; and percent responding by demographic characteristic, 2008)

	always wrong	almost always wrong	sometimes wrong	not wrong at all
TREND				
2008	71.8%	15.6%	8.1%	4.5%
1998	72.2	16.2	8.2	3.4
1988	68.5	16.4	11.6	3.5
2008 PROFILE				
Total people	**71.8**	**15.6**	**8.1**	**4.5**
Men	66.2	18.0	9.1	6.7
Women	77.0	13.3	7.2	2.5
Black	78.5	12.5	4.5	4.5
Hispanic	73.9	11.8	8.9	5.4
White	71.0	16.5	8.8	3.7
Aged 18 to 44	68.1	16.7	9.0	6.3
Aged 45 to 64	73.3	15.7	7.5	3.6
Aged 65 or older	79.8	11.8	6.8	1.6
Not a college graduate	72.9	14.7	7.5	4.9
Bachelor's degree or more	68.6	18.0	9.8	3.6

Source: Survey Documentation and Analysis, Computer-assisted Survey Methods Program, University of California, Berkeley, General Social Surveys, 1972–2008 Cumulative Data Files, Internet site http://sda.berkeley.edu/cgi-bin/hsda?harcsda+gss08; calculations by New Strategist

Many Watch X-Rated Movies

One in four adults has seen an X-rated movie in the past year, according to the General Social Survey. Men are more likely to have seen a porn film than women, and young adults more than older adults. Thirty-three percent of the public think pornography should be illegal for all, while a larger 64 percent think it should be illegal only for people under age 18.

(percent of people aged 18 or older who have seen an X-rated movie in the past year, by sex, 2008)

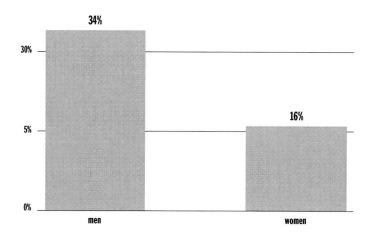

Table 9.4 Seen X-Rated Movie, 1978 to 2008

"Have you seen an x-rated movie in the last year?"

(percent of people aged 18 or older responding, 1978 to 2008; and percent responding by demographic characteristic, 2008)

	yes	no
TREND		
2008	24.2%	75.8%
1998	24.8	75.2
1988	27.6	72.4
1978	16.1	83.9
2008 PROFILE		
Total people	**24.2**	**75.8**
Men	34.0	66.0
Women	15.5	84.5
Black	34.2	65.8
Hispanic	32.1	67.9
White	22.2	77.8
Aged 18 to 44	37.1	62.9
Aged 45 to 64	14.1	85.9
Aged 65 or older	7.0	93.0
Not a college graduate	24.9	75.1
Bachelor's degree or more	22.1	77.9

Source: Survey Documentation and Analysis, Computer-assisted Survey Methods Program, University of California, Berkeley, General Social Surveys, 1972–2008 Cumulative Data Files, Internet site http://sda.berkeley.edu/cgi-bin/hsda?harcsda+gss08; calculations by New Strategist

Table 9.5 Laws against Pornography, 1978 to 2008

"Which of these statements comes closest to your feelings about pornography laws?
  1) There should be laws against the distribution of pornography whatever the age;
  2) There should be laws against the distribution of pornography to persons under 18;
    3) There should be no laws forbidding the distribution of pornography."

(percent of people aged 18 or older responding, 1978 to 2008; and percent responding by demographic characteristic, 2008)

	illegal to all	illegal under 18	legal
TREND			
2008	32.5%	64.0%	3.4%
1998	37.8	58.6	3.6
1988	43.8	51.2	5.1
1978	43.3	49.6	7.1
2008 PROFILE			
Total people	**32.5**	**64.0**	**3.4**
Men	23.9	71.6	4.5
Women	40.1	57.4	2.5
Black	22.3	70.0	7.7
Hispanic	26.8	68.9	4.3
White	34.6	62.7	2.7
Aged 18 to 44	23.1	74.1	2.7
Aged 45 to 64	35.9	59.6	4.5
Aged 65 or older	54.9	41.8	3.3
Not a college graduate	33.5	62.9	3.6
Bachelor's degree or more	30.0	67.0	3.1

Source: Survey Documentation and Analysis, Computer-assisted Survey Methods Program, University of California, Berkeley, General Social Surveys, 1972–2008 Cumulative Data Files, Internet site http://sda.berkeley.edu/cgi-bin/hsda?harcsda+gss08; calculations by New Strategist

Most Say Sex before Marriage Is OK

Attitudes toward premarital sex have changed greatly in the United States over the past few decades. Today, the 55 percent majority says premarital sex is "not wrong at all," up from 40 percent in 1978. The public has not budged on its attitude toward extramarital sex, with 84 percent saying it is "always wrong."

(percent age of people aged 18 or older who think premarital sex is not wrong at all, 1978 to 2008)

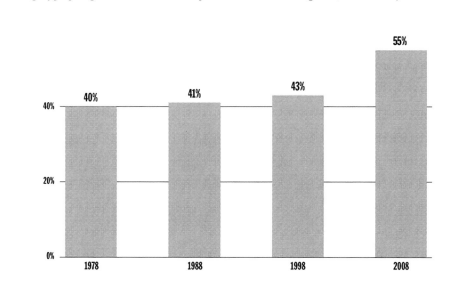

Table 9.6 Premarital Sex, 1978 to 2008

"If a man and woman have sex relations before marriage, do you think it is always wrong, almost always wrong, wrong only sometimes, or not wrong at all?"

(percent of people aged 18 or older responding, 1978 to 2008; and percent responding by demographic characteristic, 2008)

	always wrong	almost always wrong	sometimes wrong	not wrong at all
TREND				
2008	22.6%	7.2%	15.4%	54.8%
1998	27.0	8.7	21.1	43.2
1988	26.2	10.2	22.2	41.4
1978	28.2	11.5	20.2	40.1
2008 PROFILE				
Total people	**22.6**	**7.2**	**15.4**	**54.8**
Men	20.4	5.8	15.8	58.0
Women	24.7	8.4	15.0	51.9
Black	29.2	9.9	9.1	51.7
Hispanic	17.9	9.5	9.3	63.2
White	21.7	6.7	16.4	55.2
Aged 18 to 44	19.3	6.1	16.0	58.6
Aged 45 to 64	23.5	6.7	14.0	55.7
Aged 65 or older	30.8	11.5	17.2	40.5
Not a college graduate	23.1	7.4	14.9	54.5
Bachelor's degree or more	21.2	6.5	16.7	55.6

Source: Survey Documentation and Analysis, Computer-assisted Survey Methods Program, University of California, Berkeley, General Social Surveys, 1972–2008 Cumulative Data Files, Internet site http://sda.berkeley.edu/cgi-bin/hsda?harcsda+gss08; calculations by New Strategist

Table 9.7 Extramarital Sex, 1988 to 2008

"What is your opinion about a married person having sexual relations
with someone other than the marriage partner?"

(percent of people aged 18 or older responding, 1988 to 2008; and percent responding by demographic characteristic, 2008)

	always wrong	almost always wrong	sometimes wrong	not wrong at all
TREND				
2008	84.2%	9.2%	5.3%	1.3%
1998	80.5	11.7	5.5	2.3
1988	80.7	12.3	5.1	1.9
2008 PROFILE				
Total people	**84.2**	**9.2**	**5.3**	**1.3**
Men	80.2	11.2	6.8	1.8
Women	87.6	7.4	4.1	0.9
Black	85.2	4.3	9.0	1.5
Hispanic	89.3	7.2	3.2	0.2
White	84.2	10.3	4.1	1.5
Aged 18 to 44	83.4	10.4	5.0	1.2
Aged 45 to 64	85.7	7.5	5.2	1.6
Aged 65 or older	83.3	8.9	6.6	1.2
Not a college graduate	88.5	6.1	4.5	0.9
Bachelor's degree or more	71.7	18.0	7.8	2.5

Source: Survey Documentation and Analysis, Computer-assisted Survey Methods Program, University of California, Berkeley, General Social Surveys, 1972–2008 Cumulative Data Files, Internet site http://sda.berkeley.edu/cgi-bin/hsda?harcsda+gss08; calculations by New Strategist

Young Adults Are Far More Accepting of Gays and Lesbians

Although most still say homosexual relations are always wrong, the share has fallen steeply over the past two decades from 77 to 52 percent. A growing share (38 percent in 2008) says homosexuality is not wrong at all. Young adults are far more open minded than older generations. Forty-nine percent of people aged 18 to 44 think gays and lesbians should have the right to marry, compared with 22 percent of people aged 65 or older.

(percentage of people aged 18 or older who think homosexual couples should have the right to marry, by age, 2008)

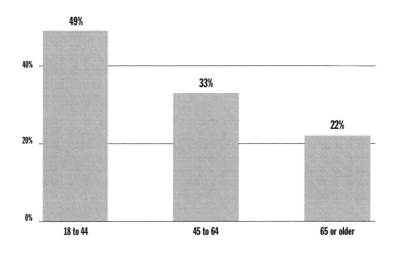

Table 9.8 Homosexual Relations, 1988 to 2008

"What about sexual relations between two adults of the same sex?"

(percent of people aged 18 or older responding, 1988 to 2008; and percent responding by demographic characteristic, 2008)

	always wrong	almost always wrong	sometimes wrong	not wrong at all
TREND				
2008	52.4%	3.1%	6.7%	37.8%
1998	58.5	5.9	7.3	28.3
1988	77.4	4.4	5.5	12.7
2008 PROFILE				
Total people	**52.4**	**3.1**	**6.7**	**37.8**
Men	56.9	3.4	6.3	33.3
Women	48.4	2.7	7.0	41.8
Black	71.6	2.7	3.2	22.4
Hispanic	51.1	6.7	5.0	37.2
White	49.4	3.0	7.3	40.3
Aged 18 to 44	44.6	2.9	5.1	47.4
Aged 45 to 64	52.8	3.3	9.9	34.0
Aged 65 or older	74.5	3.1	4.4	18.0
Not a college graduate	59.1	3.0	6.4	31.5
Bachelor's degree or more	33.5	3.3	7.4	55.7

Source: Survey Documentation and Analysis, Computer-assisted Survey Methods Program, University of California, Berkeley, General Social Surveys, 1972–2008 Cumulative Data Files, Internet site http://sda.berkeley.edu/cgi-bin/hsda?harcsda+gss08; calculations by New Strategist

Table 9.9 Gay Marriage, 2008

"Do you agree or disagree? Homosexual couples
should have the right to marry one another."

(percent of people aged 18 or older responding by demographic characteristic, 2008)

	strongly agree	agree	neither agree nor disagree	disagree	strongly disagree
Total people	**15.4%**	**23.9%**	**13.0%**	**15.6%**	**32.1%**
Men	12.2	22.9	13.2	16.2	35.5
Women	18.1	24.7	12.8	15.1	29.4
Black	9.0	17.3	13.3	24.6	35.7
Hispanic	11.3	29.1	14.8	17.2	27.5
White	16.6	24.4	12.8	13.5	32.7
Aged 18 to 44	20.9	28.6	13.2	10.9	26.4
Aged 45 to 64	12.6	20.8	14.7	19.5	32.3
Aged 65 or older	4.9	16.6	9.0	20.4	49.1
Not a college graduate	12.1	23.8	12.9	15.8	35.4
Bachelor's degree or more	24.7	24.2	13.3	15.1	22.7

Source: Survey Documentation and Analysis, Computer-assisted Survey Methods Program, University of California, Berkeley, General Social Survey, 2008 Cumulative Data Files, Internet site http://sda.berkeley.edu/cgi-bin32/hsda?harcsda+gss06; calculations by New Strategist

Most Americans Have Had Only One Sex Partner in the Past Year

The 69 percent majority of Americans have had only one sex partner in the past year. Fifty-nine percent have had only one partner in the past five years. Ninety-two percent said the last time they had sex they were in a relationship with their partner. Twenty-four percent used a condom.

(percent distribution of people aged 18 or older by number of sex partners in past year, 2008)

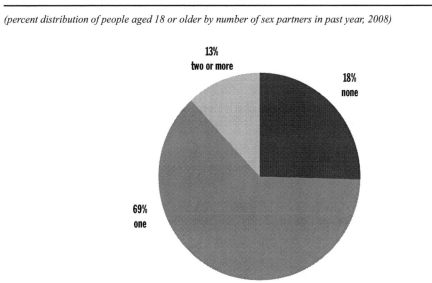

Table 9.10 Sex Partners in Past Year, 1988 to 2008

"How many sex partners have you had in the last 12 months?"

(percent of people aged 18 or older responding, 1988 to 2008; and percent responding by demographic characteristic, 2008)

	none	one	two	three	four or more	one or more, don't know number
TREND						
2008	18.0%	68.8%	6.5%	2.2%	3.9%	0.6%
1998	17.4	70.6	6.0	2.2	3.3	0.5
1988	19.8	66.5	5.0	3.2	4.8	0.7
2008 PROFILE						
Total people	**18.0**	**68.8**	**6.5**	**2.2**	**3.9**	**0.6**
Men	15.0	68.6	7.0	2.4	6.5	0.5
Women	20.6	69.0	6.0	2.1	1.7	0.6
Black	16.7	58.7	12.8	3.6	7.9	0.2
Hispanic	14.1	63.1	13.0	3.3	5.6	0.9
White	18.1	70.7	5.4	1.8	3.9	0.1
Aged 18 to 44	8.6	68.9	11.1	3.7	7.2	0.4
Aged 45 to 64	19.0	76.3	2.2	1.1	1.0	0.3
Aged 65 or older	46.8	50.5	0.9	0.0	0.2	1.6
Not a college graduate	18.2	66.9	7.4	2.6	4.3	0.6
Bachelor's degree or more	17.4	74.1	3.8	1.3	3.1	0.4

Source: Survey Documentation and Analysis, Computer-assisted Survey Methods Program, University of California, Berkeley, General Social Surveys, 1972–2008 Cumulative Data Files, Internet site http://sda.berkeley.edu/cgi-bin/hsda?harcsda+gss08; calculations by New Strategist

Table 9.11 Sex Partners in Past Five Years, 1998 and 2008

"How many sex partners have you had in the last five-year period?"

(percent of people aged 18 or older responding, 1998 and 2008; and percent responding by demographic characteristic, 2008)

	none	one	two	three	four or more	one or more, don't know number
TREND						
2008	11.0%	59.1%	9.0%	6.2%	11.6%	3.1%
1998	11.2	58.9	9.2	6.0	13.2	1.5
2008 PROFILE						
Total people	**11.0**	**59.1**	**9.0**	**6.2**	**11.6**	**3.1**
Men	8.6	54.9	9.0	7.4	16.9	3.2
Women	13.1	62.8	8.9	5.1	7.2	3.0
Black	10.5	42.0	14.8	8.5	19.0	5.1
Hispanic	6.9	46.0	13.6	11.7	16.7	5.0
White	10.9	62.7	7.0	5.5	11.4	2.5
Aged 18 to 44	3.9	49.9	12.3	10.0	20.3	3.6
Aged 45 to 64	9.9	72.9	7.6	3.0	4.7	2.0
Aged 65 or older	37.0	56.3	0.9	1.2	0.2	4.4
Not a college graduate	11.3	56.3	9.7	6.6	12.5	3.6
Bachelor's degree or more	10.0	66.7	7.0	5.1	9.4	1.8

Source: Survey Documentation and Analysis, Computer-assisted Survey Methods Program, University of California, Berkeley, General Social Surveys, 1972–2008 Cumulative Data Files, Internet site http://sda.berkeley.edu/cgi-bin/hsda?harcsda+gss08; calculations by New Strategist

Table 9.12 Frequency of Sex during Past Year, 1998 and 2008

"About how often did you have sex during the last 12 months?"

(percent of people aged 18 or older responding, 1998 and 2008; and percent responding by demographic characteristic, 2008)

	not at all	once or twice	once a month	two to three times a month	weekly	two to three times per week	four or more times per week
TREND							
2008	19.4%	9.1%	10.6%	14.8%	19.4%	19.8%	6.9%
1998	18.2	7.6	11.3	16.5	19.5	21.3	5.7
2008 PROFILE							
Total people	**19.4**	**9.1**	**10.6**	**14.8**	**19.4**	**19.8**	**6.9**
Men	14.4	9.8	11.3	14.7	21.8	20.3	7.7
Women	23.9	8.5	10.0	14.9	17.3	19.3	6.1
Black	16.4	8.2	6.0	17.8	15.0	27.1	9.5
Hispanic	10.9	12.0	6.6	13.4	18.8	25.6	12.7
White	20.4	9.1	11.7	14.3	20.1	18.3	6.1
Aged 18 to 44	7.7	9.1	8.4	16.0	21.2	27.0	10.7
Aged 45 to 64	19.8	9.0	14.3	14.7	21.2	16.6	4.3
Aged 65 or older	57.5	9.4	9.0	11.4	9.5	2.9	0.4
Not a college graduate	19.7	9.1	10.0	14.9	19.1	19.2	8.0
Bachelor's degree or more	18.3	9.1	12.3	14.7	20.3	21.4	3.8

Source: Survey Documentation and Analysis, Computer-assisted Survey Methods Program, University of California, Berkeley, General Social Surveys, 1972–2008 Cumulative Data Files, Internet site http://sda.berkeley.edu/cgi-bin/hsda?harcsda+gss08; calculations by New Strategist

Table 9.13 Relationship with Last Sex Partner, 1998 and 2008

"The last time you had sex, was it with someone that you were in an ongoing relationship with, or was it with someone else? Remember that by sex we mean only vaginal, oral, or anal sex."

(percent of people aged 18 or older responding, 1998 and 2008; and percent responding by demographic characteristic, 2008)

	yes, in relationship	no, not in relationship
TREND		
2008	92.2%	7.8%
1998	89.9	10.1
2008 PROFILE		
Total people	**92.2**	**7.8**
Men	89.1	10.9
Women	94.9	5.1
Black	89.4	10.6
Hispanic	90.6	9.4
White	93.0	7.0
Aged 18 to 44	90.8	9.2
Aged 45 to 64	94.9	5.1
Aged 65 or older	90.1	9.9
Not a college graduate	91.7	8.3
Bachelor's degree or more	93.6	6.4

Source: Survey Documentation and Analysis, Computer-assisted Survey Methods Program, University of California, Berkeley, General Social Surveys, 1972–2008 Cumulative Data Files, Internet site http://sda.berkeley.edu/cgi-bin/hsda?harcsda+gss08; calculations by New Strategist

Table 9.14 Condom Use, 1998 and 2008

"The last time you had sex, was a condom used?
By sex we mean vaginal, oral, or anal sex."

(percent of people aged 18 or older responding, 1998 and 2008; and percent responding by demographic characteristic, 2008)

	used	not used
TREND		
2008	24.0%	76.0%
1998	18.8	81.2
2008 PROFILE		
Total people	**24.0**	**76.0**
Men	26.1	73.9
Women	22.2	77.8
Black	39.1	60.9
Hispanic	38.6	61.4
White	20.2	79.8
Aged 18 to 44	35.0	65.0
Aged 45 to 64	14.1	85.9
Aged 65 or older	11.7	88.3
Not a college graduate	24.1	75.9
Bachelor's degree or more	23.7	76.3

Source: Survey Documentation and Analysis, Computer-assisted Survey Methods Program, University of California, Berkeley, General Social Surveys, 1972–2008 Cumulative Data Files, Internet site http://sda.berkeley.edu/cgi-bin/hsda?harcsda+gss08; calculations by New Strategist

Few Have Ever Strayed

When asked whether they have ever had sex with someone other than their spouse while married, 85 percent of ever-married Americans say no. While this is probably an underestimate of infidelity, it is still a testament to the essentially monogamous nature of human sexuality. Only 9 percent of the public has ever paid or been paid for sex—16 percent of men and 3 percent of women.

(percent of ever-married people aged 18 or older who have ever had sex with someone other than their spouse while married, by sex, 2008)

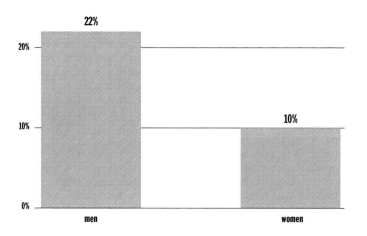

Table 9.15 Ever Had Sex Outside Marriage, 1998 and 2008

"Have you ever had sex with someone other than
your husband or wife while you were married?"

(percent of ever-married people aged 18 or older responding, 1998 and 2008; and percent responding by demographic characteristic, 2008)

	yes	no
TREND		
2008	15.2%	84.8%
1998	16.6	83.4
2008 PROFILE		
Total people	**15.2**	**84.8**
Men	21.7	78.3
Women	10.0	90.0
Black	21.3	78.7
Hispanic	15.7	84.2
White	14.6	85.4
Aged 18 to 44	11.3	88.7
Aged 45 to 64	17.9	82.1
Aged 65 or older	16.8	83.2
Not a college graduate	15.9	84.1
Bachelor's degree or more	13.5	86.5

Source: Survey Documentation and Analysis, Computer-assisted Survey Methods Program, University of California, Berkeley, General Social Surveys, 1972–2008 Cumulative Data Files, Internet site http://sda.berkeley.edu/cgi-bin/hsda?harcsda+gss08; calculations by New Strategist

Table 9.16 Ever Paid for Sex, 1998 and 2008

"Thinking about the time since your 18th birthday, have you ever
had sex with a person you paid or who paid you for sex?"

(percent of people aged 18 or older responding, 1998 and 2008; and percent responding by demographic characteristic, 2008)

	yes	no
TREND		
2008	9.0%	91.0%
1998	7.3	92.7
2008 PROFILE		
Total people	**9.0**	**91.0**
Men	16.4	83.6
Women	2.6	97.4
Black	13.4	86.6
Hispanic	5.8	94.2
White	8.5	91.5
Aged 18 to 44	7.5	92.5
Aged 45 to 64	11.4	88.6
Aged 65 or older	7.9	92.1
Not a college graduate	9.1	90.9
Bachelor's degree or more	8.9	91.1

Source: Survey Documentation and Analysis, Computer-assisted Survey Methods Program, University of California, Berkeley, General Social Surveys, 1972–2008 Cumulative Data Files, Internet site http://sda.berkeley.edu/cgi-bin/hsda?harcsda+gss08; calculations by New Strategist

Few Identify Themselves As Gay or Lesbian

Fully 97 percent of adults aged 18 or older identify themselves as heterosexuals. Only 1.6 percent say they are gay or lesbian and another 1.1 percent are bisexuals. Among women, 94 percent say they have had sex only with men since the age of 18. Among men, 96 percent have had sex only with women. Among gays and lesbians, 40 percent say they knew of their orientation before age 14, most came out after age 18, and 16 percent have never come out.

(percent distribution of people aged 18 or older by sexual orientation, 2008)

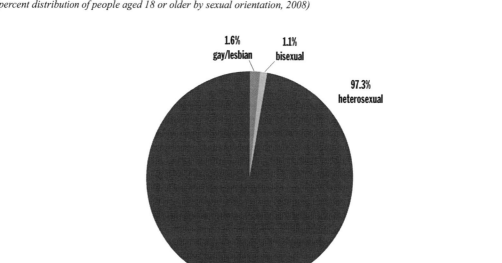

Table 9.17 Sexual Orientation, 2008

"Which of the following best describes you?"

(percent of people aged 18 or older responding by demographic characteristic, 2008)

	gay, lesbian or homosexual	bisexual	heterosexual or straight
Total people	**1.6%**	**1.1%**	**97.3%**
Men	1.4	0.7	97.8
Women	1.7	1.5	96.8
Black	2.3	2.2	95.4
Hispanic	0.2	1.5	98.3
White	1.5	0.8	97.7
Aged 18 to 44	1.9	2.0	96.1
Aged 45 to 64	1.6	0.3	98.0
Aged 65 or older	0.4	0.4	99.3
Not a college graduate	1.1	0.7	98.2
Bachelor's degree or more	3.0	2.3	94.7

Source: Survey Documentation and Analysis, Computer-assisted Survey Methods Program, University of California, Berkeley, General Social Survey, 2008 Cumulative Data Files, Internet site http://sda.berkeley.edu/cgi-bin/hsda?harcsda+gss08; calculations by New Strategist

Table 9.18 Sex of Partners in Past Year, 1988 to 2008

"Have your sex partners in the last 12 months been . . . ?"

(percent of people aged 18 or older responding, 1988 to 2008; and percent responding by demographic characteristic, 2008)

	exclusively male	both male and female	exclusively female
TREND			
2008	50.4%	0.6%	49.1%
1998	53.8	1.0	45.3
1988	53.2	0.2	46.7
2008 PROFILE			
Total people	**50.4**	**0.6**	**49.1**
Men	1.7	0.2	98.1
Women	96.1	0.9	3.0
Black	48.6	0.9	50.5
Hispanic	47.6	1.3	51.1
White	50.6	0.5	48.9
Aged 18 to 44	51.4	0.9	47.6
Aged 45 to 64	48.7	0.3	51.1
Aged 65 or older	50.0	0.0	50.0
Not a college graduate	49.9	0.3	49.8
Bachelor's degree or more	51.7	1.3	47.0

Source: Survey Documentation and Analysis, Computer-assisted Survey Methods Program, University of California, Berkeley, General Social Surveys, 1972–2008 Cumulative Data Files, Internet site http://sda.berkeley.edu/cgi-bin/hsda?harcsda+gss08; calculations by New Strategist

Table 9.19 Sex of Partners in Past Five Years, 1998 and 2008

"Have your sex partners in the last five years been . . . ?"

(percent of people aged 18 or older responding, 1998 and 2008; and percent responding by demographic characteristic, 2008)

	exclusively male	both male and female	exclusively female
TREND			
2008	50.4%	1.2%	48.3%
1998	53.5	1.5	45.1
2008 PROFILE			
Total people	**50.4**	**1.2**	**48.3**
Men	1.5	0.9	97.6
Women	95.9	1.5	2.5
Black	49.8	2.3	48.0
Hispanic	47.7	1.0	51.2
White	50.7	1.0	48.3
Aged 18 to 44	50.1	1.9	48.0
Aged 45 to 64	50.4	0.6	49.0
Aged 65 or older	51.7	0.0	48.3
Not a college graduate	50.4	0.9	48.7
Bachelor's degree or more	50.6	2.0	47.4

Source: Survey Documentation and Analysis, Computer-assisted Survey Methods Program, University of California, Berkeley, General Social Surveys, 1972–2008 Cumulative Data Files, Internet site http://sda.berkeley.edu/cgi-bin/hsda?harcsda+gss08; calculations by New Strategist

Table 9.20 Sex of Partners since Age 18, 2008

"Since the age of 18, have your sex partners been . . . ?"

(percent of people aged 18 or older responding by demographic characteristic, 2008)

	only men	some women, but mostly men	equally men and women	some men, but mostly women	only women	no sex partners
Total people	**50.5%**	**1.5%**	**0.3%**	**0.7%**	**45.0%**	**2.0%**
Men	0.7	0.8	0.2	0.4	95.5	2.4
Women	94.1	2.1	0.4	1.0	0.8	1.6
Black	52.0	1.4	0.6	0.8	44.4	0.8
Hispanic	48.9	0.8	0.0	0.6	48.1	1.7
White	50.7	1.6	0.2	0.7	45.1	1.7
Aged 18 to 44	48.2	1.9	0.5	0.9	45.4	3.2
Aged 45 to 64	50.8	1.4	0.0	0.8	46.0	1.0
Aged 65 or older	57.3	0.4	0.4	0.0	41.3	0.7
Not a college graduate	50.9	1.2	0.2	0.4	45.2	2.1
Bachelor's degree or more	49.3	2.1	0.7	1.7	44.4	1.8

Source: Survey Documentation and Analysis, Computer-assisted Survey Methods Program, University of California, Berkeley, General Social Survey, 2008 Cumulative Data Files, Internet site http://sda.berkeley.edu/cgi-bin/hsda?harcsda+gss08; calculations by New Strategist

Table 9.21 Gay and Lesbian Experiences, 2008

(percent of gays and lesbians aged 18 or older responding, 2008)

	under 14	14 to 18	19 to 25	26 or older	never told
"At what age were you first sexually attracted to someone of the same sex?"	40.3%	37.3%	13.5%	8.8%	–
"At about what age were you when you first told someone that you were gay or lesbian?"	4.7	20.5	37.4	21.6	15.8

	all	more than half	about half	less than half	none
"About how many of your coworkers know that you are gay or lesbian?"	20.1%	8.3%	3.4%	30.9%	37.3%

Note: "–" means not applicable.
Source: Survey Documentation and Analysis, Computer-assisted Survey Methods Program, University of California, Berkeley, General Social Survey, 2008 Cumulative Data Files, Internet site http://sda.berkeley.edu/cgi-bin/hsda?harcsda+gss08; calculations by New Strategist

Sexual Harassment at Work Is Common

Twenty-three percent of people aged 18 or older say they have been sexually harassed at work. The figure is a higher 27 percent among women and a substantial 19 percent among men. Only 2 percent of adults say they have been sexually harassed by religious leaders, but a larger 9 percent know adults who have been harassed by religious leaders.

(percent of people aged 18 or older who have been sexually harassed at work, by sex, 2008)

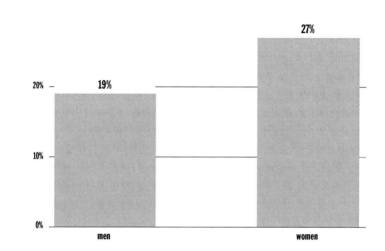

Table 9.22 Sexual Harassment at Work, 2008

"Sometimes at work people find themselves the object of sexual advances or propositions from supervisors. The advances sometimes involve physical contact and sometimes just involve sexual conversations. Have you experienced such advances?"

(percent of people aged 18 or older responding by demographic characteristic, 2008)

	yes	no
Total people	**23.4%**	**76.6%**
Men	19.1	80.9
Women	27.2	72.8
Black	22.2	77.8
Hispanic	14.6	85.4
White	24.3	75.7
Aged 18 to 44	25.0	75.0
Aged 45 to 64	24.3	75.7
Aged 65 or older	16.3	83.7
Not a college graduate	24.7	75.3
Bachelor's degree or more	19.9	80.1

Source: Survey Documentation and Analysis, Computer-assisted Survey Methods Program, University of California, Berkeley, General Social Survey, 2008 Cumulative Data Files, Internet site http://sda.berkeley.edu/cgi-bin/hsda?harcsda+gss08; calculations by New Strategist

Table 9.23 Sexual Harassment by Religious Leaders, 2008

"Now think about church, synagogue, or other religious settings. Since you turned 18, have you ever found yourself the object of sexual advances or propositions from a minister, priest, rabbi, or other clergyperson or religious leader?"

(percent of people aged 18 or older responding by demographic characteristic, 2008)

	yes	no
Total people	**2.4%**	**97.6%**
Men	0.9	99.1
Women	3.6	96.4
Black	6.9	93.1
Hispanic	2.6	97.4
White	1.6	98.4
Aged 18 to 44	2.0	98.0
Aged 45 to 64	2.4	97.6
Aged 65 or older	3.8	96.2
Not a college graduate	2.9	97.1
Bachelor's degree or more	0.8	99.2

Source: Survey Documentation and Analysis, Computer-assisted Survey Methods Program, University of California, Berkeley, General Social Survey, 2008 Cumulative Data Files, Internet site http://sda.berkeley.edu/cgi-bin/hsda?harcsda+gss08; calculations by New Strategist

Table 9.24 Know Others Who Were Sexually Harassed by Religious Leaders, 2008

"Do you know of other people who, as adults, were the object of advances
or propositions from a minister, priest, rabbi, or other clergyperson or
religious leader in a place you were attending religious services?"

(percent of people aged 18 or older responding by demographic characteristic, 2008)

	yes	no
Total people	**9.3%**	**90.7%**
Men	8.0	92.0
Women	10.5	89.5
Black	14.7	85.3
Hispanic	3.6	96.4
White	8.9	91.1
Aged 18 to 44	7.7	92.3
Aged 45 to 64	12.5	87.5
Aged 65 or older	6.5	93.5
Not a college graduate	7.9	92.1
Bachelor's degree or more	13.2	86.8

Source: Survey Documentation and Analysis, Computer-assisted Survey Methods Program, University of California, Berkeley, General Social Survey, 2008 Cumulative Data Files, Internet site http://sda.berkeley.edu/cgi-bin/hsda?harcsda+gss08; calculations by New Strategist

Most Support Abortion in Some Circumstances

The majority of the American public thinks legal abortion should be available to women whose health is endangered by pregnancy, to rape victims, and if there is a serious defect in the baby. Large minorities would also permit legal abortions if a family cannot afford more children, a married woman does not want more children, or a woman is single. Forty-one percent of Americans support legal abortion for any reason.

(percent of Americans who think abortion should be legal in selected circumstances, 2008)

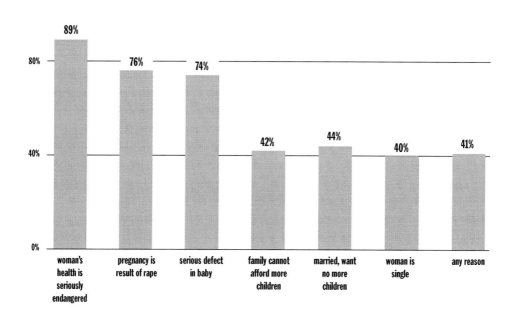

Table 9.25 Abortion for Serious Defect in Baby, 1978 to 2008

"Please tell me whether or not you think it should be possible for a pregnant woman to obtain a legal abortion if there is a strong chance of serious defect in the baby."

(percent of people aged 18 or older responding, 1978 to 2008; and percent responding by demographic characteristic, 2008)

	yes	no
TREND		
2008	73.7%	26.3%
1998	77.5	22.5
1988	78.6	21.4
1978	81.6	18.4
2008 PROFILE		
Total people	**73.7**	**26.3**
Men	74.9	25.1
Women	72.7	27.3
Black	73.1	26.9
Hispanic	60.1	39.9
White	74.8	25.2
Aged 18 to 44	69.8	30.2
Aged 45 to 64	78.3	21.7
Aged 65 or older	74.7	25.3
Not a college graduate	70.3	29.7
Bachelor's degree or more	83.4	16.6

Source: Survey Documentation and Analysis, Computer-assisted Survey Methods Program, University of California, Berkeley, General Social Surveys, 1972–2008 Cumulative Data Files, Internet site http://sda.berkeley.edu/cgi-bin/hsda?harcsda+gss08; calculations by New Strategist

Table 9.26 Abortion If Married and Wants No More Children, 1978 to 2008

"Please tell me whether or not you think it should be possible for a pregnant woman to obtain a legal abortion if she is married and does not want any more children."

(percent of people aged 18 or older responding, 1978 to 2008; and percent responding by demographic characteristic, 2008)

	yes	no
TREND		
2008	43.7%	56.3%
1998	41.2	58.8
1988	39.9	60.1
1978	39.9	60.1
2008 PROFILE		
Total people	**43.7**	**56.3**
Men	47.0	53.0
Women	40.8	59.2
Black	46.1	53.9
Hispanic	31.3	68.7
White	44.1	55.9
Aged 18 to 44	41.7	58.3
Aged 45 to 64	50.3	49.7
Aged 65 or older	34.1	65.9
Not a college graduate	38.5	61.5
Bachelor's degree or more	58.8	41.2

Source: Survey Documentation and Analysis, Computer-assisted Survey Methods Program, University of California, Berkeley, General Social Surveys, 1972–2008 Cumulative Data Files, Internet site http://sda.berkeley.edu/cgi-bin/hsda?harcsda+gss08; calculations by New Strategist

Table 9.27 Abortion If Woman's Health Is Seriously Endangered, 1978 to 2008

"Please tell me whether or not you think it should be possible for
a pregnant woman to obtain a legal abortion if the woman's
own health is seriously endangered by the pregnancy."

(percent of people aged 18 or older responding, 1978 to 2008; and percent responding by demographic characteristic, 2008)

	yes	no
TREND		
2008	88.6%	11.4%
1998	87.6	12.4
1988	88.7	11.3
1978	90.5	9.5
2008 PROFILE		
Total people	**88.6**	**11.4**
Men	89.3	10.7
Women	88.0	12.0
Black	91.3	8.7
Hispanic	80.1	19.9
White	88.8	11.2
Aged 18 to 44	87.7	12.3
Aged 45 to 64	90.3	9.7
Aged 65 or older	87.1	12.9
Not a college graduate	87.3	12.7
Bachelor's degree or more	92.4	7.6

Source: Survey Documentation and Analysis, Computer-assisted Survey Methods Program, University of California, Berkeley, General Social Surveys, 1972–2008 Cumulative Data Files, Internet site http://sda.berkeley.edu/cgi-bin/hsda?harcsda+gss08; calculations by New Strategist

Table 9.28 Abortion If Can't Afford More Children, 1978 to 2008

"Please tell me whether or not you think it should be possible for
a pregnant woman to obtain a legal abortion if the family
has a very low income and cannot afford any more children."

(percent of people aged 18 or older responding, 1978 to 2008; and percent responding by demographic characteristic, 2008)

	yes	no
TREND		
2008	42.3%	57.7%
1998	43.0	57.0
1988	41.9	58.1
1978	47.3	52.7
2008 PROFILE		
Total people	**42.3**	**57.7**
Men	44.2	55.8
Women	40.7	59.3
Black	42.8	57.2
Hispanic	27.3	72.7
White	42.7	57.3
Aged 18 to 44	42.0	58.0
Aged 45 to 64	45.8	54.2
Aged 65 or older	34.8	65.2
Not a college graduate	37.4	62.6
Bachelor's degree or more	56.6	43.4

Source: Survey Documentation and Analysis, Computer-assisted Survey Methods Program, University of California, Berkeley, General Social Surveys, 1972–2008 Cumulative Data Files, Internet site http://sda.berkeley.edu/cgi-bin/hsda?harcsda+gss08; calculations by New Strategist

Table 9.29 Abortion If a Woman Is Pregnant as a Result of Rape, 1978 to 2008

"Please tell me whether or not you think it should be possible for a pregnant woman to obtain a legal abortion if she became pregnant as a result of rape."

(percent of people aged 18 or older responding, 1978 to 2008; and percent responding by demographic characteristic, 2008)

	yes	no
TREND		
2008	75.6%	24.4%
1998	80.1	19.9
1988	81.1	18.9
1978	83.1	16.9
2008 PROFILE		
Total people	**75.6**	**24.4**
Men	78.0	22.0
Women	73.4	26.6
Black	75.0	25.0
Hispanic	57.0	43.0
White	76.9	23.1
Aged 18 to 44	76.2	23.8
Aged 45 to 64	74.4	25.6
Aged 65 or older	76.1	24.0
Not a college graduate	73.4	26.6
Bachelor's degree or more	81.7	18.3

Source: Survey Documentation and Analysis, Computer-assisted Survey Methods Program, University of California, Berkeley, General Social Surveys, 1972–2008 Cumulative Data Files, Internet site http://sda.berkeley.edu/cgi-bin/hsda?harcsda+gss08; calculations by New Strategist

Table 9.30 Abortion If a Woman Is Not Married, 1978 to 2008

"Please tell me whether or not you think it should be possible for a pregnant woman to obtain a legal abortion if she is not married and does not want to marry the man."

(percent of people aged 18 or older responding, 1978 to 2008; and percent responding by demographic characteristic, 2008)

	yes	no
TREND		
2008	40.3%	59.7%
1998	41.1	58.9
1988	39.2	60.8
1978	41.8	58.2
2008 PROFILE		
Total people	**40.3**	**59.7**
Men	43.7	56.3
Women	37.4	62.6
Black	36.7	63.3
Hispanic	24.9	75.1
White	41.2	58.8
Aged 18 to 44	39.5	60.5
Aged 45 to 64	43.0	57.0
Aged 65 or older	35.3	64.7
Not a college graduate	33.8	66.2
Bachelor's degree or more	58.9	41.1

Source: Survey Documentation and Analysis, Computer-assisted Survey Methods Program, University of California, Berkeley, General Social Surveys, 1972–2008 Cumulative Data Files, Internet site http://sda.berkeley.edu/cgi-bin/hsda?harcsda+gss08; calculations by New Strategist

Table 9.31 Abortion for Any Reason, 1978 to 2008

"Please tell me whether or not you think it should be possible for a pregnant woman to obtain a legal abortion if the woman wants it for any reason."

(percent of people aged 18 or older responding, 1978 to 2008; and percent responding by demographic characteristic, 2008)

	yes	no
TREND		
2008	41.2%	58.8%
1998	39.9	60.1
1988	36.4	63.6
1978	33.6	66.4
2008 PROFILE		
Total people	**41.2**	**58.8**
Men	42.4	57.6
Women	40.2	59.8
Black	38.0	62.0
Hispanic	28.8	71.2
White	42.7	57.3
Aged 18 to 44	41.5	58.5
Aged 45 to 64	44.2	55.8
Aged 65 or older	33.3	66.8
Not a college graduate	35.8	64.2
Bachelor's degree or more	56.8	43.2

Source: Survey Documentation and Analysis, Computer-assisted Survey Methods Program, University of California, Berkeley, General Social Surveys, 1972–2008 Cumulative Data Files, Internet site http://sda.berkeley.edu/cgi-bin/hsda?harcsda+gss08; calculations by New Strategist

Appendix: Question Variable Names

For those who want to further explore the General Social Survey questions shown in this book, below are the variable names of the questions by chapter and table number.

Chapter 1. The Public Arena

1.	Confidence in executive branch	confed
2.	Confidence in congress	conlegis
3.	Confidence in Supreme Court	conjudge
4.	Confidence in banks	confinan
5.	Confidence in companies	conbus
6.	Confidence in organized labor	conlabor
7.	Confidence in science	consci
8.	Confidence in medicine	conmedic
9.	Confidence in education	coneduc
10.	Confidence in organized religion	conclerg
11.	Confidence in military	conarmy
12.	Confidence in press	conpress
13.	Confidence in television	contv
14.	Federal income tax too high	tax
15.	Taxes on rich	taxrich
16.	Rich share of taxes	taxshare
17.	Differences in income	incgap
18.	Courts harsh	courts
19.	Death penalty	cappun
20.	Afraid to walk at night	fear
21.	War in ten years	uswary
22.	Gun permits	gunlaw
23.	Gun owned	owngun
24.	Hunt	hunt
25.	Legalizing marijuana	grass
26.	Euthanasia	letdie1
27.	Allow anti-religionist to teach	colath
28.	Allow anti-religionist book in library	libath
29.	Allow racist to speak	spkrac
30.	Allow racist to teach	colrac
31.	Allow racist books in library	librac
32.	Allow communist to speak	spkcom
33.	Allow communist to teach	colcom
34.	Allow communist book in library	libcom
35.	Allow militarist to speak	spkmil
36.	Allow militarist to teach	colmil
37.	Allow militarist book in library	libmil
38.	Allow homosexual to speak	spkhomo
39.	Allow homosexual to teach	colhomo
40.	Allow homosexual book in library	libhomo

Chapter 2. Government and Politics

1.	Political leanings	polviews
2.	Political party	partyid
3.	Women not suited for politics	fepol
4.	Vote for woman for president	fepres

5.	Vote for black for president	racpres
6.	Should government do more	helpnot
7.	Should government pay medical	helpsick
8.	Should government help poor	helppoor
9.	Should government reduce income differences	eqwlth
10.	Spending on education	nateduc
11.	Spending on environment	natenvir
12.	Spending on drug problem	natdrug
13.	Spending on crime prevention	natcrime
14.	Spending on urban issues	natcity
15.	Spending on health care	natheal
16.	Spending on blacks	natrace
17.	Spending on military	natarms
18.	Spending on foreign aid	nataid
19.	Spending on welfare	natfare
20.	Spending on space program	natspac
21.	Spending on mass transit	natmass
22.	Spending on roads and bridges	natroad
23.	Spending on Social Security	natsoc
24.	Spending on national parks	natpark
25.	Spending on science	natsci
26.	Spending on child care	natchid

Chapter 3. Science

1.	Internet access at home	intrhome
2.	Hours spent watching TV	tvhors
3.	How often read a newspaper	news
4.	Main source of news	newsfrom
5.	Main source science news	scifrom
6.	Where look for science news	seeksci
7.	Science creates opportunity for youth	nextgen
8.	Science benefits outweigh costs	scibnfts
9.	Science makes things change too fast	toofast
10.	Science does more harm than good	harmgood
11.	Quality of science and math education	scimath
12.	Government should support science	advfront
13.	Experiments on animals	anscitst
14.	Is astrology scientific	astrosci
15.	Clear understanding of science	scistudy
16.	Center of earth is hot	hotcore
17.	Radioactivity is man-made	radioact
18.	Father decides sex of child	boyorgrl
19.	Mother decides sex of child	maboygrl
20.	Lasers focus sound waves	lasers
21.	Electrons smaller than atoms	electron
22.	Antibiotics kill viruses	viruses
23.	Big bang theory	bigbang
24.	Continents are moving	condrift
25.	Evolution	evolved
26.	Earth revolves around sun	earthsun
27.	How long for earth to move around sun	solarrev
28.	Interest in international issues	intintl
29.	Interest in farm issues	intfarm
30.	Interest in local school issues	inteduc
31.	Interest in science	intsci

32.	Interest in economic issues	intecon
33.	Interest in technology	inttech
34.	Interest in medical discoveries	intmed
35.	Interest in space exploration	intspace
36.	Interest in environmental issues	intenvir
37.	Interest in military	intmil

Chapter 4. Religion

1.	Religion in which raised	relig16
2.	Religious preference	relig
3.	How often attend religious services	attend
4.	How often pray	pray
5.	Belief in God	god
6.	Has belief about God changed	godchnge
7.	Life is meaningful because God exists	godmeans
8.	Believe in life after death	postlife
9.	Belief in heaven	heaven
10.	Belief in hell	hell
11.	Belief in miracles	miracles
12.	Feelings about Bible	bible
13.	Prayer in public schools	prayer
14.	Clergy influence government decisions	clerggov
15.	Clergy influence voters	clergvte
16.	Consider self religious	relpersn
17.	Consider self spiritual	sprtprsn
18.	Has a religious experience changed life	relexp
19.	Born again	reborn
20.	Try to convince others about Jesus	savesoul
21.	Carry religion into other dealings	rellife
22.	Trust in science or religion	trustsci
23.	Truth in religion	reltruth
24.	Less committed to religion	relneg
25.	Relgious people are intolerant	religint
26.	Religion brings more conflict than peace	religcon
27.	Sinners must be punished	punsin
28.	God concerned with humans personally	theism
29.	Right and wrong have shades of gray	blkwhite
30.	Mortality is personal	permoral
31.	Immoral person corrupts society	rotapple

Chapter 5. Work and Money

1.	Satisfied with job	satjob
2.	Likely to lose job	joblose
3.	Could find equally good job	jobfind
4.	Ever unemployed in last ten years	unemp
5.	Health insurance through employer	emphlth
6.	Full-time jobs in past three years	work3yrs
7.	How has pay changed	paychnge
8.	Starting pay at current/past job	pastpay
9.	More trade, fewer jobs	moretrde
10.	How often meet with customers	meetf2f1
11.	How often meet with co-workers	meetf2f2
12.	How often meet foreign co-workers	intlcowk
13.	Own a business	ownbiz
14.	Paid employees	paidemps

Chapter 6. Family and Friends

Chapter 7. Race

8.	Should blacks work their way up	wrkwayup
9.	Affirmative action for blacks	affrmact
10.	Whites hurt by affirmative action	discaff
11.	Blacks in neighborhood	raclive
12.	Open housing laws	racopen
13.	Favor half-black neighborhood	liveblks
14.	Favor half-white neighborhood	livewhts
15.	Favor relative marrying Asian	marasian
16.	Favor relative marring black	marblk
17.	Favor relative marying Hispanic	marhisp
18.	Favor relative marrying white	marwht
19.	Income of blacks	wlthblks
20.	Income of whites	wlthwhts
21.	Intelligence of blacks	intlblks
22.	Intelligence of whites	intlwhts
23.	How close to blacks	closeblk
24.	How close to whites	closewht

Chapter 8. Personal Outlook

1.	Is life exciting	life
2.	Happiness	happy
3.	Happiness	hapunhap
4.	Health status	health
5.	Are people helpful	helpful
6.	Are people fair	fair
7.	Can people be trusted	trust
8.	Life serves no purpose	nihilism
9.	Life meaningful only if you provide meaning	egomeans
10.	People cannot change their lives	fatalism
11.	Speak other language	othlang
12.	Should immigration be increased	letin
13.	Visit an art museum	visart
14.	Visit a natural history museum	visnhist
15.	Visit a zoo	viszoo
16.	Visit a science museum	vissci
17.	Visit a public library	vislib
18.	Developed emergency plans	done911a
19.	Stockpiled supplies	done911b
20.	Purchased things for safety	done911c
21.	Know where to get information	done911d
22.	Duplicated documents	done911e
23.	Reduced air travel	done911f
24.	Reduced train travel	done911g
25.	Reduced use of public transportation	done911h
26.	Changed mail handling	done911i
27.	Become more aware	done911j
28.	Avoided certain cities	done911k
29.	Avoided tall buildings	done911l
30.	Avoided national landmarks	done911m

Chapter 9. Sexual Attitudes and Behavior

1.	Sex education in school	sexeduc
2.	Birth control for teenagers	pillok
3.	Sex between teens OK	teensex

4.	Seen x-rated movie	xmovie
5.	Pornography should be illegal	pornlaw
6.	Sex before marriage	premarsx
7.	Sex outside marriage	xmarsex
8.	Homosexuality	homosex
9.	Gay marriage OK	marhomo
10.	Sex partners in past year	partners
11.	Sex partners in past five years	parnrs5
12.	Frequency of sex	sexfreq
13.	Relationship with last sex partner	relatsex
14.	Condom use	condom
15.	Ever had extramarital sex	evstray
16.	Ever paid for sex	evpaidsx
17.	Sexual orientation	sexornt
18.	Sex of sex partners in past last year	sexsex
19.	Sex of sex partners in past five years	sexsex5
20.	Sex of sex partners since age 18	sexsex18
21.	Gay and lesbian experiences	attractd
22.	Sexually harassed at work	harsexjb
23.	Sexually harassed by clergy	harsexcl
24.	Know others sexually harassed by clergy	knwclsex
25.	Abortion, if defect in baby	abdefect
26.	Abortion, if woman wants no more children	abnomore
27.	Abortion, if woman's health endangered	abhlth
28.	Abortion, if woman is poor	abpoor
29.	Abortion, if woman has been raped	abrape
30.	Abortion, if woman is single	absingle
31.	Abortion, for any reason	abany

Index

ability as reason for differences between
    blacks and whites, 248, 250
abortion
    for any reason, 350, 357
    for serious defect in baby, 350–351
    if woman cannot afford more children, 350, 354
    if woman is unmarried, 350, 356
    if woman wants no more children, 350, 352
    if woman was raped, 350, 355
    if woman's health is endangered, 350, 353
addiction to drugs, government spending on, 68, 70
affirmative action, 192–195, 256, 258–260
African Americans. *See* Blacks.
airplane travel, reduced as response to terrorism,
    303, 309
American Dream, 204, 207
animals, scientific research on, 102, 105
antibiotics, 116
art museum, frequency of visiting, 297–298
Asian Americans, opinion of marrying, 266
astrology, 106–107
atheist, allow to speak, publish, 39–41
atoms, 115
awareness, greater because of terrorism, 303, 313

banks, confidence in, 6, 10
bars, frequency of socializing at, 241, 245
Bible
    feelings about, 147–148
    in public school, 147, 149
big bang theory, 117
birth control
    condom use, 331, 336
    for teenagers, 318, 320
bisexual orientation, 340–341
blacks
    affirmative action for, 256, 258–260
    as share of workplace, 256–257
    feelings of closeness to, 275–276
    for President, 59, 62
    government spending to improve conditions
      of, 68, 75
    in neighborhood, 261–262
    income, opinion of, 270–271
    intelligence, opinion of, 270, 273
    living in neighborhood with, opinion of,
      261, 264
    marrying, opinion of, 261, 267
    reason for differences from whites, 248–252
    work hard, 253–254
books, as source of information, 93, 95–96

born again, 152, 156
born in the United States, 217–220
bridges, government spending on, 68, 81
Buddhism, 135–136
buildings avoided in response to terrorism,
    303, 315
business
    confidence in, 6, 11
    own, 186–191

capital punishment, 25, 27
Catholic religion, 135–136
change, possibility of, 290, 293
child care, government support for, 68, 85
children
    ideal number of, 232–233
    relationship with working mother, 226,
      229–230
    should aged share home with grown, 221, 225
    should learn obedience, 232, 234
    should learn to be popular, 232, 236
    should learn to help others, 232, 238
    should learn to think for themselves, 232, 235
    should learn to work hard, 232, 237
    spanking, 239–240
    standard of living, 204, 206
church attendance, 134, 137
cities
    avoided in response to terrorism, 303, 314
    government spending on problems of, 68, 73
    lived in at age 16, 210–212
civil liberties
    allow atheist, 39–41
    allow communist, 39, 45–47
    allow homosexual, 39, 51–53
    allow militarist, 39, 48–50
    allow racist, 39, 42–44
class identification, 201–202
communist, allow to speak, publish, teach, 39,
    45–47
companies, confidence in, 6, 11. *See also* Industry.
condom use, 331, 336
confidence in institutions, 6–19
Congress, confidence in, 6, 8
conservative political leaning, 56–57
continental drift, 118
contraception. *See* Birth Control.
courts
    confidence in, 6, 9
    treatment of criminals, 25–26
crime, government spending on controlling, 68, 72